The Bourbons
The History of a Dynasty

J. H. Shennan

continuum

Continuum UK, The Tower Building, 11 York Road, London SE1 7NX
Continuum US, 80 Maiden Lane, Suite 704, New York, NY 10038

www.continuumbooks.com

First published 2007

Reprinted 2009

British Library Cataloguing-in-Publication Data
A catalogue record for this book is available from the British Library.

ISBN 978 1 84725 200 5

Typeset by Egan Reid Ltd, Auckland, New Zealand
Printed in Great Britain by the MPG Books Group, Bodmin and King's Lynn

Contents

Illustrations

Preface

The ancient house of Bourbon succeeded to the throne of France at the end of a protracted period of confessional and tribal conflict. It lost the crown two centuries later in the course of the French Revolution, the even more violent harbinger of a new political order. In between, the Bourbons sought to restore the prestige of the monarchy – for so long the chief source of national identity – and thereby to sustain the power of their state. In this enterprise, the metaphor for their achievement is to be found in the iconic palace of Versailles. In a brief historical moment the family itself was swept aside by forces which it neither identified nor understood. But its former home, one of the wonders of the modern world, remains, and its DNA survives in the body politic of modern France.

I am grateful to Professor Nigel Saul for the invitation to contribute to his series of dynastic histories, and to two Hambledon stalwarts, Tony Morris for his long-term support and Martin Sheppard for his invaluable editorial advice.

Louis IX (St Louis) (1214–70)
|
Robert (1256–1318) = Beatrice de Bourbon
count of Clermont |
|
Louis I (1279–1342)
1st duke of Bourbon

Pierre (1311–56)   Jacques (c. 1315–61)
duke of Bourbon   count of La Marche

Charles (1490–1527)   François (1470–95)
duke of Bourbon   count of Vendôme

Charles (1489–1537)
duke of Vendôme
|
Antoine (1518–62) = Jeanne d'Albret
|
Henry IV (1553–1610) = Marie de' Medici
|
Louis XIII (1601–43) = Anne of Austria

Louis XIV (1643–1715) = Maria Teresa   Philippe I (1640–1701)
| duke of Orléans
Louis (1661–1711) = Marie-Anne |
Grand Dauphin | of Bavaria   Philippe II (1674–1723)
                                                    duke of Orléans, regent

Louis (1682–1712)   Philippe (1683–1746)   Charles
duke of Burgundy   duke of Anjou   (1686–1714)
| Philip V of Spain   duke of Berry
Louis XV = Maria
(1710–74) | Lesczinska   Louis-Philippe-Joseph
Louis (1729–65)   (1747–93)
Dauphin   duke of Orléans
                                                    Philippe Egalité
                                                    |

Louis XVI = Marie-   Louis-Stanislas-Xavier   Charles   Louis Philippe
(1754–93)   Antoinette   count of Provence   count of Anjou   (1775–1850)
| Louis XVIII   Charles X   king of the French
Louis XVII   (1755–1824)   (1757–1836)
(1785–95)

1

Antecedents

Long before the first Bourbon ascended the throne in 1589, kingship in France had become a family business. The three royal dynasties – Capetian, Valois and Bourbon – which ruled in an unbroken line of succession between the late tenth century and the French Revolution all benefited from that fact, though in the end it proved to be a fatal inheritance. The nature of family government required the sovereign to rule in person, surrounded by his chief relatives and, at one remove, by his extended family, the country's leading nobility, whose duty it was to advise and assist him. At each king's death the royal relative ordained to succeed him inherited the same set of responsibilities. But ruling the kingdom of France attracted a degree of prestige not ordinarily associated with even the grandest of family concerns. Paradoxically, therefore, successive kings were able to consolidate their authority, in part at the cost of distancing themselves from their natural supporters. The tensions thereby created troubled the monarchy down the centuries.

In the beginning, the founder of the dynasty, indeed of the state of France, Hugh Capet, owed his royal status to election. He was one of a small number of influential landowners, counts and dukes, seeking to impose order on that part of the former Carolingian Empire known as Western Francia. His domains were restricted to a thin sliver of land, including Paris and Orléans, at the heart of what became known as the Île de France. He was simply *primus inter pares*, first among equals, an uncomfortable position from which he began to distance himself forthwith. If the magnates who elected him had no thought of establishing a new dynasty, the same could not be said of their nominee, who in the very year of his election succeeded in having his son, Robert, crowned as co-ruler with his father. The date of the ceremony, Christmas Day 987, was deliberately chosen to suggest an underlying continuity between the new royal house and its Carolingian predecessors, for Charlemagne himself had been famously crowned emperor by the pope in Rome on Christmas Day 800.

The practice of designating a successor son during the reigning king's lifetime persisted for the first two and a half centuries of Capetian rule. Thereafter, when some of the giants of the line ruled France, including Louis IX (Saint Louis, 1226–70), and Philip IV (the Fair, 1285–1314), the hereditary principle in favour of the eldest son seemed to have been securely established. When, however, Philip the Fair's son, Louis X, died without leaving a male heir, he was succeeded by his brother, Philip V, rather than by his daughter. Philip was likewise succeeded by a third brother, Charles IV, who claimed precedence over Philip's daughters. But when Charles IV died childless in 1328 there were no more brothers left to inherit. In the absence of clear juridical guidance, it was necessary to resort once more to election. The Notables convened to judge between the three candidates in an updated version of the Assembly of 987, were not on this occasion choosing from an open list. Over the intervening centuries the Capetians had firmly established the principle of heredity in the male line where the king's immediate relatives were concerned. What remained to be decided was the question of whether more distant claims to the throne could be transmitted through the female line.

The Assembly of 1328 faced a tricky political decision as one of the candidates was the king of England, Edward III, who was Philip IV's grandson. He was not nominated, the choice instead falling on Philip, count of Valois, grandson of Philip the Fair's father, Philip III (the Bold). This decision, coming on the eve of the Hundred Years War, was unsurprisingly political and practical. Yet a significant die had been cast. Philip VI, the first Valois king, shared with his Capetian predecessors a title to the throne entirely dependent upon male forbears, whereas Edward III's claim was through his mother, Isabel, daughter of Philip IV and sister of the last three Capetian kings. There was no reference at this time to the Salic Law which would later be appropriated by royal lawyers to add gravitas to the decision. Yet, for all its pragmatism, this judgement of 1328 shaped the course of French history for almost half a millennium. It ordained that kings of France would be summoned to the throne by a law which had operated since the reign of Hugh Capet, in favour of the eldest male heir in the direct line of descent. That law would survive until the Revolution brought down the monarchy itself. Its effect was to concentrate authority in the person thus nominated to govern the state, and thereby to legitimize the political order. Challenges to royal authority, therefore, were less likely to come from rival dynasties or institutions, as happened periodically across the Channel, than from internal disquiet about how that authority was being exercised. For inevitably the king's critics resented any royal manipulation of the status quo, just as the crown in its turn found it necessary from time to time to push its authority to new limits.

At the heart of the matter lay the issue of personal relationships. It has been truly observed that the middle ages defy understanding if the essential role of the personal and the familial is not given pride of place.[1] As the royal domain expanded, the Capetians sought to secure their kingdom with the help of key members of their clan. They created a system of apanages, or land endowments, in the hope of persuading ambitious siblings that collaboration in the family business was preferable to fratricidal strife. Thus, for example, between 1227 and 1241 Louis VIII bestowed upon his three sons the lands of Artois; Poitou and

Auvergne; and Anjou and Maine respectively. Among many such grants were two which would have particularly long-term consequences. Robert, the younger son of Saint Louis, received as an apanage the county of Clermont in Beauvaisis. Following his marriage in 1272, it became part of the domain of future kings of France, for his wife, Beatrice, was heiress to the lordship of Bourbon and his son its first duke. Similarly, the royal house of Valois owed its title to the apanage land north east of Paris which Philip III had bestowed upon the father of the first Valois king.

This habit of parcelling out portions of the royal domain to younger brothers, sons or grandsons, was not limited to the Capetians. Their Valois and Bourbon successors both continued the practice. Indeed, as late as 1766 the king's right to establish apanages was proclaimed a fundamental law of the monarchy, the argument being that the younger sibling's renunciation of his claim to succeed his father required compensation.[2] By the late eighteenth century, the relationship between the crown and the holders of these fiefdoms no longer represented a series of potential fault lines on the political landscape. Nevertheless, the legal position was unchanged: the kingdom of France remained the patrimony of its kings.

This highly personalized perception of royal authority was buttressed by the residual feudalism which even in the eighteenth century continued to underpin the ownership of land. As kings, Hugh Capet and his successors were not the vassals of any great lord. On the contrary, they received the homage of men who were powerful enough to have overthrown them. That the latter preferred homage to rebellion is an indication of why the *Regnum Francorum* survived. It also provides an essential clue to an understanding of French history down to the Revolution. All those who held landed property, the seigneurs, continued to be contracted into personal relationships with both their lord and tenants. Although that contract lost its original justification, namely the obligation to render military service, it retained, even in an attenuated form, its power to provide social cohesion. In one form or another, therefore, it continued to inhibit the half-hearted attempts of Bourbon rulers to modernize the French state, by making government more impersonal and bureaucratic.

For a period of some eight hundred years the kings of France, Capetian, Valois and Bourbon, worked hard at the business of overawing their subjects. Their claim that the law summoned them to rule was a powerful weapon in their armoury, but more potent still was the aura conferred by the act of coronation itself. In the feudal world of lord and vassal an exception was made for the king, who, uniquely, was not required to pay homage for any lands he might acquire. That begs the question of why he should have been so exempted. The justification echoed down the ages and gave meaning to a world only recently vanished: kings were God's lieutenants, exercising His power on earth. That power was conferred at the king's coronation when he was consecrated with holy oils. This unction transformed Hugh Capet and all his successors into quasi-sacerdotal figures, setting them apart from their greatest subjects. Each ritual inauguration dramatically reinforced the king's majesty, colouring it with the divine. The permanent home of the king's coronation became the cathedral of Reims. There in 1825 the last Bourbon king, Charles X, his dynasty briefly restored to the throne after the turmoil of the Revolution, went through a ceremony which would have been familiar and rather more credible to his predecessor, Louis IX, Saint Louis, who had been crowned in the same great Gothic cathedral six hundred years before.[3]

The most convincing demonstration of the alliance between the Almighty and the kings of France was the latter's power of healing. Hugh Capet's son, Robert the Pious, was the first Capetian to cure his subjects of disease by the miracle of the royal touch. Later, when that disease became the specific scourge of scrofula, royal miracle-working became a highly charged part of the ritual of court life. Important church festivals were the preferred occasions for these gatherings, Christmas Day, Palm Sunday, Easter Sunday, Pentecost, when the sovereign would lay his hands on hundreds of his suffering subjects in turn, saying over them: 'The king touches thee, and God heals thee.' The practice continued through the eighteenth century, though by then an aristocratic gossip like the duke of Saint-Simon was beginning to doubt 'the pretended miracle attached to the king's touch'.[4]

The powerful mystique of kingship had its counterpoint in the ultimate crime of *lèse-majesté*. Regicide was considered so heinous an offence that even capital punishment seemed inadequate retribution unless accompanied by a cocktail of the most savage tortures. In 1757, when enlightened European minds were beginning to question the justification for such barbarism, Robert Damiens suffered the most brutal of public deaths in Paris for inflicting a superficial knife wound upon the person of Louis XV. Four horses tearing apart his tortured body provided the climax to an orgy of retribution in the place de Grève. By then the nature of the punishment reflected less the awesome power of the regime than its extreme vulnerability. For the rich apparel in which the monarchy had been decked was becoming threadbare. So well had the rulers of France succeeded in increasing their authority that ultimately it became unsustainable.

This crucial issue has often been analysed in the following terms: did the king possess the crown, and therefore the kingdom, in the same way as he owned the royal domain; or was kingship an office imposing obligations on its holder which were not purely possessory? Put another way, was the king both a public and private person? Surely he was. The Capetians administered their royal domains according to precisely the same private law as that regulating the ownership of land anywhere else in the kingdom. But their 'ownership' of the kingdom involved a dual public obligation: to provide security and justice. The real problem was that these public and private functions were not as easily separated as medieval lawyers were inclined to imply.[5]

The imposition and maintenance of a just regime, reflecting the divine justice of their patron, was considered the primary public responsibility of French kings. The king was represented therefore as a judge on Hugh Capet's royal seal, not as a warrior. Yet, because a just regime could never endure in an insecure world, all rulers ex officio also shouldered the paramount obligation of guaranteeing their subjects' security. That complementary public task, with its overtones of coercion, did not always sit easily with the image of the royal justiciar, and the Bourbon kings of France would have their difficulties in reconciling these twin roles.

The chief problem in providing security, however, was the practical one of the cost. The Capetians accepted the traditional view that kings should live off their own resources, those drawn from the royal domain. This did not prove to be a major burden for the early Capetians. Their relations with the great feudal vassals, who paid homage for their lands in Normandy, Brittany, Anjou, Aquitaine, Toulouse, Flanders, Champagne and Burgundy, were for the most part mutually beneficial; indeed, these acts of personal fealty provided the sole measure of the kingdom's identity. In the final century of Capetian rule that identity became more recognizable as a number of these fiefs became part of the royal domain. By 1328, the process of centralizing the realm was well under way. That is to say, the kingdom of France was becoming increasingly identified with those lands and rights directly possessed by the monarch as seigneur. To avoid anachronism, it should be stressed that the centralization referred to was not of an impersonal French state but of the king's own estates. The Capetians felt no need to secure a perfect match between the royal domain and the kingdom of France, between their private and public interests. They were content to allow three of the most powerful fiefs, Flanders, Brittany and Burgundy, to remain outside their directly administered domain, and they were perfectly willing to alienate parts of that domain in the form of apanages. They were fortunate too in that this territorial expansion was largely achieved by pacific, and therefore relatively inexpensive, means. Nevertheless, in due course the tensions generated by the kings' two roles, personal and private on the one hand, personal and public on the other, would risk crippling the body politic. In 1328 the family's obligations were inherited by its junior branch, the Valois. The new dynasty was plunged almost at once into the episodic conflict with England known as the Hundred Years War. In retrospect it is clear that this struggle, which began in 1337 and ended with the English defeat at Castillon in 1453, marked a turning point in the development of western European states. At its outset political behaviour was governed by personal obligations of fidelity and service, the feudal code binding lord and vassal together. Indeed, the war remained a dispute between the chiefs of the Valois and Plantagenet houses. Over time, however, it threatened to become something more.

The success of the Capetians in extending the frontiers of their royal domain, as well as their authority over a greater France, led inexorably to a showdown with the other major ruler in the region, the Angevin king of England. When the first Valois king, Philip VI, succeeded to the French throne his greatest vassal and rival was the duke of Aquitaine, who also happened to be the king of England. Extraordinary as it appears to those wedded to the idea and ideal of the nation state, Edward III duly rendered personal homage to his liege-lord, Philip, in 1329. The greater reality, however, was that Capetian expansion had made the king of France a significant figure on the international stage and rendered the old order suspect. Edward III's conviction that he and not Philip, was the rightful king of France did nothing to reduce the rising level of tension.

It was not long before the two rivals, Philip and Edward, embarked on that series of military adventures which would only end in 1453, in the reigns of Charles VII and Henry VI respectively. The Hundred Years War changed the perceptions both of the French crown and of its politically aware subjects. It brought home to the former the fact that its obligation to guarantee the security of its subjects could not be built exclusively upon the resources of the royal domain, however extensive.

In truth, that had been obvious for some time, for the gathering of the kingdom beyond the Île de France was only possible with the assistance of an army of officials charged with the tasks of extending the king's justice and garnering his finances. The chief town of the Capetians on the banks of the Seine was gradually transformed into the capital city of France. Paris became the headquarters of a burgeoning royal bureaucracy. It also grew into one of the great centres of Christendom, enhancing in the process the reputation of the ruling dynasty. In the very heart of Paris, on the Île de la Cité, the cathedral of Notre Dame was completed during the reign of the first Valois king; only yards from the church of Sainte-Chapelle, which still stands, an ethereal masterpiece of Gothic architecture, built a century earlier as a royal chapel for Saint Louis. Close to both, on the Seine's left bank, the university of Paris, forever associated with Louis's erstwhile chaplain, Robert de Sorbon, was already famous enough in the saint-king's lifetime to include Thomas Aquinas among its teachers. By 1400 this great city had a population of some 150,000, perhaps 50,000 more than inhabited contemporary London, and its relative sophistication indicated the growing complexity of the political order in France.[6]

The authority of the king as a public figure was threatening to challenge his role as head of the dynasty. Indeed, that process was already well advanced in the judicial sphere. Before the end of the twelfth century the first Capetian ordinances, intended to apply to the whole country, had appeared during the reign of Louis VII. The revival of Roman law influences in the following century further enhanced the king's legislative role and the prestige of the *curia regis*, the supreme court of justice. In fact, it became impossible for the *curia* to cope with the volume of specialized legal business coming before it. The result was the gradual emergence from the royal court of a new judicial body, the parlement of Paris, which enjoyed an independent existence from some time during the second half of the thirteenth century. Later this body would come to play a highly significant political role in the history of Bourbon France. But even at the time of its foundation the parlement already represented a social and political step forward from the rudimentary basis of Capetian kingship. The royal judges in the *palais de justice* in Paris owed their prestige to the exercise of high office, not to a land-holding relationship with the king. The king's justice was therefore independent of the dominant feudal ties which otherwise bound him.

His growing authority as a public figure did not free the king from the obligations which he continued to owe, as suzerain of the land, to his chief subjects. On the contrary, that relationship inhibited the further development of a public persona. In particular it prevented the king's subjects from feeling any obligation in normal circumstances to provide him with financial support above and beyond what he could properly extract from the royal domain. Even by the seventeenth century this feeling had not changed very much. The concept of a permanent state revenue that could provide for the needs of an ever more complex political organization simply did not exist. Because of this, from a very early stage the rulers of France were forced to employ a variety of stratagems to finance their kingdom. As a result, their control over affairs was periodically prejudiced.

Their subjects were a little more forthcoming when France was at war. The Hundred Years War could not have been sustained without subsidies, so the concept of 'extraordinary' taxation was born. This allowed for additional money to be raised beyond the 'ordinary' income available from the royal domain when the realm was at risk. Even this grudging concession, however, was frequently subjected to further hair-splitting qualifications: the need for the king to be present in person at the head of his army; or the maintenance in the field of an army of specified size. In 1354 the town of Montpellier in Languedoc went so far as to suggest that any necessity for additional subsidies would not be evident unless Edward III led the English army in Gascony in person.[7]

This final example may imply that the French king was doubly constrained, by a shortage of funds and by a quasi-constitutional bridle manipulated by the estates of the realm. Such an implication would be grossly misleading, for it is a critical characteristic of late medieval France that the king was not required to seek consent for his taxes from any representative body. The Roman law principle of *quod omnes tangit ab omnibus approbetur*, 'no taxation without representation', which would cause so much trouble to the old enemy across the Channel, did not register prominently on the French political scale.[8]

There are several reasons why this should have been so. In the first place France was, and in many respects still is, a country of regions. It also became, particularly after the expulsion of the English, a kingdom of great size and scope, encapsulating a multitude of customs, loyalties and traditions. The great linguistic schism of the *langue d'oil* and the *langue d'oc* divided the country, while dialects differed by neighbourhood. The king's subjects were hardly French, unless they were denizens of Paris or the Île de France, and not even Norman, Breton or Gascon except when so viewed by outsiders. The touchstone of identity was essentially local.[9] This characteristic of late medieval France owed a great deal to the Capetian ethos of state-building, which was not a novel centralizing policy. It was simply a matter of extending the areas of fealty due by landowners to their liege lord. As part of that relationship was the obligation to offer counsel when required, by the thirteenth century the great feudal dignitaries, lay and clerical, were in the habit of convening their followers, mirroring their own expectation of a royal summons. Such local and regional assemblies proliferated, providing the model for the emergence during the following century of more formal provincial estates. These were the bodies made responsible for voting the extraordinary revenues regularly and urgently needed by the Crown. They shared two characteristics: a preoccupation with local issues; and a mission to offer counsel, not to command consent.

That extraordinary taxation should habitually be settled at a local level rather than in a national assembly highlights both the essential relationship between the king and his great vassals, and the deeply held and persistent belief that such taxes were no more than temporary expedients, levied to counter an immediate and unmistakable threat. The insistence that they should cease as soon as the emergency they were intended to combat was over localized the concept of 'evident necessity' and made a national assembly superfluous. The estates general duly appeared in the fourteenth century but failed to establish a significant political role thereafter.

Another reason for the French king's increasing divergence from the path of their English rivals lies in the legitimacy of the Capetian–Valois line. It is difficult to exaggerate the degree of honour and dignity, deriving from the legality of his inheritance, which the French king enjoyed within his kingdom. This level of continuity was in marked contrast, as the French themselves were quick to point out, with the experience of English kings, who frequently became the victims of regicidal mania. In the four centuries between the fracture of the ruling line in 1066 and the late fifteenth century, when the Hundred Years War came to an end, the succession of England's kings had not proceeded smoothly. Stephen met a natural death despite usurping the throne in 1135; Edward II, who was his father's legal heir, was murdered in 1327; Richard II was deposed and subsequently murdered by the usurper Henry Bolingbroke, who in 1399 became Henry IV; the last Lancastrian king, Henry VI, was murdered in the Tower of London; the young king Edward V was murdered by his uncle, Richard duke of Gloucester; who became Richard III, and the Wars of the Roses ended in 1485 with Richard's death in battle. Impressive as this sequence of royal disaster stories was, some Frenchmen still found it necessary to overplay it. In 1484 the French Chancellor, Jean Masselin, claimed to identify twenty-six changes of dynasty since the foundation of the English monarchy, an assertion difficult to sustain even with the inclusion of a number of seventh-century kings of Northumbria.[10] There was, however, a serious point being made by this distinguished French lawyer. In France the king's position was secure because the law of succession had identified him and called him to rule. His regime was therefore just and he personally represented the source of justice in his state. His counterpart in England could make no such claims.

It did not follow that the greater security of the French king's position rendered him more powerful in his country than the king of England was in his. It did mean that the evolving French state would owe its cohesion to the king's role as the fount of justice. It also meant that that very role would inhibit as much as assist the development of the central government ethos needed to sustain the emerging power of the state. For the king's justice essentially reflected the social and regional privileges upon which the Capetian dynasty had been built.

The problem of how to justify the collection of state revenues was a case in point. The traditional view that 'extraordinary' royal taxation was a temporary imposition survived to the very end of the *ancien régime*. In some cases, of course, temporary measures were persisted with until they became permanent. This was the case with the most unpopular of all such taxes, the *gabelle* or salt tax. Introduced in 1341 by the first Valois king, Philip VI, as a temporary expedient, in the course of the following four and a half centuries it became a synonym for oppression. The subjects' obligation to purchase a vital commodity at a higher price than most could afford to pay may have helped to replenish the royal coffers, but it did nothing to integrate the wider authority of government with the king's role as the source of all justice.

Characteristically, the *gabelle* originated as a seigneurial right: the Capetians' exploitation of salt pans in southern France, acquired as the kingdom expanded. Initially this right was simply extended as a measure of 'extraordinary' taxation. Despite its longevity, the *gabelle* remained a grossly inefficient tax. This was because until very late in the *ancien régime* all such additional revenues continued to display the ad hoc nature of their origins. Put another way, the concept of efficiency in tax gathering suggests a state machine geared to maximizing income. The reality was quite different: it was about the king's often desperate need to procure financial resources, from whatever source, however justified. In this instance the abiding regionalism of the country ensured that incompetence was piled upon inefficiency.

In the original homeland of the Capetians around the Île de France, the so-called *pays de grande gabelle*, salt was extremely expensive to buy. It was less expensive in the south east of the country, bordering the Mediterranean, and cheaper still in the south west, in the former English possessions of Armagnac and Aquitaine. In Brittany it was entirely tax free. In addition, there were geographical pockets of privilege – Paris was a prominent example – where salt could be bought at a more favourable rate than in the surrounding region. The multi-bordered salt map of the kingdom was an open invitation to smugglers, who responded enthusiastically, inhibited only by the draconian penalties, including death, for those apprehended. Salt-tax revenue was further lowered by the privilege of *franc-salé*. Those who possessed this right had a reduced level of obligation, in whatever region they lived. They included the members of the First and Second Estates (nobility and clergy), certain royal officers and the communities of some charitable institutions like hospitals and convents.[11]

The *gabelle*'s bewildering configuration as a source of indirect taxation was mirrored in the equally convoluted structure of the kingdom's chief direct tax, the *taille*. This was also the product of a piece of 'extraordinary' legislation, the 1439 ordinance of Charles VII. The *taille* was intended to support a modern royal army raised during the final stage of the Hundred Years War, replacing the old feudal host and the dangerously unpredictable mercenary bands. Both the army and the tax would become permanent.

The manner in which the *taille* was assessed and collected is indicative of the true nature of French government and society for much of the *ancien régime*. The history of the French state under the Capetians, Valois and Bourbons was not about the gradual centralization of power under an absolute ruler. Rather, and far less dramatically, it was about the efforts of successive kings to add much needed muscle to their undoubted moral authority. This was a difficult balancing act to perform since that authority was based upon their obligation to dispense justice, which meant primarily the need to maintain the bewildering collection of diverse rights and privileges customarily enjoyed by their subjects. Only against that background is it possible for modern observers to make any sense of the *taille*.

First of all, it was not a fixed tax. Nevertheless its expected yield could still be calculated in advance because each year the king's council decided on the global sum to be raised, before instructing the royal officials to organize the collection. The grand total was divided first by *généralité* and then subdivided by *élection*. Finally an assessment of each individual's contribution was made at parish level. The exercise was highly arbitrary, imprecise and impressionistic, resting upon government needs in a particular year and making little effort to take into account the ability to pay. Equality of treatment in particular was not on the agenda of the *ancien régime*, even for those subjected to the tax.

Those who were exempt from the *taille* were precisely the people best equipped to contribute to it, the nobility and the clergy; because the *taille* was in essence a military tax, neither group, for diametrically opposed reasons, could be included. Nobles because their vocation was to fight for the king, clerics because they had no part to play in war. There were many other exemptions too: royal officials, members of the legal profession and of the universities, mayors and corporations, even whole urban communities – there were nine of these in Normandy alone. Then there were the widows of those who had been legally entitled to exemption, and, less legally but just as certainly, members of communities enjoying the patronage of powerful local seigneurs. By and large this list suggests that the more affluent members of the Third Estate were the beneficiaries of exemption.

This complex procedure for levying or not levying the *taille* was further complicated by two other factors. The first was the distinction made between the *taille personelle* and the *taille réelle*. The former, a tax on individuals, was levied in the north and centre of the country. The latter was a tax on land, levied in Languedoc, Provence and the south west. The significance of the land tax was that it was attached to estates that had been designated *roturier*, non-noble, whether the owners belonged to the first, second or third estate. The final confusion was rendered by a profound difference in the manner of collection, between the regions called *pays d'états* and those called *pays d'élections*. In the *pays d'état* the provincial estates survived and voted the equivalent of the *taille* in the form of a so-called *don gratuit*, or free gift. Over time this gift tended to become the precise amount required by the king's council. Nevertheless, the *pays d'états* possessed an autonomous financial organization, a fact which probably allowed them to contribute proportionately less than the *pays d'élections*. The number of provincial estates declined during the reigns of the Bourbons. At the beginning of the sixteenth century there were fifteen, but that number was gradually reduced until by the end of the eighteenth century only four remained: the great *pays* of Brittany, Burgundy, Languedoc and Provence.

These tax-collecting procedures highlight the mosaic character of the French state. Its chief claim to unity down to the Revolution was through the focus of the crown, which continued to provide the impetus for political action and to give point to social aspirations. The later Capetians and their successors were able through their public role to identify with the nation at large and, at least *in extremis*, to generate a patriotic fervour which offset the country's inherent particularism. They owed their success in this to the exploitation of a variety of interwoven aspects of religion and the law.[12]

The consecration which formed part of their coronation admitted kings of France into a rarefied, spiritual, miracle-working domain which impressed even their most powerful vassals. As the kingdom acquired a clearer geographical identity it began to reflect something of its ruler's special relationship with the Almighty. After all, it was surely unthinkable that the people over whom God had called His anointed line of Christian kings to rule would not themselves be exceptional in their Christian commitment. By the time the Valois succeeded the Capetians, theologians and chroniclers were routinely acknowledging the special status of France as 'the Most Christian' kingdom, and the French as latter-day Hebrews, God's chosen people. Early in the fourteenth century the first of the Avignon popes, Clement V, solemnly proclaimed in the bull *Rex gloriae* that, 'like the people of Israel, the kingdom of France, as a peculiar people chosen by the Lord to carry out the orders of Heaven, is distinguished by marks of special honour and grace'. Presiding over this Promised Land was His Most Christian Majesty, *rex christianissimus*.[13] The religion of monarchy thus provided an early manifestation of French nationalism.

The first victim of this vibrant religious nationalism was the Universal Church in France. Although the crystallizing out of separate states in Europe had undermined the old duumvirate of empire and papacy, the pope was still inclined to view Christendom as his oyster, especially in matters of taxation. In 1296 one of the great medieval battles between church and state began. The pope, Boniface VIII, published a bull, *Clericis laicos*, excommunicating any secular ruler who taxed the clergy within his domains without the approval of the Holy See. Philip the Fair was adamant that not even the successor of Saint Peter could be allowed to interfere with the government of his kingdom. The feud culminated in 1302 with the publication of the most celebrated manifesto of the middle ages in favour of papal supremacy, the bull *Unam sanctam*. Subsequently, the king was excommunicated and his subjects declared free of their obligation to obey him. This was the last throw of the papal dice since Philip, the grandson of Saint Louis and the first Capetian to insist that his subjects address him as 'Most Christian King', held both the moral high ground and the armed forces needed to seize and incarcerate the pope. Boniface died shortly after his brief imprisonment, having made his unwitting contribution to the emergence of a powerful Gallican Church which would remain symbiotically linked with the crown for the duration of the *ancien régime*.

The rise of Gallicanism also affords a reminder of the fact that by this time the chief agents of the crown's expanding authority were not feudal levies or mercenary troops but canon and Roman lawyers. By the thirteenth century concepts of Roman law, rediscovered in the sixth-century *Corpus juris civilis* of the Emperor Justinian, had reached northern Europe, at about the same time as Thomas Aquinas was reconciling Aristotelian ideas of a secular state with the medieval preoccupation with the City of God. The result was a quickening of the process whereby the king's justice helped to define and unify the state. The Roman law revival enabled rulers like Philip the Fair to insist that membership of the French state or *patria* imposed certain obligations on all the subjects: to fight in its defence; and to contribute taxes for that purpose. For his part, the ruler was entitled in times of crisis to summon all his subjects to defend the homeland, ignoring traditional feudal bonds in the process.[14]

The fundamental importance of the law in state affairs was reflected in the increasing significance of the parlement of Paris, whose history demonstrated the continuity of royal justice from the reign of Saint Louis to that of Louis XVI, and therefore the legitimacy of their monarchical authority. The parlement began its judicial conquest of France by validating customary laws. These oral traditions were strictly local, often limited by natural features such as the course of a stream or the slope of a mountainside. After investigation by the king's judges, royal declarations would translate the accepted customs into writing. The influence of Roman, written law stimulated jurists to integrate and codify these traditions in the form of *coutumiers*. This practice began in the thirteenth century with the *Grand coutumier de Normandie* and the incomparable *Coutumes de Clermont en Beauvaisis*. The latter was the work of a royal bailiff, Philippe de Beaumanoir, who as a legal thinker merits comparison with Montesquieu. The *Grand coutumier de France*, containing the custom of Paris, appeared in the fourteenth century. Finally, in 1454 at the end of the Hundred Years War, in an effort to introduce a degree of regulation though not uniformity to the process, Charles VII decreed in his ordinance of Montils-les-Tours that all the customs of the kingdom should be approved by the royal judges, set down in writing and legally enforced in the particular area from which they came.

In this way customary law became the king's justice. The nation's identity was revealed in the sovereign's unique responsibility for promulgating and validating the law. In 1436 the parlement of Paris reviewed a case involving the confiscation of a couple's property in the capital. The parlement approved the action because the Italian husband had links with the English enemy. Indeed, the court went much further. For her action in joining her husband and the English, the French wife was accused of the crime of *lèse-majesté*, and of later compounding her offence by bearing several children, thereby adding to the sum total of the king's enemies. What the parlement's register was proclaiming in this case was that in wartime the king's law defined the national interest.[15]

The identification of the king with the national interest was already being reflected more generally in the parlement's jurisprudence. Certain cases, wherever they originated, were reserved exclusively for trial in a royal court with final appeal to the parlement. These so-called *cas royaux* included *lèse-majesté* or high treason, debasement of the royal coinage, and forgery of the royal seal.

With the passage of time and the increasing acceptance of the king's public role, however, the list of *cas royaux* steadily lengthened to include any activity likely to threaten or undermine the integrity of the state: illicit assembly, sedition, popular disturbance, heresy, the malpractice of royal officials.

As a court of law, the parlement of Paris played a crucial part in buttressing the monarchy's unique function, though in its quasi-political guise its contribution turned out to be more equivocal. With the king's writ running more freely across the kingdom the parlement was joined in its judicial endeavours by similar provincial organizations. First came the parlement of Toulouse (1443), established by Charles VII to apply the predominantly written law of the Midi, which he confirmed in the same way as he would shortly validate the customary laws of the north at Montils-les-Tours. Next came Dauphiné (1456), followed by Bordeaux (1467), Burgundy (1476), Rouen, for Normandy (1499), and Aix, for Provence (1501). That most independent of provinces, Brittany finally agreed to the establishment of a provincial parlement at Rennes in 1553.

Despite this prolonged stimulus to the national pulse, the body politic remained distinctly uncoordinated. Royal approval of the country's multifarious collection of customs pointed up the enormous variations in the law, a factor bound to limit central government attempts at regulation and control. In the sixteenth century jurists like Charles du Moulin dreamt of producing a unified code of customary law for the whole kingdom. 'Nothing could be more worthy nor more useful and desirable for the whole république', he wrote, 'than to reduce all the unsystematized and often futile variations of this kingdom's customs to a single concise, clear and equitable harmony.'[16] But such aspirations remained unfulfilled at the close of that century, by which time the first Bourbon had ascended the throne.

A closer examination of the laws collated by the parlements demonstrates the meaninglessness of the concept of national identity except under royal patronage. For the subjects of the king of France were not all equal before the law, or in the eyes of the tax-collectors, or in any other way. They were not equal as individuals at all because no concept of individualism existed. Everybody was placed in an estate or order and usually into smaller sub-categories. But all owed their rights and privileges to their group affiliation.

The lowly village *curé* had little in common with the archbishops and bishops, usually noblemen, whose seats were the great Gothic cathedrals, but he shared with all the members of the First Estate the prestige attached to their calling, the benefits of an autonomous tax regime, and an independent judicial organization. The nobility, members of the Second Estate, likewise enjoyed their collective privileges. Whether princes of the royal blood or the neediest of *hobereaux* from the Auvergne, whether scions of ancient noble houses like the Montmorency and the La Rochefoucauld or new men holding high judicial office in the parlement of Paris, they were all deeply conscious of their membership of an exclusive club. And of the privileges accompanying that membership: in financial terms, exemption from the personal *taille* and the *gabelle*; in judicial terms, the right to have cases tried in the first instance at least at the level of bailiwick, the tribunal immediately below the parlement; and on a personal level, a host of honorific rights at any public gathering.

Finally, the overwhelming masses of the Third Estate were for the most part characterized by the absence of special rights. There were, however, exceptions. The *bourgeois* of Paris, for example, were permitted, like the nobility, to bear arms. They were freed from the obligation to billet the king's troops and to pay the *taille*. They also possessed the legal privilege of not having to respond to any legal summons issued outside the capital. Most members of the Third Estate, however, lived in rural communities which were organized and administered by their own assemblies, meeting regularly after mass on Sundays. These bodies preserved the routines of daily life in their localities, protecting crops and cattle, keeping a look-out for fires, maintaining roads and bridges, sometimes fixing the level of local wages. They also appointed the local collectors of the *gabelle* and the *taille*. This latter assignment was particularly unappealing, hence the grudging list of exemptions which included the syndic (the assembly's elected agent),the churchwarden, the schoolmaster, persons over seventy, the incurably sick, beggars, and fathers of at least eight children![17] In this regard the structure of royal justice was given a helping hand at a crucial point in the tax-raising procedure. The assemblies assisted similarly in the compilation of local customs though that very fact underlines the immense diversity of customary law.

These rural assemblies had no judicial powers of their own, but depended on the court of the local seigneur. The significance of that fact cannot be overstated. Coexisting with the king's regional courts, the bailiwicks and seneschalcies (the latter to be found largely in the south but also in Brittany) were the ancient seigneurial courts which impinged far more directly than the royal courts on most people's lives. There the communities' agrarian disputes were settled, boundaries agreed, the payment of dues enforced. Most of the suits were about land, as land tenure was at the heart of French society. For the original feudal concept survived, that the granting of land bore with it the acquisition of a series of rights and obligations. Possession of a seigneury conferred upon the seigneur powers of high, middle or low justice. Those with powers of high justice, dukes, marquises, counts, had all received their seigneury directly from the king. Their judicial powers were considerable and significant. In criminal matters they wielded powers of life and death, and could impose an array of harsh penalties, including mutilation and banishment. They had cognizance in civil matters of all cases involving nobles living in their seigneury. Indeed, nobles were not allowed to reject their jurisdiction, even though they could refuse to plead before royal judges below bailiwick level. In fact, by the sixteenth century many royal judges had acquired seigneuries themselves, thereby helping to form closely knit legal networks in the localities. Land and its forensic implications remained the warp and weft of French society.[18]

In sum, the responsibility of the parlement of Paris and of the other royal courts of justice was to reinforce the king's authority as head of state while at the same time acknowledging the existence of fundamental legal constraints. There was no intellectual problem about this. Neither the Capetians nor the Valois were modernizers, much less authoritarian tyrants, set upon a policy of centralizing power at all costs. They supported the legal status quo because it justified their dominion. At the same time, they were bound to take pragmatic measures to maintain their control when extraneous circumstances threatened to blow the ship of state off course. During these tricky navigational manoeuvres the parlement of Paris continued to claim a prominent role as pilot.

This was because the parlement was beginning to establish an advisory position comparable in some respects with the work of elected assemblies in some other west European countries. Linguistically of course the parlement and the high court of parliament over the Channel clearly had much in common. But the parlement of Paris was an unelected body whose political role was limited to keeping the king on the legal straight and narrow, by reminding him of the law and of his dependence upon it. It appeared to be a restricted, almost pedantic function. It had future potential, however, and in due course the parlement would be cast as the nemesis of kings, programmed to point fatefully back to an ever more unsustainable past.

The origin of this political check lay in the king's need to publicize and authenticate his laws by having them registered in the parlement. The latter then began, with royal approval, to identify flaws in the legislation. The sovereign's response was either to agree to the proposed changes or, if he found the objections unconvincing, to insist that registration go ahead. The procedure was finalized in the reign of Louis XI (1461–83). By this time it had become elaborate and potentially confrontational. Remonstrances might be presented verbally or in writing. If in the latter form a sub-committee of the court produced a draft for approval at a plenary session. A group of deputies was then nominated to present the remonstrances to the king. Then came the royal reply and the debate upon it, which might be followed by immediate registration or by further remonstrance repeated up to five or six times. The king might expect to get his way by issuing *lettres de jussion*, ordering immediate and unqualified registration. Sometimes, however, even that measure did not quell the opposition and the king would then be forced to attend the parlement himself in order to reclaim his delegated authority as the unique source of justice in the kingdom. At these solemn sessions, called *lits de justice*, the royal judges had no alternative but to acknowledge the king's right to impose his will in this way.[19]

Religion, always at the heart of royal authority in France, provided the first major demonstration of the growing ambiguity in the relationship between the king and his chief law court. The famous quarrel between Philip the Fair and Boniface VIII had set the scene for a protracted struggle between king and pope for the headship of the French church. The bonds between the secular and spiritual power, which were traditionally very close, included the king's sworn support of the French church's right to self-government and his own right to summon and preside over the prelates of his kingdom to discuss their relations with Rome. Naturally this rapport was reflected in the parlement's jurisprudence.

This tradition of self-government within the Gallican Church reached its apogee in 1438 with the publication of the Pragmatic Sanction of Bourges which forbade the pope to nominate new bishops and archbishops to French dioceses and to extract payment from the French clergy in return. Gallicanism never threatened to become a breakaway movement of the kind that would shortly produce the English Reformation. That was because French kings already possessed a relationship with their church which strengthened their position vis-à-vis the papacy as well as their own authority at home. However they would later decide that the Pragmatic Sanction was not the best means of tightening their grip. This brought them into serious conflict with their loyal *parlementaire* judges, who took a different view of the crown's best interests.

Towards the close of the fifteenth century relations between states changed. Renaissance princes were coming into their own and international rivalry was about to become the chief catalyst for change in Europe. Across the Channel in England Henry Tudor's victory at Bosworth in 1485 enabled him to consolidate his power after the Wars of the Roses. In Spain the union of the kingdoms of Aragon and Castile under Ferdinand and Isabella in 1479 was followed by the conquest of Granada in 1492. On France's eastern and north-eastern frontiers the Emperor Maximilian inherited Franche-Comté and the Netherlands to set alongside his native Habsburg lands in Austria. The expansion of European frontiers threatened a thousand confrontations as one proud dynasty challenged another. Nowhere was this more evident than in Italy, where there was little room for manoeuvre. There, out of the need to maintain a balance of power and to avoid a perpetual state of war, modern diplomacy was born.

This pattern of Italian politics was quickly imitated in the rest of Europe. Yet diplomacy was a surrogate for war and its spread simply demonstrated what a dangerous place Europe was becoming in this age of dynastic competition. No longer so preoccupied with the issue of internal security, great princes were freer to concentrate their attention on their primary ambition, to bequeath an undiminished patrimony to their heirs. By this time the genealogies of ruling families, the foundation stones of dynastic statehood, were so intertwined as to provide endless justification for legally based titles to foreign inheritance. In the case of France the die was cast in 1494 when Charles VIII invaded Lombardy en route to Naples, a kingdom to which he could lay claim through his Angevin forbears.

The military adventurism of Charles, and of his two successors, Louis XII and Francis I, was an updated version of old feudal relationships. As seigneur of all France, the king was the greatest nobleman of all. He shared with his noble cousins the ethos of nobility, service and obligation, and expected them to act accordingly in the interests of the dynasty. Especially in the second generation of the Renaissance power struggle, when the stage was dominated by the giant figures of Francis I, Henry VIII and the emperor, Charles V, the cult of princely personality reached an unprecedented level, inflating personal and dynastic considerations above all others.

The long struggle against the English in the Hundred Years War had made French kings anxious to improve on the hiring of unreliable mercenaries and the summoning of the feudal host. The core of their new royal army consisted of the *compagnies d'ordonnance* and the *maison du roi*. The latter formed the king's personal bodyguard and included the French and Swiss Guards, light cavalry and musketeers. All these cavalry troops had to be noblemen. In addition, there were non-noble infantrymen, volunteers from regions like Gascony and Picardy, and foreign mercenaries from wherever they could be recruited.

The size and therefore the cost of these forces steadily increased. In the mid-fifteenth century the army's core was between 10,000 and 15,000 men, but that number had grown to near 20,000 when Charles VIII crossed the Alps in 1494. Francis I was briefly able to put 70,000 men in the field in the first half of the sixteenth century.[20] The army was also becoming technically more advanced. In particular, the French artillery, with its light and flexible cannon that could fire missiles at the speed of sound, acquired a formidable reputation in siege warfare. But how was all this to be paid for? Besides the cost of the new technology, soldiers had to be paid, provisioned, equipped and billeted, and on occasion transported long distances to foreign fields. When Charles VIII embarked on his Italian adventure in 1494, total military expenditure for that year amounted to 1.5 million *livres*; by 1553 it had reached 12.5 million. Only a few years later, during the reign of the first Bourbon king, Henry IV, it was consuming one third of the king's annual budget.[21]

These figures make very clear what Francis I was quite capable of working out for himself, namely that the old distinction between the monarch's 'ordinary' and 'extraordinary' revenues had become a fiction. The king permanently needed both, then more besides. In 1523 Francis established a new central treasury, the *trésor de l'Epargne*, into which all his revenues were to be paid, whatever their origin. This decision highlighted a growing emphasis upon the king's public nature without in any way diminishing the importance of his personal role. The consequence was that in seeking greater control over the country's resources than had previously been contemplated, French kings were inclined to interpret the public good in terms of their own personal dynastic aspirations, emphasizing their needs rather than their subjects' rights. Since under Francis I Habsburg encirclement posed a real threat to France's security nobody doubted the king's right to demand additional financial sacrifices from his subjects. His public persona as the guardian of his state's integrity was justification for that.

The two mutually incompatible concepts which lay at the heart of French kingship were at last having to be addressed. Was the king the family inheritor of the French state and therefore its effective owner; or was he rather its chief officer, inheriting more obligations than rights? The most dextrous of legal minds sought to reconcile the two positions. To justify Francis I's imposition of additional taxes his chancellor, Poyet, argued that the monarch was the proprietor of the kingdom and therefore entitled to his subjects' property when the need arose. Later in the century another, more famous chancellor, Michel de l'Hôpital, added a gloss to his predecessor's explanation. He maintained that, though kings could indeed claim ownership of the throne without threatening their subjects' property, the latter would not be available for the king's own use but only for the public good. In raising extra revenue the king was invoking the authority of his royal office, not his proprietary rights. By the same token the principle, generally accepted in the late middle ages, that the lands forming the kingdom of France could not be alienated, became law in 1566 with the promulgation of the edict of Moulins. The monarch was deemed to hold his kingdom in trust, an idea given symbolic support by a sixteenth-century amendment to the royal coronation ceremony. When Henry II was crowned in 1547, a ring placed on his finger represented his marriage to the kingdom, and the dowry he received was the inalienable domain of France.[22]

Whatever the concept of kingship, the machinery of government was becoming more complex. Consequently, the sovereign had to rely on the support of increasing numbers of skilled officials. These men were not to be compared, however, to the salaried servants of the modern state. Most had bought their office as an investment for themselves and their families. This practice of venality, which burgeoned from the early sixteenth century, left its mark on the political, social and economic life of France down to the Revolution.

Sale of office had been practised since the fourteenth century. For a long time, though with diminishing enthusiasm, French kings legislated against it until eventually they recognized its potential as a source of revenue. From the reign of Francis I venality became a royal industry. Both existing and newly created administrative, financial and judicial offices were made available for purchase. Furthermore, an office could be sold on during the lifetime of the office-holder as a means of allowing families to hold on to their offices in perpetuity – on condition that the vendor was willing to hand over a proportion of the agreed sum to the royal exchequer. In 1522 Francis I established the *Recette des Parties Casuelles* to receive the increasingly rich pickings available from this source.

As well as helping to keep the king solvent, the presence of these venal officials reinforced the idea that running the government was becoming a professional matter not to be left in the hands of amateurs, however wellborn. At the apex of this new proto-bureaucracy were the royal secretaries of state, whose very title might suggest an obligation to serve the king their master through a less personal relationship. In law, however, office-holders were simply deemed to exercise the king's delegated authority, transmitted to them in the interests of good government. They had no right to qualify how it should be applied. In any case, they remained strongly influenced by the ethos of possessory kingship, a view reflected in their treatment of office as private property, eligible for sale or inheritance.

As the sixteenth century progressed, the dazzling cult of royal personality increasingly threatened to blind observers to the king's wider obligations. There is no better example of this phenomenon than the Field of Cloth of Gold (1520), where Francis I spent 200,000 *livres* that he could ill afford in seeking to impress his rival monarch, Henry VIII. He succeeded so well in alarming the king of England with his magnificence that two years later Henry joined the third great warlord of the day, the Emperor Charles V, in attacking France. This particular set-piece was an expensive failure, but it symbolized the Renaissance princes' world. Their public appearances were contrived and theatrical, spotlighted against sumptuous backcloths, with casts of supporting players whose deference enhanced their easy domination of the stage. The political life of Europe was beginning to throb to the pulse of the royal courts.[23]

By the reign of Francis I the French court had become a formal body governed by a set of rules. It was, however, still peripatetic, moving mainly between Paris and the châteaux of the Loire and the Île de France, a world within a world, reflecting the domestic arrangements of the Valois family as much as the preoccupations of the king of France. The court attracted all the senior members of government but its nucleus remained the king's household, and its fascination lay in the public projection of private concerns. Head of this 'showcase of royal power', as it has been called, was the grand master, one of the great officers of the crown.[24] Through his work with the king on a day to day basis he wielded enormous political influence, though his office never became a formal part of the government establishment. For a significant part of the sixteenth century the office was held by a member of one of France's most ancient noble families, Anne de Montmorency. As constable, another office emanating from the king's household, he would also play a prominent role in the Wars of Religion, the prologue to the triumph of the Bourbon line.

Already the cynosure of all eyes at the heart of their court, the French monarchs of the Renaissance worked assiduously to embellish their self-image. Under the influence of Italian humanism princes were being admonished to pay as much regard to the letters of Homer as to the arms of Achilles. Francis I, a supreme propagandist, knew how to add to his already formidable reputation. He rebuilt the old château of Fontainebleau to provide a fitting setting for his court, his collection of paintings and sculpture, and the library which would later form the nucleus of the Bibliothèque Nationale. With a shrewd appreciation of genius, and of glory by association, the king persuaded Leonardo da Vinci and the Florentine goldsmith, Benvenuto Cellini, to visit him. He failed with similar invitations to Raphael, Michelangelo and Titian, though the latter responded with a portrait of Francis modelled from a royal medallion, which is now in the Louvre. Fontainebleau, adorned with the salamander emblem of the great Valois king, was the prototype for Louis XIV's Versailles, with its sun king imagery. The monarch's Olympian reputation was further enhanced during the reign of Francis's son, Henry II. This time the medium was literary rather than artistic: the leader of the poets of the Pléiade, Ronsard, eulogizing the king as Jupiter's mirror image.[25]

Even when the court was on the move there were excellent opportunities for ostentatious royal display. In progresses through the kingdom, like that undertaken by Francis I between 1531 and 1534 and in the solemn entries to towns the cult of kingship was extravagantly served. Yet amidst all this mundane magnificence with its increasingly classical allusions, the spiritual inheritance of French kingship continued to exercise its dominion over the subjects' imagination. For the king of France, every king of France was *rex christianissimus*, the consecrated inheritor of a God-given kingdom.

That powerful image of kingship was to some extent compromised by the Pragmatic Sanction of Bourges (1438), which, although it confirmed the Gallican Church's independence from Rome, also reiterated its freedom from royal interference in the appointment of its priests and prelates. Louis XI, who ascended the throne in 1461, decided that he could more effectively control the Gallican Church by restoring both papal and royal authority. The Pragmatic Sanction was therefore jettisoned in favour of a Concordat allowing the pope to appoint to major benefices but only on the king's recommendation. This decision, and subsequent royal policy, reflected not only the growing royal cult of personality but also the sovereign's increasing inclination to eschew the limitations imposed by tradition, when his public role as representative of the nation required him to act. The danger was, paradoxically, that such actions might undermine the essential character of the nation's identity, which was of a regime validated by the king's law.

The king and his legal watchdog, the parlement of Paris, fell out badly over this issue. Royal legislation on the issue of Gallicanism was of two kinds: that which fitted readily into traditional French law and jurisprudence, and was supported by broadly based opinion and by the formality and publicity surrounding its registration in the parlement; and that which depended for its efficacy solely upon the royal will. The Pragmatic Sanction itself was the prime example of the former kind. The judges in the parlement sought to counter the second kind of legislation by arguing that laws which had not been sent to the court for registration were of dubious validity and this for very practical reasons. Without a record in the parlement's registers how was the court to know what the law was, and how was that law to be publicised so that everybody else knew it and recognized it as authentic? There was, of course, behind this argument about the mechanics of the legislative process a constitutional issue. What the magistrates in the parlement wanted was *free* registration, implying the right to object when legislation ran contrary to the jurisprudential record enshrined in their registers.

There was nothing revolutionary about this. The great fifteenth-century French humanist and theologian, Jean Gerson, chancellor of the university of Paris, distinguished plainly and frequently between the tyrannical state, which tended to the destruction of all political life, and the monarchical state, which was submitted to such legal constraint that, as he put it, even the king cannot slay any man except by process of law. Almost a century later, in 1519, Claude de Seyssel, a faithful servant of the house of Valois, published his *Great Monarchy of France*, in which he identified three limitations upon the exercise of royal power in France: religion, which was fundamental to the whole concept of kingship and which imposed a set of values and a standard of conduct which could be universally recognized; justice, which required the king to obey the same laws as his subjects; and 'police', by which he meant the law and customs of the kingdom made sacred by their enduring observance, the rights of the various estates and the opinions of royal advisers, princes, prelates and magistrates, representing 'the political intelligence of the community'.[26] Seyssel was writing for the instruction and edification of the young king Francis I. The latter's subsequent relations with the parlement, however, especially over the disputatious issue of Gallicanism, suggest that he had been a somewhat sceptical reader.

Following the example of his predecessor, Louis XI, Francis decided that an alliance between king and pope would leave him in a more powerful position to control the French church than if he continued to support the traditional

Gallican liberties. He therefore agreed a Concordat with the pope, Leo X, at Bologna in 1516 which once again condemned the Pragmatic Sanction and confirmed the exercise of royal control over appointments to major benefices. Both king and pope then looked to the parlement to register the agreement as law. Francis was in no mood for forensic argument, however well founded, and his attitude towards his legal advisers became both threatening and arbitrary. He sent his uncle, René of Savoy, who had no standing in the parlement, to 'assist' in its deliberations and report back on what he heard, with the implication that recalcitrant magistrates would have to be removed. It was therefore a particularly courageous decision of the judges to refuse to register the Concordat, and to reassert the validity of the Pragmatic Sanction. No doubt they were emboldened to do so by the knowledge that their own records allowed them no alternative; and perhaps too by a realization that the king's dismissive attitude towards both the law and the lawyers was dangerously innovative and had to be challenged. In any event, having taken the decision, they enthusiastically and comprehensively condemned the Concordat as being against the honour of God, the liberties of the church, the honour of the king and the wellbeing of his kingdom. They then added insult to injury by criticizing Francis for his habit of appointing bishops from among his cronies at court.

The king's response to this challenge to his authority was to remind the magistrates that there was but one sovereign in France, not a senate as in Venice, and if they did not recognize that fact very swiftly they would suffer in one of two ways. Either they would be forced to leave their permanent home in Paris to follow the king on his peripatetic journeys through his kingdom, or they would be replaced altogether by a new law court sitting in Orléans. The parlement recognized that it was time to compromise, and an extraordinary solution was worked out. The Concordat was duly registered, on 22 March 1518, *de expresso mandato regis iteratis vicibus facto*, a formula intended to indicate that the magistrates had acted under duress. The parlement, however, went further. In its decree of 18 March, indicating the conditions on which the Concordat would be registered, it stipulated that beneficial cases would continue to be judged according to established jurisprudence. It also entered a secret protestation in its registers, reiterating that registration of the Concordat was not the will of the parlement but of the king, and that the parlement intended to continue to pronounce its judgements according to the dictates of the Pragmatic Sanction.

This was a bizarre dénouement to the whole protracted episode. Nobody denied, least of all the royal magistrates, that the king was the sole source of law in the state, and that their opposition was founded upon the need to preserve that authority inviolate. Were it to be exercised as the whim of a strong man, careless of the processes through which it was usually moderated, the king could be portrayed as a despot, and despotism was anathema to the spirit of French kingship. On the other hand, it could be argued that Francis, in his public role as king, was doing what was necessary to strengthen and secure his state. The difficulty was that there was as yet no justification for such action. Francis himself was content with the parlement's registration of the Concordat of Bologna, ambiguous and equivocal though it was, because he recognized the potency of established procedures.[27]

The leading English historian of the reign of Francis I has concluded that the Concordat 'was not just a feather in the king's cap; it was also a jewel added to the papal tiara'.[28] For the currents pulling national churches away from their universal anchorage were quickening. Less than six months before the parlement's registration of the Bologna Concordat, Martin Luther had published his *Ninety-Five Theses* in Wittenberg, and by 1519 Lutheranism had reached Paris. Heresy was in the air, and the fracturing of the universal church would profoundly affect the French state in the dying years of the Valois dynasty.

The greater threat to the Gallican church came not from the German professor of biblical studies in Wittenberg but from much closer to home. From his base in Geneva, the French theologian John Calvin sent scores of his countrymen back into their native land as missionaries on his behalf. From 1555 French Calvinism, or Huguenotism, became a profoundly destabilizing force, influencing Henry's decision to bring an end to the Italian wars which had begun in 1494 when Charles VIII led his troops into Lombardy. But within three months of the signing of the peace of Cateau-Cambrésis (1559) the king was dead, killed in a celebratory joust, and Calvinist infiltration became a torrent. The challenge to the monarchy was apparent but nobody could have anticipated the imminence or the scale of the assault about to be launched upon the French state.

Tipping the Balance

2

France in Peril

The presence of an alternative, subversive creed in France challenged six hundred years of Capetian–Valois rule. For the union of the lawful king and his people under the banner of *rex christianissimus*, had long guaranteed the integrity of the state. Suddenly that idea was under pressure as John Calvin's missionaries made their clandestine way from Geneva into France. Henry II sensed the danger and increased the level of persecution against the Protestants. He established a new tribunal in the parlement of Paris to deal with the heretics, with the menacing title of *chambre ardente* (burning chamber). But it was already too late. Between the signing of the treaty of Cateau-Cambrésis in April 1559 and the king's death in July the first national synod of the French Calvinist churches met in secret, not in some relatively secure provincial hideout but in the rue Visconti in the heart of Paris.[1]

In the aftermath of Henry's unexpected death the scale of the crisis became clearer as the dominant king was replaced by a sixteen-year-old youth, Francis II, who lacked the charisma and energy of his father and grandfather, the latter his namesake, Francis I. In the course of those two previous reigns the nobility had become increasingly uncertain of its role. Both Francis and Henry were strong personalities, unwilling to brook opposition in their quest for additional resources and greater control over their kingdom. But in the absence of a perceived doctrine of state authority it seemed to many that these powerful personalities were pushing their powers beyond traditional limits, and doing so in no other interest but that of their own dynasty: precisely because Francis and Henry were such formidable personalities the institutional aspect of their kingly office faded from view. What the great noble families observed, therefore, was the ever widening gap between the old days of *primus inter pares* and the new world dominated by the strong-arm tactics of Francis and Henry, climaxing in the latter's savage assault upon French Protestantism.

The sudden death of Henry II offered an unexpected opportunity to redress the balance. Francis II was old enough to rule without a regent but too young and immature to know how to handle those powerful elements now seeking to regain the political centre-stage. Below the level of the *grands* a variety of discontented groups would become foot soldiers for one side or the other. The dispossessed were to be found at every level of society. The Italian wars of

Francis I and Henry II coincided with a period of inflation severe enough to merit the description of price revolution. The wars themselves had to be financed by increased taxation. The *taille*, the direct tax exacted from unprivileged groups, rose from four million *livres* towards the end of Francis I's reign to near seven million by the end of Henry's. The ramifications of this fact were felt higher up the social scale, by those impoverished tenants who could not meet their feudal obligations. Some younger sons and lesser noblemen especially found it increasingly difficult to swim against the rising tide of prices. Additionally, the noble class had made unprecedented financial contributions to the war effort in the shape of forced loans and investments in royal schemes which paid no interest because by 1557 Henry II was bankrupt. Cateau-Cambrésis dashed the hopes of the few who dreamt of recouping their financial losses in a successful campaign, though in reality the emergence of a large, professional armed force, paid for by the state, had already underlined the fact that for many noble families, riding to war on the king's behalf was no longer part of their agenda.[2]

What transformed these myriad dissatisfactions into a full-blown crisis was the so-called Reformed Religion (Religion Prétendue Réformée), which from about 1560 acquired the etymologically mysterious name of Huguenotism.[3] In organizational terms Calvinism was always more likely than Lutheranism to take root in France: the latter needed the prince's support whereas Calvinism could operate as a resistance movement against a hostile government. Nevertheless, the process of religious conversion remains ultimately unknowable, despite the accompanying social and sociological indicators. In mid-sixteenth-century France the attractions of Calvin's proposed new world order appealed equally to aspiring newcomers, seeking to climb the social ladder – members of the printing fraternity are the most-quoted example – and to those threatened with the loss of their established place. Both groups might expect their due reward, in the next world if not in this.[4] Huguenotism established itself more firmly in the towns than in the countryside, among the educated elite who were inclined to question the Establishment's conservative values. At the same time the movement acquired rural roots through the conversion of a significant number of nobles. Their traditional seigneurial and client relationships became highly significant, for although the mass of the peasant population remained faithful to the old church, pockets of protestant loyalists especially in the south, reflected the religious convictions of their noble lords. Among the *grands*, converts included some of the greatest names in France, Bourbon, Condé, La Rochefoucauld. Because of the prevailing culture of clientage the effect of these conversions was to cause whole sections of the political establishment to follow suit immediately.

The first of the great nobility to take advantage of Henry II's fatal accident were the Guise clan. Originally from Lorraine they were officially foreign princes though by 1559 they were well established in France and married into

Europe's ruling houses. Francis II's wife, Mary Stuart, later to become more famous across the channel as the Queen of Scots, was the niece of the head of the family, François, duke of Guise. He himself married a granddaughter of the Valois king Louis XII, and in order to cover all eventualities one of his brothers married a daughter of King Henry's influential mistress, Diane of Poitiers. Another brother, Charles, the cardinal of Lorraine, headed the French delegation at the Council of Trent. He and the duke became the real rulers of France when Henry II died. The new king's court was set up in the Louvre where the Guise were already in residence, and their most serious rival for power, the constable, Anne de Montmorency, was forced to hand over his office of grand master to Duke François. The Guise were an ambitious and formidably cohesive family during a time of fractured loyalties. They assembled a vast network of clients and supporters for whom François became a national hero, a distinguished soldier and a brave and chivalrous knight.

This fervent support, however, provoked an equally tribal reaction from those outside the Guise magic circle, particularly from the Huguenots. For apart from family ambition, the chief motivation driving the Guise was their intense loathing of the Protestant movement and their determination to enforce Henry II's legislation against heresy. The man who emerged as leader on the Huguenot side was in many ways the mirror image of François de Guise. He was Louis de Bourbon-Condé, younger brother of the first prince of the blood and king of Navarre, Antoine de Bourbon. The Bourbons believed that the Guise, who were essentially foreigners, had usurped the authority of the crown's natural advisers and even that of the crown itself. Personal jealousies mixed with religious fanaticism presaged a desperate dénouement.

For the second time in the sixteenth century a representative of the house of Bourbon found himself at the sharp end of national politics. Much earlier, following the marriage between Louis IX's son, Robert de Clermont and Beatrice, heiress to the lordship of Bourbon, the family had prospered. Their son became the first duke of Bourbon in 1327; the stronghold over which he presided, the Bourbonnais, was centred on the modern city of Moulins in the heart of France. From this base the family acquired additional lands including, most notably, the county of Vendôme, which lay to the northwest of the River Loire. By the beginning of the sixteenth century the Bourbonnais represented a formidable state within the state, where the duke could dispense justice, levy taxes and raise troops. In a political world still comprehended in terms of suzerainty this was not an unacceptable state of affairs. Although relationships between the Valois kings and their cadet cousins, common heirs of Saint Louis, had never been particularly relaxed neither had they ever descended into open conflict. That situation changed during the reign of Francis I. Initially the king heaped favours upon the Bourbon family. Vendôme was translated into a duchy for a representative of the junior line, and Charles, duke of Bourbon, already at the age of twenty-five a military veteran, was appointed constable of France. He immediately enhanced his reputation by playing a leading role in the battle of Marignano (1515), which re-established a French foothold in northern Italy. His relations with Francis soured, however, after the death of his wife Suzanne in 1521, when the king and his mother, Louise of Savoy, attempted to sequestrate parts of the Bourbon domain which Suzanne, herself a Bourbon, had brought to the marriage. This legal chicanery was trumped by Bourbon's treachery in agreeing to join Henry VIII and the emperor in a triple armed assault upon the French king. That attack failed and Bourbon fled the country. His last, most spectacular action was to lead the imperial troops against Rome in 1527. He was killed in the act of scaling the walls of the Eternal City, and therefore could not be blamed for the infamous sack that followed.

Francis was free to indict the duke before the parlement of Paris, sitting as the court of peers, and there Bourbon became a non-person. Having failed to answer the summons to appear at the bar of the court, an absence easily explained by his death two months earlier, his coat of arms was effaced, his property confiscated and fiefs, which testified both to his own standing and to his obligation to his sovereign, were annexed to the royal domain. The episode captured the changing relationship established during the sixteenth century between the king and his great vassals. In the political drama of Renaissance kingship the constable was simply being written out of the script. For the Bourbon family the effect was to transfer seniority to the dukes of Vendôme, who henceforth became the premier princes of the blood outside the immediate royal family. In 1527 their head was Charles, the governor of Paris and then of Picardy. He was succeeded as duke a decade later by his eldest son, Antoine.

For quite another reason the year 1527 is hugely significant in the history of the house of Bourbon. It marks the marriage between King Francis's sister, Marguerite d'Angoulême, and Henri d'Albret, king of Navarre. The paramount importance of the part played by women at key moments in the dramatic history of the Bourbon dynasty was to be a recurring theme in the years ahead. Marguerite was one of a small group of noblewomen who played a disproportionate enabling role in the early history of French Protestantism. Her influence, however, was more widely felt. She has been called 'the most prominent "career woman" in Europe', because of the range of her political activities.[5] She was an independent and courageous spirit, commanding admiration across Europe for her pilgrimage to Madrid in 1525 in an effort to gain her brother's freedom after his capture at the battle of Pavia. But it was her response to the religious earthquake beginning to fracture the surface of Christendom in the early sixteenth century that characterized her authentic individualism. Marguerite was a humanist who favoured religious reform but saw no reason why it should not come from a multitude of sources.

Though she indignantly insisted on distinguishing between the word of God and heresy, in truth a grey area had invaded the religious spectrum by the 1520s, where moderate reformers met and exchanged ideas with potential radicals. Marguerite d'Angoulême was close to such a group around Guillaume Briçonnet, the bishop of Meaux.

The fact that Marguerite was the king's sister was highly relevant to her interest in religious reform. Francis I, though similarly disinclined to go along with the reactionary attitudes of the Sorbonne and the parlement of Paris, knew as well as his sister that his subjects' religious convictions could not be a matter of personal choice. The stability of his state depended in part upon maintaining the special and intertwined identity of a Christian kingdom and His Most Christian Majesty. Reform of the Gallican Church was one thing – and a Lutheran stimulus to greater piety might be one way to accomplish it – but religious revolution was quite another, and appeared certain to provoke the crown's implacable hostility. The luxury enjoyed by Marguerite of practising a faith described as neither Catholic nor Lutheran but a mixture of the two, would not outlast her generation. Her grandson, the first Bourbon king, Henry IV, would have great difficulty in reconciling the old faith with the militant Protestantism emanating from John Calvin's Geneva.

Following the death of her first husband, the duke of Alençon, Marguerite married the king of Navarre. The title was more impressive than the reality. Most of the kingdom of Navarre lay south of the Pyrenees and had been annexed by King Ferdinand of Aragon in 1512. What remained in the north was mostly the province of Béarn with its capital city of Pau, Henri d'Albret's inheritance through his mother, the countess of Foix. The strategic location of this otherwise insignificant kingdom commanded, however, the attention of both France and Spain, and in Henri it acquired a ruler shrewd enough to exploit its importance in the interests of his house. Henri was also a Gascon, a prototype all-action d'Artagnan figure, who escaped from captivity after the battle of Pavia by means of a convenient rope ladder. His union with the king of France's sister was one of the great social events of the decade.

In religious matters d'Albret was less adventurous than his wife; indeed by the mid-1530s they were coming to literal blows over her support for the unorthodox Gérard Roussel, her chaplain on whose behalf she later used her influence to help him become bishop of Oloron in Béarn. Yet in later life Henri d'Albret reversed the normal human inclination to grow more conservative with age. He allowed Roussel to retain his see even after Marguerite's death and, despite the bishop's continuing difficulties with the Sorbonne, refrained from implementing his own anti-heresy legislation. His calculation appears to have been that political tranquillity mattered more than strict religious conformity, and that therefore a degree of religious tolerance was necessary in his kingdom. When faced with a comparable dilemma, though on a far larger scale, his grandson would follow a similar path.

The king and queen of Navarre had only one child who survived to adulthood. Jeanne d'Albret was born in November 1528 and lived only forty-three years. In that life-span, however, and from a power base far less commanding than that enjoyed by two other contemporary political women, Elizabeth I of England and Catherine de' Medici, she gained a formidable European reputation as a Protestant champion. From the moment of her conversion, on Christmas Day 1560, Jeanne remained a convinced Huguenot for the rest of her life. In defending that position against her many political enemies she revealed great courage but also an intransigence and bitterness which made reconciliation well-nigh impossible. Her mistrustful and generally jaundiced view of the world was the result of personal betrayals: her mother's acquiescence in Francis I's demand that she should be betrothed at the age of twelve to the duke of Clèves (a marriage annulled four years later), and the perennial apostasies and infidelities of her second husband, Antoine de Bourbon, whose most improbable achievement was to father one of France's greatest kings.

Antoine died ten years before his wife, succumbing to wounds received at the siege of Rouen during the first War of Religion. With his marriage to Jeanne, Antoine had shifted his family's power base once more, this time from Vendôme in the heart of Valois France to the Pyrenean kingdom of Navarre. His desire to acquire the title of king through his wife's inheritance is revealing. Antoine was ambitious but lacked the self-belief to make his mark at the highest level. A lifetime spent in conspiring to reunite the divided kingdom of Navarre suited him better than playing for the higher stakes which his proximity to the French throne made possible. Despite his seniority as the first prince of the blood, he put up no opposition to the Guise when they seized power after Henry II's death. Later, when Francis II died, he renounced his superior claim to the regency in favour of the queen mother. His religious vacillation merely symbolized his obsession with acquiring, by whatever means, a kingdom and a title of his own to go with it. The father of France's first Bourbon king was not devoid of personal qualities. He was a fine soldier and a brave one, and he possessed an affability and charm that won him many friends. But he lacked the heroic virtues of magnanimity and imagination which enabled his son to succeed at a far more august level than he had ever contemplated.

In December 1560 Francis II died at the age of sixteen. He was succeeded by his ten-year-old brother, who became Charles IX. Their mother, Henry II's widow Catherine de' Medici, acted quickly to seize the regency, seeking to establish an independent position for the crown between Guise and Bourbon. Catherine remains an enigmatic figure but there is no mystery about the motivation which consistently governed her actions. When her husband died Catherine was left with four sons, three of them under the age of ten, and the fourth, who succeeded his father as Francis II, a weakling of fifteen. Francis was followed as king by his two brothers, Charles IX (1560–74), and Henry III (1574–89). The youngest sibling, the duke of Alençon, died in 1584 of natural causes, an unusual end for a clan leader in this violent age. Catherine devoted all her considerable energies to the task of ensuring that her sons were not deprived of their legitimate inheritance. She had after all spent fourteen years at the court of her father-in-law, Francis I, a hot-house of dynastic self-esteem where the cultivation of the king's personality obscured the significance of the monarchical office. Catherine had greatly admired her father-in-law and was determined that his grandsons should follow in his footsteps. Unfortunately for her ambitions they turned out to be an unprepossessing set of heirs, and her desperate endeavours on their behalf eventually implicated her in one of the bloodiest crimes of the century.

Initially, however, her search for compromise between the Scylla and Charybdis of Bourbon and Guise was statesmanlike. Her moderation was shared by the head of the third great political family, Anne de Montmorency, the aged constable and governor of Languedoc. Montmorency lacked the intellect to become a moderate by conviction, remaining a fervent Catholic though without the Guise fanaticism. Despite the fact that the Guise had deprived him of his influential position of grand master he decided to bury his differences with them in the interests of the Catholic cause. He remained a significant figure in his own right, with an impressive curriculum vitae of service to the crown which included being taken prisoner with Francis I at Pavia in 1525. Unlike the Guise, however, Montmorency's family was deficient in ideological purity. Several of his sons embraced a policy of religious toleration, and his nephew, Admiral Coligny, eventually became the Huguenot leader.

In an era characterized by varying shades of intolerance the only truly tolerant voice, however, was that of Catherine de' Medici's first chancellor, Michel de l'Hôpital. He believed that the king's pre-eminent obligation remained what it had always been, to maintain a regime of peace, order and justice throughout his kingdom. But he also maintained that such a task was no longer viable unless both religions were tolerated. Because the threat posed by the religious schism to the integrity of the state was so powerful and unprecedented, l'Hôpital sought an adequate counterbalance, and found it in the unfettered power of the sovereign. The authority to act without constraint in order to preserve the security and liberty of all the subjects would have seemed arbitrary government if exclusively associated with the king's person; but as a function of the office of kingship the idea presaged the concept of unlimited state power, most strikingly captured later during the Religious Wars in the writings of Jean Bodin, and later still in Thomas Hobbes' *Leviathan*. Before the butchery of the Wars of Religion finally ended, l'Hôpital's radical ideas had become attractively mainstream. In the short term, however, he was a prophet with diminishing honour in his own country, retiring from public life in 1568.[6]

Meanwhile, mutual hatreds easily overcame any instinct for toleration as France was plunged into an episodic Grand Guignol of carnage, decades of slaughter which accounted for the chieftains as well as their followers. Antoine de Bourbon, king of Navarre, died before Rouen in 1562. In the following year François, duke of Guise, was assassinated while besieging Orléans. The septuagenarian constable, Anne de Montmorency, died of wounds received in the battle of Saint-Denis in 1567, and Prince Louis de Bourbon-Condé was murdered after the battle of Jarnac in 1569. All of these deaths pale into insignificance, however, in comparison with the assassination of Admiral Coligny in Paris in 1572. The Massacre of Saint Bartholomew's Day represented the high point of the bloodletting in the Religious Wars, and one of the most shameful episodes in European internecine conflict. Early in the morning of 24 August, Saint Bartholomew's Day, members of the royal guard, led by Henri, duke of Guise, the son of the murdered Duke François, burst in on the Huguenot leader, Gaspard de Coligny, and assassinated him in his residence. This act sparked off a witch hunt leading to the mass murder of Huguenots in Paris and in other cities across the country including Rouen, Lyon, Bordeaux and Toulouse. The effect of the Massacre was not sufficiently traumatic to force the protagonists to disarm, but it did provoke an intellectual backlash which would have important political consequences.

In 1576 a moderate supporter of the Catholic cause, Jean Bodin, published his *Six Books of the Republic*. Bodin's belief, like l'Hôpital's, that the survival of the French state was more important than the victory of one confession over the other led to the elaboration of his famous doctrine of sovereignty, with its emphasis upon the ultimately unchallengeable nature of the power exercised by the sovereign prince. The word 'ultimately' is significant in this context, for in most respects Bodin's work drew heavily on the Scriptures, Greek philosophy, Roman law and the comparative legal history of nations ancient and modern. The attributes of sovereignty according to Bodin – the power to make laws, levy taxes, declare war and peace, coin money and regulate weights and measures – were unremarkable. But with a sharp eye on the contemporary French scene he was prepared to contemplate any additional action that the sovereign might have to take in the interests of his state's security. 'In matters of state', he observed, 'it can be taken as an unquestionable rule that he who is master of the armed forces is master of the state.' Though the patrimonial idea of kingship is not lost in Bodin its impact is greatly reduced. For him the royal domain, once both the heart of the country and the prince's private estate, was the public domain. Bodin took l'Hôpital's thinking to a new level: from that moment it became increasingly clear that behind even the most principled and law-abiding of regimes there lurked the justification for state tyranny.[7]

After the Saint Bartholomew's Day massacre new and revolutionary ideas also began to find their way into the Huguenot vocabulary. It seemed clear that a king who was willing to preside over such slaughter of his subjects must be a tyrant, and killing a tyrant, even though he wore a crown, was justified in the sight of God. The mystique and cult of personal kingship was thus stripped away, leaving the crown's Protestant subjects to ponder where, as French men and women, their loyalty now lay. They found their answer in distinguishing between a patriotic attachment to France and its people, and an implacable hostility to tyranny. The most famous statement of their position was the pamphlet of 1579, the *Vindiciae contra tyrannos*. Among the contradictions and illogicalities which abound in the argument it is possible to glimpse a decisive shift in the balance between prince and subject. The state, so the argument ran, is not the ruler's patrimony; it was originally established by the community for its own good, and government exists simply to implement the community's wishes. The crown is not, therefore, an inherited piece of personal property like other parts of Valois real estate; it is an office, legitimately exercised by kings in the ruling line only so long as they eschew tyranny. The conclusion reached by the author of the *Vindiciae* on the issue of princely power was diametrically opposed to those of l'Hôpital and Bodin. But all three commentators were united in interpreting kingship primarily as an office. Whether that evolving view would help to restore the dignity and integrity of the French state would depend on the actions of the kings themselves.

Since 1562 the periodic conflict had raged over the whole country, but following the Saint Bartholomew's Day massacre the focus of military operations moved south of the River Loire. There were new leaders in the field too. Henri, duke of Guise succeeded his father as the head of the ultra-Catholic party; the duke of Montmorency-Damville, son of the long-lived constable, Anne de Montmorency, followed his father as governor of Languedoc, inheriting, too, a more moderate stance towards his Huguenot opponents; and in 1569, upon the death of Louis de Bourbon-Condé, his fifteen-year-old son, Henri, and the sixteen-year-old son of Jeanne d'Albret, Henri, prince of Navarre, became the joint titular chiefs of the Huguenot forces. The zealots on each side continued to be sustained by the emotions of religious triumphalism. For their leaders, however, whatever the extent of their own commitment, there was a second preoccupation. Related to each other by blood or marriage they were party to a family quarrel over a rich inheritance. Beyond their allegiance to Rome or Geneva lay the troublesome question of the succession to the throne of Saint Louis.

Henri of Navarre understood this very well. So indeed did his mother, whose unshakeable loyalty to the Huguenot cause was matched by her determination to defend her son's position of premier prince of the blood. Jeanne shared the fierce maternal feelings of her arch-enemy, Catherine de' Medici. She was eventually persuaded, therefore, to agree to the queen mother's suggestion that, in the interests of religious harmony, her son should marry Catherine's daughter, Marguerite de Valois. The idea of a mixed Catholic–Huguenot wedding, to be celebrated in the 'great temple' of Notre Dame, was not a prospect to which the queen of Navarre looked forward, but she appreciated that it might well be to her son's political advantage.[8] In fact, she did not live to witness the wedding – or the fateful repercussions that followed six days later on Saint Bartholomew's Day. Jeanne d'Albret died just over two months earlier in Paris, on 9 June 1572.

Living under duress at the court of Charles IX Henri was persuaded, not for the last time, to renounce his Protestant faith. For some years he remained in gilded captivity, well aware that political anonymity was the price of his survival. His situation became even more vulnerable in 1574 with the death of Charles IX, still only a young man of twenty-three, and the succession of his brother as Henry III. At that moment, according to the law of succession, only the youngest son of Henry II and Catherine, François, now duke of Anjou, stood between Henri of Navarre and the French crown.

Two years later Henri succeeded in fleeing the royal court, and set out to re-establish his political identity. He found himself in a country on the brink of disintegration. The Protestants had remained strong in the South and West despite the massacre. In 1573 Charles IX had failed to take the Huguenot seaport fortress of La Rochelle, and in Languedoc both Montaubon and Nîmes strengthened their semi-independent Protestant status. The position of La Rochelle posed a particular threat to the French government. Huguenot privateers operating out of La Rochelle helped to finance the costs of the conflict by their raids on Catholic shipping, forging a formidable partnership with the Protestant Dutch Sea Beggars.[9] Indeed, the danger of France becoming the victim of international predators became a serious prospect. Early in 1576 twenty-five thousand German cavalry from the Calvinist Palatinate invaded eastern France in support of their Protestant co-religionists, while the already dire situation was made even more perilous by the bizarre behaviour of the latest heir to the throne, François, the new duke of Anjou. Sustained by delusions of grandeur he first took up the Huguenot cause in France before accepting an invitation from William of Orange to become the defender of the liberties of the Netherlands against the tyranny of the Spaniards and their allies. His final *folie des grandeurs* was to imagine that Elizabeth I of England might be persuaded to marry him.

After making good his escape from Paris Henri of Navarre reverted to the Protestant faith and headed for his family lands in Béarn. What he discovered in the south and south west of the kingdom was virtually a Huguenot state, the United Provinces of the Midi. This Protestant republic employed the traditional administrative organization of towns, villages and estates, newly reinvigorated by the doctrine of Calvinism and given military backing by a Protector whose authority would nevertheless be subject to that of a General Assembly. In July 1574, while Navarre was still a comfortable captive at the French court, the role of 'head and general of the Reformed churches of France' was bestowed upon Henri de Bourbon-Condé, son of the victim of Jarnac. Condé, who was Henri of Navarre's first cousin, had inherited all his father's devotion to the Huguenot cause, and was ready to sacrifice the peace and even the integrity of the kingdom in the pursuit of a Protestant victory. By the time that Henri of Navarre had re-established himself in Béarn, this policy of adamantine exclusivity was being mirrored in the north of the country where the Catholic League was in the process of being formed.

This movement began in Picardy in 1576 and rapidly spread through the kingdom. Its godfather was Henri, duke of Guise, who was quick to seize the opportunity to put himself at the head of an intransigent Catholic party. One of the compelling features of this period of civil war was the generational replication of its commanders. Henri de Guise emerged as heir to his assassinated father, François, in the leadership of the Catholic cause in much the same way as the Huguenot Condé had succeeded his father. Born only two years apart they were also near contemporaries of the king, Henry III, whom they both held in contempt. All three would die in 1588, as the unsurpassed savagery of the time reached its climactic dénouement. Henri of Navarre had more in common with another second-generation chieftain, the Catholic governor of Languedoc, Henri de Montmorency-Damville, who shared Navarre's preference for reconciliation. Damville followed Condé and preceded Navarre as protector of the Protestant churches in the Midi. The king of Navarre had his own agenda, of course, instilled into him by his mother. In a letter written in 1576 he remarked that 'after the person of my lord the king and Monsieur his brother, I have a greater interest than anyone else in the preservation and restoration of the realm'.[10]

By the early 1580s the very survival of the kingdom seemed questionable. Warlords controlled their territories as the great feudatories of earlier generations had done, and even the royal family threatened to implode as Anjou's machinations risked provoking the formidable king of Spain into a declaration of war. France was in danger of separating into a loose federation of mutually hostile zealots under the nominal authority of a discredited regime. Anjou's death in June 1584 at least halted a disastrous foreign enterprise. For many, however, it also threatened a calamity of seismic proportions, for it made Henri, the Protestant king of Navarre, heir to the Capetian throne of France.

It is impossible to overstate how close France would come to dissolution in the years that followed, as a tragedy of Shakespearean proportions was played out between mutually irreconcilable forces. In the semi-detached south, Navarre found himself leading a political organization which in many respects imitated that of the republican rebels in the Spanish Netherlands, though he himself remained single-minded in his determination to safeguard that fragile line of inheritance which linked him to Saint Louis. In the north, the position of the king, Henry III, who was destined to be the last of the Valois, reflected that of his Bourbon cousin. Though staunchly Catholic, he shared Navarre's belief in the ineluctable rights of hereditary succession. Also like Navarre he depended on supporters whose interests did not coincide with his own. Chief among them was the party of Henri, duke of Guise, the scion of a brave and chivalrous yet ultimately fanatical family, that threatened briefly and bloodily to change forever the character of the French monarchy.

The chosen vehicle for the delivery of Guise ambitions was the Catholic League. The avowed intention of this association was to remove Henri of Navarre from his position as heir to the throne, substituting his uncle, the Cardinal of Bourbon, the next in line. How far the Guise clan itself, with its impressive genealogy reaching back to Charlemagne, also harboured designs on the throne, remains unclear. What is certain, however, is that the League's religious fanaticism released politically destabilizing forces which threatened not only the Protestant heir to the throne but also its zealously Catholic incumbent. When Henry III moved elements of the royal army into Paris in May 1588 to secure his authority against Henri of Guise, the capital's de facto rulers, later to be known as the Committee of the Sixteen, organized the erection of street barricades against them.[11] This was the first example of what would become a popular Parisian pastime, invariably signalling the breakdown of political authority, and in this first instance marking a further dramatic stripping away of the mystique of monarchy.

One of France's leading historians has recently drawn attention to the parallel between the aspirations of the Catholic League and the events which took place in England a hundred years later leading to the so-called Glorious Revolution.[12] In both countries an attempt was made to effect a minimal change in the royal line of succession in order to exclude a rightful heir who espoused the wrong religion. Had the Catholic League succeeded in substituting the Cardinal of Bourbon for Henri of Navarre, the revolution in France would have been no less dramatic and far-reaching than that presided over by William of Orange a century later. Not that it was at all surprising that the League should have put so much emphasis upon the king's Catholicity, for the continuing authority of the Capetian and Valois dynasties had been heavily dependent upon their title of *rex christianissimus*. The coronation service in Reims Cathedral centred upon the new king's consecration with Holy Oil, would have been a meaningless ritual for a Huguenot, particularly since in the course of that ritual he would also be required to swear to defend the Catholic faith and protect the church's possessions.

Yet it was no less difficult to contemplate the destruction of the Salic Law. Although there was more than a hint of *post hoc ergo propter hoc* about it, the law had nevertheless provided a mechanism for guaranteeing centuries of lawful royal succession in France, in contradistinction to the English experience, as French commentators were happy to observe. (For the French, what happened in England in 1688 would be merely the latest chapter in an all too familiar story.) In 1588, however, there was a strong possibility that the French political nation would begin to read from the same text as the English. For the first time, two fundamental aspects of the French monarchical tradition appeared to be mutually exclusive: one would turn out to be less fundamental than the other, with enormous implications for the monarchy's future.

The scenario offered by the Guisards was an attempt to restore more than the nation's religious homogeneity. It harked back to a quasi-feudal, decentralized world where the old nobility of the sword held sway. The Guise family had already made a good start in this direction, Duke Henri and his brother, the duke of Mayenne, being governors of Champagne and Burgundy respectively, and their cousin, the duke of Mercoeur, governor of Brittany. The return to power of the *grands* would be at the expense of the administrative and legal office-holders who formed the new professional nobility. The king's right to tax his subjects beyond the traditional limits would also be challenged. The estates general, meeting every third year, would authorize any necessary taxation, and by their permanent existence inhibit the dangerous growth of central government power. Finally, the pope would reassert his ultramontane authority over a French church deprived of its tradition of Gallican independence.[13]

Although these proposals fell short of constituting a revolutionary – or reactionary – programme, they did further undermine the crown's already shaky political authority. And that authority was increasingly scorned by Parisian demagogues during the rule of the Sixteen, who in the name of the Catholic religion began to contemplate tyrannicide just as Huguenot writers had done in the aftermath of the Saint Bartholomew's Day massacre. In addition, because the crown was traditionally the sole focusing lens for the expression of patriotic sentiment, the extremists on both sides were forced to adopt an anti-patriotic stance in support of their creed. Thus the *Vindiciae contra tyrannos* answered in the affirmative the question of whether foreign princes were bound to intervene in defence of their oppressed Protestant brethren in France; while Parisian League propaganda demanded rhetorically whether it was not better to be a Spaniard than a Huguenot.[14]

The king of Navarre instinctively understood the need to play the patriotic card. His preference, and initially Henry III's, was to join forces against the Guise. When the French king was forced into an unwilling alliance with the Catholic League by the treaty of Nemours (1585), Navarre responded by pledging his opposition to the treaty, calling it a peace with the House of Lorraine at the expense of the House of France, and asking for the support of 'all true Frenchmen without regard to religion, since at this time it is a question of the defence of the state against the usurpation of foreigners'.[15] This was an observation of great significance for the future. For the implication was clear, that it was the supreme responsibility of the rightful inheritor of the crown, a right acquired without regard to religious conviction, to lead the national effort to secure the integrity of the French state. The idea of the king as the proprietor of the land, the heir to the family fortune, was thereby much diminished. Indeed, the future Henry IV's accession by virtue of the Salic Law, coupled with the need to mend the deep divisions brought about by the Wars of Religion, would just about tip the scales. Subsequently, French kingship would be perceived in the last resort as a public office, though one still entirely dependent upon personal relationships.

That accession was precipitated by further acts of personal savagery and fanaticism which overwhelmed two of the three leading players. First, the king, determined to rid himself of the charismatic and dangerously popular leader of the League, the duke of Guise, had him and his brother, the Cardinal of Lorraine, assassinated in December 1588. That act led to the rapprochement with Navarre that Henry III had long favoured but had been prevented from achieving because of the power of the Guise and the Catholic League. In April 1589 the two men agreed a truce and aimed their combined forces towards Paris. Several months later a twenty-two-year-old Dominican friar, Jacques Clément, himself a victim of the League's virulent propaganda, made his unique mark on French history by assassinating the last Valois king. It was the ultimate sign that the mystique of kingship, which had helped to preserve all Henry's predecessors from a like fate, had lost its potency. That was not a comfortable thought for Henri de Bourbon, king of Navarre, who at the moment of his predecessor's death on 2 August 1589, by virtue of the Salic Law, became King Henry IV of France.

3

Henry IV

FOUNDING FATHER: A REAL BÉARNAIS

The future Henry IV was born in the château of Pau in December 1553, heir
to an independent kingdom in the shadow of the Pyrenees, far away from the
traditional nexus of French royal power between the Île de France and the Loire.
He was a Gascon, a real Béarnais, as his deliriously happy grandfather, Henri
d'Albret, put it on the morning of his birth.[1] Henri spent most of his first eight
years at home in the countryside of his native south west, untouched by the
royal court and the affectations of courtly life. In this relatively poor but fiercely
proud region he began to acquire characteristics traditionally associated with
Gascony: an air of hail-fellow-well-met; and a paradoxical tendency to be both
boastful and parsimonious. When he came to Paris, however, he showed no signs
of an inferiority complex. On the contrary, his Gascon wit proved a rapier in his
hand, and his aura of self-confidence was as discernible as his lingering odour
of garlic. He was precocious, quick-witted and remarkably relaxed, considering
the dangerous future he faced.

The single most important fact about his childhood was that it coincided with
the establishment of French Calvinism in the south west. His view of the world
and of his role in it, the significance of his reign, even the nature of his death,
are all related to that seminal influence. Jeanne d'Albret embraced Huguenotism
with all the fervour of a convert, while her husband's flirtations with the reformed
religion were prompted by self-interest alone. The impressionable young Henri
was more influenced by his mother's conviction, but the reality of his situation
gradually cautioned him against pursuing a policy of religious exclusivity. In 1562
he found himself at the royal court, separated from his mother and forced by his
capricious father to abjure his Protestantism. This first abjuration was followed
by a number of others. Between 1563 and 1572 he resumed his Huguenot
faith; reverted to Catholicism after the massacre of Saint Bartholomew's Day;
rediscovered his Protestantism after escaping from the court in 1576; and finally,
and most famously, he embraced the old religion as King Henry IV in 1593. It
might well be assumed from the evidence of this record that Henri was a serial

opportunist who had inherited his father's vacillating character. Antoine de Bourbon's reputation had been forever damaged by the single word, *ondoyant*, which the great essayist Michel de Montaigne used to define his character. In Henri's case, however, the changeability was all on the surface. There was an underlying certitude which he owed to his mother, acquired not from her belief in the rightness of the Protestant cause, but from her determination that he should realize his inherited destiny. This conviction was a compass guiding him through dangerous times and pointing him, in the words of his most recent biographer, towards 'une vision de la France'.[2] It complemented his personal courage, and was reflected in the daunting power of his personality. None of his contemporaries could have saved France, and none of his royal successors had to work so hard to maintain their state.

Henri's pursuit of women was, in a minor key, the second recurring theme of his life. In this too he was his father's son, but he had more to lose than Antoine, and on occasion his inability to master his feelings and cope with the sexual politics involved left him more politically vulnerable than he should have allowed himself to be. But those problems lay in the future. In 1572 the young man in love with life was making the best of his situation as a privileged prisoner at the royal court, newly married to the king's sister and reconverted to the Catholic faith. There he encountered the first in a long line of recorded mistresses, Charlotte de Sauve, who also included among her lovers the king's youngest brother, the duke of Alençon, and Henri, duke of Guise, Navarre's former classmate and leader of the extreme Catholic party. No doubt this example of ecumenism contributed to Henri's increasingly pragmatic view of the world. It was only after his escape from the court, however, that his pragmatism began to reveal itself as more statesmanlike than selfish, less *ondoyant* than *politique*.

When Navarre successfully fled Paris in 1576 in order to re-establish his own political identity, the *Politique* party did not yet exist. The hostility to religious fanaticism which would provide the new group's *raison d'être* was, however, beginning to assert itself. Both L'Hôpital and Bodin were powerful advocates of the *politique* position, as were countless townspeople and lesser nobility who sought peace for their families and security for their property. There were those too who believed that the Massacre of Saint Bartholomew's Day, and the near-permanent condition of civil war which it symbolized, blackened the name of France among civilized nations.[3] It gradually became clear that Henri of Navarre shared these sentiments.

His escape from Paris was quite lacking in Gascon bravura. Indeed, it is quite possible that the whole episode was stage-managed by the queen mother herself. To the surprise of many on the Huguenot side it was not until four months later, at Niort near La Rochelle in June 1576, that Henri formally renounced his Catholicism and regained his leading position in the Protestant camp. He was finally pushed into that decision by his sister, Catherine, who had inherited all her mother's religious enthusiasm. But the true reason for his prevarication was clear to his closest comrades, both Catholic and Huguenot. His intention was to uncouple religious conviction from personal relationships, assuring one of his Catholic lieutenants in a memorable phrase that 'those who unswervingly follow their conscience are of my religion, as I am of all those who are brave and virtuous'.[4]

Henri headed to the south west, first to Guyenne where he had been confirmed as governor in the Peace of Monsieur in May 1576, before travelling home to Béarn. The Peace of Monsieur was a milestone on the road to toleration along which Henri of Navarre was embarked. Its terms, embodied in the edict of Beaulieu, stipulated that the Protestants would be granted eight so-called places of security across the south, and would be free to worship in any town outside Paris. Most significant was Henry III's public condemnation of the 'disorders and outrages committed on 24th August and days following at Paris and in other cities and places of our realm'.[5] This virtually unheard of *mea culpa* was, however, more a recognition of the limits of intolerance than a plea for religious toleration. Henri quickly came to appreciate that fact in seeking to re-establish his credentials as the broadminded champion of the Huguenot party.

Though willing to become the *ex officio* leader of the reformed churches throughout the south, Henri of Navarre operated in a relatively relaxed environment, far from the febrile atmosphere of Paris. But he was unhappy both with the quasi-republican sentiments adopted in the so-called United Provinces of the Midi, from Guyenne and Gascony to Languedoc and Provence, and with Guise's 1576 Catholic League formula which envisaged a role for the estates general in restricting royal authority. Despite his easy hedonism – or perhaps because of it since there was no room in his make-up for fanaticism, Henri being a Huguenot by inheritance rather than conviction – he believed that the future viability of the kingdom depended not on the Reformation principle of *cuius regio eius religio* but on a secular union between king and people. Though not a disinterested view, this degree of lateral thinking identified the king of Navarre as an exceptional product of his turbulent age.

Meanwhile, he continued to lead his troops with bravery and élan – and with the remarkable good fortune to remain unscathed – through the recurring savageries of the civil wars. In 1580 he stormed Cahors in the Midi after four days of intense close combat. Seven years later he crushed the royal army commanded by the duke of Joyeuse, who was killed in the battle, at Coutras near Bordeaux. At that moment the opportunity presented itself for Navarre to press home his advantage. Not for the only time in his life, however, private passion got the better of public obligation, and he returned post-haste to Béarn to lay the captured Catholic standards at the feet of his latest mistress, Diane d'Andoins, the countess of Guiche and Gramont. His companion in arms, the future duke of Sully, remarked resignedly, that 'all the advantage of so famous a victory floated away like smoke on the wind'.[6] The romantic countess, who preferred to be known as Corisande, a name borrowed from a manual of courtly love, was also the highly intelligent friend of Michel de Montaigne. As a member of the old faith she shared Henri's view that personal relationships should not be dictated by religious convictions. *La belle Corisande* was the only intellectual soul mate of Henri's life, but even their unique relationship could not survive his dedicated promiscuity. They drifted apart during the year before Clément's dagger transformed the king of Navarre into the king of France.

Henry now found himself in a situation which none of his predecessors had faced. The crown's twin supports, its Catholicity and its legitimacy by right of lawful succession, were not both available to him at the moment of his accession. His subjects had therefore to make a choice, previously unthinkable, between the religion of Saint Louis and the Salic Law by which all the successors of that revered king had inherited the throne. His crusade to persuade his countrymen and women of the rightness of his cause changed for ever the nature of the French monarchy. For in rejecting the primacy of the divine order Henry was opting, under the aegis of man-made law, to bring his kingdom down to earth and to unify it by means of the secular doctrine of patriotism.

He was not alone in his aspirations. Astute observers of the scene realized that France was on the verge of disintegrating and that only wholehearted commitment to the new king could save it. As invariably has been the case, patriotism thrived when the enemy was at the gate. In this instance the enemy was Spain, His Catholic Majesty united with the fanatical Leaguers who would sacrifice a united kingdom for religious uniformity. Patriotic pamphleteers allowed their imaginations to explore the effects of a Spanish takeover. France would become but one more colony, with the country's youth shipped to the New World to mine the silver on which Spain's empire was built.[7] Against such a background Henri of Navarre had no difficulty in projecting himself as the champion of the embattled French nation, sharing with his subjects a common loyalty and sense of identity. He had another fight on his hands too, against another colonial power, the papacy. In March 1591 Pope Gregory XIV published a bull annulling Henry's claim to the throne and excommunicating any Frenchman who continued to support him. The parlement of Paris sitting in Tours, and detached from a minority of its members in the capital who remained supporters of the Catholic League, reacted as true patriots against this attempt by the universal church to discount the long Gallican tradition of independence. It enthusiastically condemned the papal bull as 'null, abusive, seditious, damnable, full of impiety and deception, contrary to the holy decrees, rights, privileges and liberties of the Gallican church'.[8] It was clear that Henry IV was not without formidable allies in his efforts to persuade his compatriots that the unity of the state must not depend exclusively upon religious conformity, however important a factor religion remained in state affairs.

Of course it was still of paramount importance. Indeed, that was a measure of the significance of Henry's claim to exercise legitimate power without the blessing of the Catholic Church. He recognized that in due course it would be politic for him to re-embrace the old religion in order finally to reunite the country. It was not a question of opportunism versus conviction. Henry's primary objective had long been to rally the whole country to the French cause, and that meant reconciling the two religions and subordinating both of them to the national interest. By doing that he made a unique contribution to the history of the French state, redefining its identity in terms of the union between king and people. The perception of the sovereign as the guardian rather than the owner of his state never became a transparent part of Bourbon political theory, yet from the reign of Henry IV it provided the best means of understanding Bourbon politics.

In July 1593 therefore the king formally abjured his Huguenot faith in the basilica of Saint-Denis, the last resting place of the kings of France. Some seven months later his belated coronation took place amid the Gothic splendour of the cathedral of Notre Dame at Chartres. Reims, the traditional venue for this solemn, and highly symbolic ceremony, was still in Guise hands, as was the chief prize of Paris itself. But the opposition was crumbling as more and more influential figures settled for the restoration of a pacific regime under the newly crowned, Most Christian Henry IV. Among them was the governor of Paris, the count of Brissac, who plotted the manner in which Henry would regain his capital. The plan worked near perfectly from the moment, six o'clock in the morning of 22 March 1594, when the king arrived at the Porte Neuve, the city gate guarding the southern flank of the Louvre, where the Saint Bartholomew's Day Massacre had been hatched over twenty years before. By then his troops had already secured the key areas of the capital so there was time for a decorous little ceremony at which Brissac presented a municipal sash to the king, and the mayor and aldermen handed over the keys of the city. Then Henry made his way on horseback through an increasingly noisy and enthusiastic crowd along the great sixteenth-century thoroughfare of the rue Saint-Honoré, eventually sweeping south across the Notre Dame bridge onto the Île de la Cité. At eight o'clock he entered the great cathedral where he heard mass and listened to the celebratory *Te Deum*.[9] There is no evidence that Henry ever uttered the *bon mot* that Paris was worth a mass. In fact the sentiment behind that phrase does him less than justice. As he left Notre Dame for the Louvre on that showery spring morning he might have harboured the far more worthy thought that the united kingdom of France was indeed worth a mass.

For the example of patriotism offered by the king of France and Navarre to his fellow countrymen was *sans pareil*. Ultimately it would cost him his life and immortalize his reputation. Long before his triumphant entry into Paris he had been at pains to play down the animosity between Frenchmen committed to opposing sides in the civil wars. A pamphlet celebrating Henry's famous victory on the field of Coutras alleged that the king of Navarre, though commanding superior forces, had refused to join battle earlier because he was unwilling to oppose the king, Henry III, directly. It was after this battle that stories began to circulate of Navarre's amiability towards his enemies, of his determination to treat them as Frenchmen first, whatever their religious and political affiliations. By the same token he marked his pacific conquest of Paris with a general amnesty and a chivalrous farewell to the Spanish troops who had been stationed there in support of the Leaguers.

The true measure of Henry's desire for inclusiveness would ultimately depend, however, on how he handled the Huguenot problem. His definitive response came in April 1598 with the publication of the edict of Nantes. Historians have been inclined to concentrate more on the revocation of this edict almost a century later than upon its original enactment. This is surprising, since the edict of Nantes is one of the landmark documents of European history. For the previous forty years French politics had been dominated by mutually self-righteous hatreds, a characteristic state of affairs in Europe at large, and one which still resonates four hundred years later. Nantes was imperfect in many respects. It was an edict cobbled together from earlier pieces of legislation and shaped by the needs of the moment. Its significance was not that it heralded a regime of toleration in France, but that it brought peace.[10]

At this critical juncture the king raised statesmanship to a new level. He sought the universal acceptance of his edict through free registration in the parlements, and by dint of his personal and oratorical powers persuaded a sceptical magistrature to fall into line. The bloody events of 1588 had left his chief court, the parlement of Paris, divided between its League supporters who remained in the capital, and Henry III loyalists who defected to Tours. The latter had twice proclaimed their support for Henry IV, once in 1591 against papal intervention, and again in 1593 when faced with the prospect of a Spanish-backed ruler, the daughter of the king of Spain, emerging as the successor to the murdered king. On this second occasion, in one of the parlement's most celebrated sessions, the future keeper of the seals under Henry IV, Guillaume du Vair, dramatically challenged his fellow judges to pronounce on whether the Salic Law – the adornment of the kingdom and the guarantee of its security – should be preserved, or sacrificed to the ambitions of a foreign ruler with the inevitable loss of national identity and independence. 'Therefore arouse yourselves, Sirs, and display today the authority of the laws which are in your keeping! For if this evil admits of any remedy, you alone can provide it!' His colleagues were persuaded, and the legitimacy of Henry IV's claim to the throne reinforced. Shortly afterwards the divided court was reunited in the parlement's traditional home on the Île de la Cité.[11]

Nevertheless, when it came to registering the edict of Nantes early in 1599, the parlement, initially at least, was less supportive. Its preference was to draw up remonstrances indicating its objections to the proposed legislation. Henry reacted by summoning the magistrates *en bloc* to his palace, the Louvre, where in a memorable address he both reassured and overawed them:

> You see me in my study, where I have come to speak to you not in my royal garb or with sword and cloak, like my predecessors, nor like a prince speaking to foreign ambassadors, but like the father of a family speaking informally to his children. What I want to say is that I wish you to verify the edict granted to the Protestants ... You ought to obey me if only because of my position, and the obligation which is shared by my subjects and particularly by you of my Parlement ... I am now king, and speak as king. I wish to be obeyed ... Yield up to my entreaties what you would not have given up by threats, for you will have none from me. Do what I require of you at once, I beg you; you will be doing it not only for me, but for the sake of peace.

One by one the other parlements of the realm yielded to royal pressure, exerted with more or less fierceness according to the stubbornness of the opposition. Henry's speech to the judges representing the parlement of Toulouse encapsulated his vision of the future, set out in language which brooked no opposition. It deserves to be quoted at length:

> It is strange that you cannot cast out your ill-will. I see that you still have Spanish notions in your bellies. Who, then, can believe that those who have exposed their life, property and honour for the defence and preservation of this state are not worthy of honourable public posts in it? ... But those who have done their very best to wreck the state are to be seen as good Frenchmen, worthy of such posts! I am not blind; I see through all this, and wish that those of the [Protestant] Religion should be able to live at peace in my realm and be eligible for all posts, not because they are Protestants, but because they have faithfully served me and the French crown. I wish to be obeyed, and that my edict shall be published and implemented throughout my kingdom. It is high time that all of us, drunk with war, sobered up.[12]

In legislating for the coexistence of two religions the edict of Nantes ineluctably defined the French state as essentially secular, in defiance both of France's previous history and of the Reformation doctrine of *cuius regio eius religio*. It proclaimed the credo of Henry IV that loyalty to the king, not as God's representative on earth but as the rightful inheritor and custodian of the kingdom of France, was the subjects' chief and patriotic obligation. Therefore, in order to foster that universal sense of commitment, it decreed that Huguenots holding judicial or financial office in one of the great institutions of state should continue to do so, with recourse to the king's council if their rights were denied; and that no distinctions should be made on religious grounds when admitting scholars to schools and universities, or the sick and the poor to hospitals and alms houses. In a phrase which affirms the greatness of his vision Henry exhorted all his subjects to live together in peace, as brothers, friends and fellow-citizens.[13] This was a rallying call to trouble many unquiet consciences then and thereafter.

In order to ease the edict's passage, however, Henry also issued two *brevets*, or letters of grace, providing money for the payment of Protestant pastors, and for the garrisoning of those towns in the possession of the Huguenots in August 1597, which they were to be allowed to hold for a further eight years. This was clearly unfinished business to which sooner or later Henry or his successors would have to return.

Though the old feudal ties, which had once provided the effective spine of state and society, had lost their original *raison d'être*, they continued in changed form to shape all the important political connections. And, despite Henry's state revolution, they remained highly personal: family networks built on carefully calculated marriage contracts; the territorial community based on the seigneury; the relationships between patron and client which updated the traditional hierarchical bonds uniting the old nobility.[14] None of them implied the individual subject's prior obligation to serve the state. That concept could only come about with the passage of time and changing circumstances. Henry nevertheless appreciated that the trauma of the Religious Wars had precluded the restoration of the status quo. It was necessary to provide his subjects with alternative means to achieve a sense of security and self worth, and at the same time prevent the return of anarchy. The architect of this initial attempt at Bourbon state building was Maximilien de Béthune, who in 1606 became the duke of Sully. The partnership of Henry and Sully was the prototype for a series of later such alliances between kings and ministers. Sully joined the king of Navarre as a Protestant teenager, fought alongside him at Arques (1589) and Ivry (1590), and in 1594, the year of Henry's victorious re-entry into his capital, graduated to the king's council. In 1599 this lifelong Huguenot became *surintendant des finances* and remained the king's chief minister until Henry's death in 1610.

With the signing of the treaty of Vervins (1598), ending the war with Spain which Henry had formally declared at the beginning of 1595, Sully was free to concentrate on the twin tasks of replenishing the state's coffers and reinforcing its authority. Not all his policies were innovative. His reduction of the *taille*, for example, at a time of increasing national prosperity following the stagnation of the civil war years, encouraged further economic growth and resulted in improved indirect tax returns. More ambitious, though not unprecedented, was his attempt to spread the tentacles of central government into the *pays d'états* by establishing fiscal districts known as *élections*, directly under the control of the crown. But by far the most significant and longlasting of his reforms was the introduction in 1604 of a new annual levy, the so-called *paulette*. This tax, which owed its name to the royal secretary originally responsible for its collection, was in fact a modification of existing arrangements for the sale of judicial and financial offices. It allowed office-holders to pass on their office to their heirs on condition of paying an annual sum to the crown equal to one-sixtieth of the office's value.[15] This was an astute move welcomed on both sides: by the king because, thanks to the ramshackle fiscal system, he always needed the money; and by the office-holders who wanted the associated security and prestige to be part of their family's heritage. But the *paulette* had implications extending far beyond the financial sphere. It gave the king a set of natural allies in high places, men who were satisfied that the sovereign would not interfere with their public role so long as they paid their yearly tax. This was reassuring for the sovereign too. Henry IV remembered how the duke of Guise had been able to buttress his support by the careful distribution of key offices, a strategy which the *paulette* would render otiose to future rivals.

The annual levy also provided the state with a permanent workforce of professionals capable of managing a complex organization with a competence undreamt of by their less qualified predecessors. At the upper end of this office-holding spectrum were posts bestowing nobility, and a distinction developed between the old aristocracy and the new, between the *noblesse d'épée* and the *noblesse de robe*. The lawyers who formed the core of this new nobility were servants of the state, just as their feudal forerunners had been counsellors to the king. The parallels between the two groups are a warning against the dangerous assumption that robe and sword represented altogether different species. The fact of noble status was always more important than its origins. Besides, many members of the *noblesse de robe* came from old noble stock and, conversely, many non-robe noblemen were related to one of the growing number of legal dynasties. The family background of Sully himself provides an excellent example of that phenomenon. On his father's side he claimed descent from the counts of Flanders, while his maternal background was quintessentially *robe*, including a line of *parlementaire* magistrates and a president in the *chambre des comptes*, the court ultimately responsible for auditing royal financial accounts.

The effect of the *paulette*, therefore, was to help delineate the French state by providing it with a proto-bureaucratic organization which functioned independently of the king. Indeed, one of the incipient dangers for the crown of the new system was the fact that its chief servants, as hereditary office-holders, were in a position to resist change, however necessary in royal eyes. For the moment, however, Henry and Sully had succeeded in strengthening the idea of the state without risking a social revolution; for in its updated form the second estate maintained its governing alliance with the sovereign. In truth, established attitudes in general remained powerfully resistant to new ways of political thinking, despite the radical ideas thrown up during the Wars of Religion. The new governing elite still bore the marks of that old dichotomy between private possession and public service which had characterized the French monarchy for generations. The introduction of the *paulette* was a straw in a wind yet to blow fiercely; even Thomas Hobbes' *Leviathan* was still half a century away.

In a very material sense, however, Henry did leave his mark on the incipient French state. He was a builder, not of royal palaces intended to add lustre to the royal line, but of a more broadly based nation which needed to regain its pride, its sense of identity and its security. He began with his capital city. Under Henry IV modern Paris began to emerge. For Henry understood, however imperfectly, that the identity of the kingdom's chief city reflected the state of the nation. His interest, therefore, was less in buildings per se, more about how they fitted into the overall scheme of things: he was a town planner keen to transform the accumulation of inherited jurisdictions into a designer city.

Though his achievements were relatively modest they betokened a future of grand vistas and architectural order which are still characteristic of the modern city. He was much involved, for example, with the completion of the Pont Neuf and the building of the adjacent Place Dauphine on the Île de la Cité. The latter represented something new in western European domestic architecture: rows of uniform houses, all sharing the same proportions and the same red brickwork, with white stone facings and high grey slate roofs. There was an air of spaciousness about this development which was heightened by the new bridge's novel appearance. No houses lined its sides; instead, a pavement was constructed to separate pedestrians from the busy traffic of carriages and carts. The rue Dauphine, forming an extension to the bridge onto the Left Bank, also contributed to the grandeur of the locality. In this case the king's role was to urge his minister, Sully, in his capacity as superintendent of buildings, to 'ensure that those who build here construct the façades to a common plan, because it would be very fine to look down the street from the bridge and see the uniform fronts'.[16] This observation reveals an important aspect of Henry's urban planning. It was designed as a public/private initiative. The vision was the king's, but the finances came largely out of the pockets of wealthy investors, often representatives of the new *robe* nobility, whose most prestigious institutional base, the parlement, virtually overlooked the Place Dauphine.

Henry pursued a similar line in developing the Place Royale, later the Place des Vosges, on the edge of the fashionable Marais district on the Right Bank of the Seine. Again the intention was to create an ensemble, the brick-and stone-built houses with their steeply pitched slate roofs drawn up to face each other across a vast open square. Again the inspiration came from the king and most of the resources from the *robe* nobility. The new square was on the site of a former royal residence, the Tournelles, which had been pulled down by Catherine de' Medici after the accidental death there of her husband, Henry II. Henry IV, however, was not rebuilding for the royal family. His aim was to further the alliance between crown and nobility upon which the effective running of the French state would increasingly depend. This was to be a partnership embracing the old nobility as well as the new, some of whose most distinguished representatives occupied town houses in the Marais, immediately behind the Place Royale. It appeared that the state's chief servants were to be identified less by their Bourbon livery than by their places of honour outside the royal palaces.

Henry's last great building enterprise in Paris had hardly begun before his death brought it to an end. It was to have been another spacious residential development, this time of semi-circular design, planted with imposing and matching town houses and called the Place de France. The title was significant, indicating the preoccupation of the king and his minister with the wider task of unifying the country; seeking to identify the capital city with the government of the whole nation. In the original plan the characteristic semi-circle of the Place de France, situated a little to the north of the Place Royale, was to have been pierced by a series of roads, each called after one of the country's great regions. Although the project died with the king, it is still possible to trace its broad outline in the 3rd *arrondissement* where thoroughfares bearing the names of Brittany and Normandy meet the semi-circular rue Debelleyme.[17]

If the intention behind the aborted Place de France was largely symbolic, there is abundant evidence of the practical steps taken by Sully, with his master's support, to make the unity of France a reality. Among Sully's portfolio of titles was that of *grand voyer*, or director of communications. In that capacity he established a network of regional officials to help develop and supervise a skeletal national communications system. It was skeletal because the great *pays d'états*, notably Dauphiné, Provence and Languedoc, with Brittany and Burgundy not far behind, were unwilling to countenance all the implications of Sully's centralizing policies. But elsewhere, in the *pays d'élections*, real progress was made, especially in bridge building at key river crossings including those at Bordeaux, Orléans and Rouen, and in the construction of canals, notably the Briare which joined the rivers Seine and Loire near Montargis. In making France more self-sufficient the *grand voyer* was helping the king to achieve his overriding ambition, that of giving the French state a politically coherent identity.

To achieve this Henry had to make his frontiers more secure, particularly the regions in the east and south east of the country. Sully came to his aid once more, this time wearing his hat of superintendent of fortifications. Concentrating on the four eastern frontier provinces of Picardy, Champagne, Dauphiné and Provence, he established a network of subordinates through whom to regulate central government policy. Through their efforts he presided over the construction of a line of fortresses and citadels stretching from the Channel to the Mediterranean, from Calais and Amiens in the north through Metz, Toul and Verdun down to Grenoble in the south and to the naval base at Toulon. The establishment of this iron barrier also betokened the future direction of French foreign policy down to the Revolution, its quest for secure and defensible frontiers.[18]

Henry of Navarre was a warrior but not a warmonger. Though circumstances frequently made him a soldier, in his later years especially, as undisputed king of France, he strove for peace, to restore his country's damaged economy and his countrymen's damaged morale. He was acutely aware, however, just as he had been when growing up in Béarn, of the permanent threat emanating from Madrid. His Catholic Majesty's annexation of the southern part of the kingdom of Navarre some forty years before Henry's birth, had been part of the young man's inherited baggage. During the difficult years of internecine struggle Spain had supported the Catholic League, first with subsidies and then with troops under the command of the greatest captain of the age, the duke of Parma. Even Spanish setbacks seemed to threaten France. The Revolt of the Netherlands, which gave birth to the Dutch Republic, brought large concentrations of Spanish troops close to the French frontier, with Paris uncomfortably accessible from Flanders. By the same token, however, these troops depended for their support on a hazardous and circuitous supply line from the mother country. This was the famous Spanish Road, from landfall in Genoa through Milan, Savoy, Franche-Comté, Lorraine and Luxembourg. It did not require great tactical appreciation on Henry's part to recognize that the security of French frontiers would be greatly enhanced if the Spanish Road was in regular need of repair. The conduct of Spain's allies along the route, the dukes of Savoy and Lorraine, underlined the problem. In 1588 Charles Emmanuel of Savoy invaded Saluzzo, a French possession in the Alps offering access to northern Italy. In the following year Charles, duke of Lorraine, overran the bishopric of Toul at the very heart of France's eastern frontier. Eventually, in January 1595, Henry was persuaded to convert the cold war with Spain into the real thing.

This brief conflict, which was ended by the treaty of Vervins in 1598, revolved around the Spanish capture of Amiens and Calais. Amiens was the key to Picardy, and its loss highlighted the threat to France's north-eastern frontier: hence the ferocity of the fight to regain it. The treaty virtually restored the status quo following the treaty of Cateau-Cambrésis in 1559. Calais and Toul were returned to France and Saluzzo was made the subject of papal arbitration. Henry's ultimate decision in regard to the latter territory confirmed the fact that the old Valois–Habsburg rivalry in Italy did not interest him. When the devious duke of

Savoy, backed by Spanish gold, proved difficult to shift from the marquisate of Saluzzo, Henry was forced to invade. A treaty was hastily agreed at Lyon in 1601. By its terms France relinquished Saluzzo but received in exchange the territories of Bresse, Bugey, Gex and Valromey further to the west. The king was castigated by some of his contemporaries for agreeing to this, but his critics' mindset was locked into the past. Saluzzo was indeed a handy base from which to adventure into Italy, but the new possessions secured France's eastern frontier between Dauphiné and Franche-Comté, and made it much easier for French troops to disrupt the traffic on the Spanish Road. The treaty of Lyon was a portent of how Bourbon foreign policy would operate along the whole length of France's vulnerable eastern frontier: essentially defensive in intent though often aggressive in implementation.[19]

In the last decade of the king's life a serious attempt was made to map out France's eastern frontier with more precision than previously. This project was symptomatic of Henry's governing philosophy: to make the concept of the French state reflect a three dimensional reality. It has been observed that both he and Sully preferred to employ images as a way of developing their ideas.[20] The production of up-to-date maps was the best way to comprehend the nature of the inheritance which Henry had received from his Valois predecessors; and to distinguish it from the states of his European neighbours. Catherine de' Medici had already commissioned work on mapping the French provinces, but Henry pushed government patronage of cartography to a new level. He set up craft workshops in the Louvre where map-making could flourish, and demonstrated his support by allowing a well-known cartographer to take up residence in his fashionable new Place Royale. This was Claude de Chastillon, a military engineer in charge of mapping the defensive fortifications of Champagne, who also produced large-scale maps of the province which later appeared in atlases of France. His colleagues produced similar detailed maps of Brittany, Dauphiné and Picardy. By the end of his reign Henry's vision of France was acquiring a topographical identity.[21]

The distinguishing feature of the reign of Henry IV was the street level operation of the monarchy. The king's reputation as an insatiable womanizer certainly added to his street credibility and to the reassuring sense of shared humanity with his subjects. But there was more to it than that. Henry himself did not inspire reverence. 'I have seen the king, but I have not seen His Majesty', was one noblewoman's disappointed reaction to her first sighting.[22] The atmosphere which should have enveloped the person of God's anointed was not present. Although capable of putting on a show when he thought it necessary – like the spectacular set piece marking the abjuration of 1593 – that was not his style. In the plainness of his manners and the simplicity of his eating habits – he loved onion soup and omelettes – he retained the character of a country gentleman: in his grandfather's phrase, welcoming him into the world, he was a real Béarnais.

Therein lay the origins of his legend. It was easier for the people at large to identify with the aspirations of such a king, to assume that he had their welfare at heart. His court, unlike the courts of his Valois predecessors and Bourbon successors, was not designed to transport the sovereign to some other world from which ordinary folk were excluded. It was accessible to all and its membership was astonishingly varied, impoverished visitors from Gascony mixing with soldiers and sophisticated representatives of the old Valois court. When one of the royal gardeners complained of the quality of soil in the Tuileries, Henry responded with mock resignation that he should try planting Gascons, because they sprout up everywhere![23] The first Bourbon presided over a court that still reflected the country at large, earthy and unrefined, short on regulation and ritual: it has been called the final manifestation of the age of Rabelais.[24]

At its heart was the flawed yet charismatic figure of the *vert galant* himself, short of stature, grizzled as he approached fifty at the turn of the century, but still fresh faced and vigorous. In 1599 his marriage to the childless Marguerite de Valois was finally annulled, allowing arrangements for the king's remarriage to proceed. His choice fell upon the niece of the duke of Tuscany, Maria de' Medici, whom he favoured over a German princess, confiding to Sully that if he married one of the latter he would feel as if he had a wine-barrel in bed with him. Henry and Marie (as she was to be known) were married in 1600, and in the following year a dauphin, Louis, was born to the happy couple. Henry's joy was unconfined; his wife's mingled with relief that she had done what was expected of her, and produced an heir to the throne.

Henry's predilection for allowing his sexual appetite to blunt his personal and political sensitivities became ever more conspicuous in his later years. He had been in thrall to Gabrielle d'Estrées, his most celebrated mistress, since 1590 and towards the end of the century, as the prospect of obtaining an annulment of his marriage to Marguerite increased, he began to contemplate marrying her, and legitimizing their children. This was a dangerous pipe dream, for it was inconceivable that the king's bastards would ever be recognized as heirs to the throne of Saint Louis. Nevertheless, Henry could not be dissuaded, and announced his intention to marry Gabrielle on Low Sunday, 1599, a week after Easter. But on the preceding Holy Saturday the unfortunate and pregnant bride-to-be, died from complications caused by her condition. Though momentarily heartbroken by the traumatic dénouement to his most enduring physical liaison, Henry was incapable of prolonged grief, and was soon acknowledging the narrow escape from political disaster that her death had afforded him. Besides, there was already another young lady on the horizon in the beguiling form of Henriette d'Entragues.

Henry's single-mindedness in the pursuit of sexual conquests made him vulnerable to political machinations and to the wiles of ambitious families who saw a means to make their fortune. In the 1590s Gabrielle's father became a governor and her brother a bishop. Gabrielle's near miss in just failing to become queen of France was noted by her successor's family, who planned to go one better. Only six months after Gabrielle's death Henry was assuring Henriette's father that if his daughter bore the king a son, he would marry her.[25] That promise led eventually, in 1604, to a Spanish-backed plot to replace the existing Bourbon line with a new royal dynasty headed by Henry's illegitimate son by Henriette. Despite the d'Entragues family support for Spain Henry continued to indulge his mistress, whom he had named marquise of Verneuil in 1600. Queen Marie de' Medici was embarrassed and humiliated by her continued presence at court, and by Henry's insistence that all his children, legitimate and illegitimate, should be brought up together at the château of Saint-Germain-en-Laye outside Paris. The king was not a cruel man, but his relationship with the queen inevitably suffered from his emotional preoccupations elsewhere: 'Henry's judgement was always defective when Venus had the upper hand'.[26]

Only assassination delivered him from his final female entanglement. At the time of his death he was about to embark on a war fraught with incalculable risks. In 1609 the death of the duke of Clèves-Julich, the strategically important state on the lower Rhine, threatened to upset the balance of power in Europe. The succession was disputed, so the Habsburg emperor exercised his rights of suzerainty to order the sequestration of the duchies pending a decision. Spanish troops from the southern Netherlands occupied Julich and the old fears of a Habsburg encirclement resurfaced in Paris. There was even more concern in Protestant Amsterdam, where the very survival of the newly formed Dutch Republic appeared to be at risk. Initially, the king was cautious, unwilling to plunge his country into a major war and uncertain of his allies. Then Henri II de Condé, the premier prince of the blood, who unlike his Huguenot father and grandfather had been brought up a Catholic, fled to the Spanish Netherlands and put himself under the protection of the king of Spain.

This action dramatically raised the political and emotional stakes for the king. Suddenly the nightmare years of civil war and confessional conflict seemed poised for a replay. In the wider European arena the champions of Protestantism and the Counter-Reformation were preparing for battle, while Spanish voices were reminding Condé that if the annulment of Henry IV's first marriage, to Queen Marguerite, were to be declared invalid then his second marriage, to Marie de' Medici, would be rendered null and void and their progeny illegitimate. In that case he, the prince of Condé, would become heir to the French throne. The old enemy, Spain, was again seeking to weaken France from within.[27]

But even that wasn't the whole story. For Condé's young bride, Charlotte de Montmorency, daughter and granddaughter of constables of France, was Henry's latest female object of desire. His calculation that Condé was likely to prove an amiable cuckold was spectacularly undone. Furiously, he demanded that both husband and wife should be returned forthwith, and, failing to receive satisfaction, opted for war. By early May 1610 he was ready to move. There would be three strikes, one into the Spanish Netherlands from Champagne, one into northern Italy, and one into Spanish Navarre. Before a shot could be fired, however, the king was dead. An offensive campaign which could have undone Henry's careful reconstruction of his country, and ruined his reputation, had been averted. Historians disagree over Henry's motivation in these last months of his life. In particular they have pondered the question of whether the great king was guilty of allowing lust to distort his political judgement. It would not have been the first time, and certainly his impetuosity was at odds with his previously cautious foreign policy. At the very least it seems that the flight of the desirable Charlotte added piquancy to Henry's appraisal of the situation. That was certainly the view of the Dutch ambassador in Paris at the time, Francis Aerssen, who called the princess of Condé the new Helen of Troy.

It is appropriate, therefore, that the abiding image handed down to posterity from the court of this serial philanderer should be of two naked women in a bath, one blonde and one brunette, Gabrielle d'Estrées and Henriette d' Entragues. Gabrielle has in her hand but not on her finger a wedding ring, while Henriette's outstretched hand touching the other's breast, together with the servant in the background preparing a layette, suggest that it is her turn to love the king and bear his children. Together they stare out at their audience from their place in the musée du Louvre close to where in life they captivated the incorrigible vert galant.[28]

The problem about the king's easy accessibility to his subjects was that it rendered him permanently vulnerable to attack, and Henry's chequered religious past was an invitation to fanatics from both camps to try their hand at murder. Also, his relatively ordinary lifestyle turned treason into a less breathtaking enterprise. Assassination attempts were frequent; there were nine between 1593 and 1596, and nine more after that, so that on the balance of probabilities sooner or later one of the king's subjects would achieve notorious immortality. That man turned out to be the shadowy figure of François Ravaillac, a Catholic extremist whose connections and motivation remain unclear.

His moment came on 14 May 1610, on a busy Parisian Friday afternoon. The circumstances surrounding this historic event were mundane. The king's carriage was caught in a traffic jam on the rue de la Ferronnerie as Henry made his way from the Louvre to Sully's lodgings in the Arsenal. He had forgotten his spectacles and was concentrating on listening to a letter being read to him by his travelling companion, the duke of Epernon, when the assassin, the red-headed Ravaillac, struck. Some similarities between the death of Henry IV and the murder three and a half centuries later of President John F. Kennedy have already been noticed: unbalanced assassins apparently acting alone, and countervailing conspiracy theses implicating far wider and more calculating political interests.[29] There are other parallels too. Both men aroused deep feelings of loyalty or animosity, and the killing of each in his time shook the world. Finally, the brutal and premature nature of their dying did nothing to diminish their reputations.

Indeed, it has been argued that in terms of the cultivation of his legend, Henry of Navarre could not have chosen a better moment to depart the stage.[30] It is certainly true that a bungled foreign adventure based on an affair of the heart rather than the national interest would have dented his posthumous reputation. Nevertheless, his achievement in rescuing France when the French state appeared to be beyond redemption entitles him to heroic status. His reign did not change dramatically or decisively the direction of France's political development, but it did provide a new justification for it. It offered an alternative to fratricidal strife as a means of noble advancement, and it promoted the belief that religious intolerance should not be the cornerstone of the French state. Most significantly, it sketched out the concept of a secular state, a *patrie*, in whose service government and people would be united. In 1597 a moderate Huguenot commentator, Jean de Serres, proclaimed: 'Frenchmen, are you not all patriots, are you not all subjects of the same king ... One king, one law of the state, one country.'[31] The unremitting drama of the king's life worked to fashion in his mind 'une vision de la France', a phrase, incidentally, which would have come readily to the lips of another great French patriot, Charles de Gaulle.[32] With the help of his versatile lieutenant, Sully, Henry sought to give some substance to that idea. He demonstrated the fact that France could quickly become economically prosperous again, even without radical financial reform, provided that the country remained at peace. He took steps to integrate the regions more effectively through the introduction of improved communications, and to protect them by means of foreign and defence policies designed to secure France's vulnerable eastern frontier. Although a provincial from the southwest with no great personal affection for Paris, Henry understood that the capital represented the nation, not the dynasty, and he planned to make it a modern city worthy of France's elevated place in the world. Finally, he established an understanding with the *noblesse de robe*, families with the professional expertise to run complex organizations, with the financial resources to contribute to his public/private enterprise schemes, and whose interests and outlook made them more likely to support the king's vision than to take up arms against him.

Henry of Navarre was an astute man but not an intellectual, good with words but impatient for action, brave, magnanimous, insensitive and self-indulgent; and he bequeathed to his Bourbon successors the possibility of achieving greatness.

There was one aspect of his reign, however, which did not offer encouragement to his heirs, and that was the nature of its end. The Bourbons had lost the sheen of invulnerability which had protected their Capetian and Valois predecessors. A second successive occupant of the throne of Saint Louis had been murdered, and what so recently had been unprecedented was in danger of becoming a habit. Henry IV's vision of a modern French state promised the king the exercise of unparalleled powers without the threat of retribution which all dictators face. That was because the impersonal authority of the state could not be linked to the fortunes of the ruling house. The snag was that running the kingdom of France had always been a family business, and there was no knowing whether the family, together with the other main shareholders, would agree to being bought out by France plc.

It is safe to assume that such considerations had never entered the mind of the eight-year-old boy, also called Louis, who was now summoned to take the place of his charismatic father.

Consolidating the State

4

Louis XIII: the Implacable

On the day that Ravaillac made his fatal thrust the king's heir, his eldest legitimate son, Louis, was still some months short of his ninth birthday. Since French kings did not reach their majority until their thirteenth birthday, a period of regency was inevitable and with it the threat of instability. On the evening of Henry's assassination the country's chief law court, the parlement of Paris, declared his widow, Marie de' Medici, regent of the kingdom until Louis reached his majority. On the following day she brought the new king to the Palais de Justice where he held his first *lit de justice*, a ceremony intended to confirm and solemnize his mother's title. This uncharacteristic speed of action by the parlement ensured that in the short term at least the change of regime would be peaceful.

It is instructive to reflect on the significance of these inaugural events of the reign of Louis XIII. The most important effect of the involvement of the parlement of Paris was to highlight the legitimacy of the Bourbon dynasty, heirs by virtue of the law of succession to the throne of their Capetian and Valois predecessors. That would be by far the king's greatest asset when forced to grapple with his father's unfinished business of transforming the French state. The parlement's intervention had other implications for the future, however, which were less supportive of the royal cause. The grandees of the French nobility, the peers, included among their privileges the right to sit in the parlement and to take part in its deliberations. They had neither the expertise nor the interest to attend the routine sessions of the court, but on great state occasions like that of 15 May 1610 the parlement once more became the court of peers, reminding any who cared to reflect on the matter that neither the battlefields of the Wars of Religion nor the efforts of Henry IV to encourage alternative forms of public service had quite erased the memory of that ancient feudal principle of *primus inter pares*.

Although the judges of the parlement exemplified the highest echelon of the professional *noblesse de robe*, they were outranked by the peers, descendants of warlords, who sat at the king's right hand. Amongst those present on that day was the duke of Epernon, once a favourite of Henry III and later a less than trustworthy ally of Henry IV. The latter, concerned to keep him away from his power base in Guyenne, was literally keeping an eye on him when Ravaillac struck. The duke of Guise, son of the assassinated head of the Catholic League, was also there, along with his uncle, the gout-ridden duke of Mayenne, who had taken over the leadership of the League after his brother's death. Counterbalancing the militantly Catholic Guises was the staunchly Protestant duke of Lesdiguières, unswervingly loyal to Henry IV and the virtual king of Dauphiné. Their collective presence was a reminder of the fact that there was far from universal support for the late king's patriotic agenda.

There was yet another agenda being tabled on this occasion, and that was one drawn up by the parlement itself. To be sure, this body had long maintained that it possessed a constitutional function in the state which went far beyond its role as a sovereign court of appeal. That argument was based on the assumption that the registers recording generations of *parlementaire* decisions represented a kind of blueprint for acceptable government action. However, on 14 and 15 May 1610 the parlement was presented with the opportunity to play a part at an unprecedented political level. Following Henry's murder, the queen, Marie de' Medici, and Epernon and Guise communicated with the court, requesting that it should pronounce immediately upon the pressing matter of the regency. The parlement was only too pleased to oblige, unanimously declaring the queen mother to be regent of the kingdom. The magistrates cited a number of precedents in support of their decision, including those provided by the illustrious duo of Saint Louis and his mother, Blanche of Castile, as well as by the altogether less admirable pair of Charles IX and Catherine de' Medici. The significance of the occasion was that never before had the parlement played so decisive a role. Previously the position of regent had been simply claimed by the relative next in line to the minor king, or ratified by the estates general. Sometimes the parlement had confirmed the choice expressed by the previous ruler, but on 14 May 1610 it issued an apparently binding judgement on its own account to the effect that Marie de' Medici should be recognized as regent. When that recognition was solemnized at the *lit de justice* on the following day it was not surprising that the new regent should have assured the magistrates that in the conduct of affairs she intended the king to be guided by their advice, which they were urged to proffer whenever their consciences dictated.[1]

The child king, Louis XIII, on whose behalf these elaborate ceremonies were being conducted, was already a complex personality. His early childhood has provided some commentators with an irresistible opportunity to venture into psychoanalysis, thanks to the survival of a remarkably intrusive journal written by the king's physician, Jean Héroard. No sovereign in history can have been subjected to a more exhaustive scrutiny of his childhood habits and relationships. Despite this, not all historians are convinced of the ultimately revelatory nature of psycho-history, however detailed the source material may be. There is clearly a danger in viewing Louis' future actions as king through the narrow prism of the child-rearing mores of the early seventeenth-century French court. Nevertheless, the harsh apprenticeship to which the dauphin was subjected undoubtedly left its mark on the young man. Louis proved to be a difficult child to handle, wilful, troubled, and sometimes violent. He loved his father deeply but saw him irregularly. He showed early signs of inheriting Henry's love of hunting and soldiering, but also of worrying about his father's enemies. He was aware of Henry's relaxed view of the world, and of the magnanimity with which he treated his enemies. That was not the son's style. From an early age he was determined to have his future status acknowledged, so that in the fullness of time he would be entitled to deal justly with his enemies. He was clear that this should not include giving them a second chance.

The chief pressure driving him in this direction was in fact the same irritant that had driven his mother to exchange blows with his father, namely the presence of a veritable seraglio of mistresses and their children, Louis' half-brothers and half-sisters. These included the sons of Gabrielle d'Estrées, the Vendôme brothers César and Alexandre, and Gaston-Henri de Verneuil, the son of Henriette d'Entragues. The latter was a particular bugbear, since Louis coveted the names of his father and of the gallant and chivalrous Gaston de Foix for himself. As they all grew up together at Saint-Germain Louis began to use the routine ceremonial of the royal court to underline his own superior status as dauphin. The origins of this petty rivalry lay in King Henry's provocative support for his alternative ménage, the effect of which was to make his only legitimate son deeply suspicious of the motives of those about him.[2] Perhaps for that very reason Louis was forever searching for a reassuring confidant or confidante, a quest with no happy ending. Undoubtedly, his youthful intuitions were burned into his character by the traumatic event of his father's murder.

For the immediate future, however, the royal authority which the king was so determined to defend, lay with his mother. The appointment of the regent was not a signal for universal celebration. The very name she bore was a reminder of the recent past, when her Medici predecessor had presided over decades of bloody civil war. Both queens were from the Florentine stable of Machiavellian politics, though Marie lacked Catherine's guile and subtlety. She was determined to seize her opportunity, however, having been humiliated for much of her marriage by the constant presence of her husband's mistresses and their offspring. She used her new-found authority without flair or imagination, and without Sully, dismissing her husband's trusted Huguenot counsellor in 1611. She turned instead to two unreliable members of her Florentine entourage, Concino Concini and his wife, Leonora Galigaï, whose growing influence and transparent greed helped to distance the new regime from the patriotic values established by her late husband.

Henry IV's view of France as a state whose unity and élan flowed from the universal recognition of its identity by ruler and subjects alike meant nothing to Marie de' Medici. She was not unusual in that, since the pursuit of suitable marriages for the ruling families of Europe had transformed the latter into a cosmopolitan class, who had difficulty in establishing a single-minded commitment to their state which was at the heart of Henry's vision. Marie never mastered the French language and continued to prefer the company of her Italian companions. Through her mother she claimed membership of the Austrian Habsburg dynasty. She was singularly ill-equipped to inculcate in her son the political convictions of his murdered father.

There was little more support for Henry's views immediately below the regent's level. The idea of universal loyalty was difficult for all parties to comprehend so long as the monarch had to relate to groups or orders rather than to individuals. The particular order with which traditionally the king had the closest links was the second estate of the realm, the order of nobility. The informal contract existing between king and nobility had long provided the basis for political stability. Initially that relationship had been feudal, the holding of fiefs in return for service, and that principle had been mirrored down the landholding scale. Out of these largely military alliances had developed the more sophisticated concept of seigneury, the linking of landholding with the dispensation of justice, with seigneurial courts continuing to constitute an important part of the social fabric. To hold a title, an office or a seigneury was a source of honour in seventeenth-century France, as the great jurist Charles Loyseau (1564–1627) observed.[3]

The greatest source of noble prestige remained military service. The royal army was officered by noblemen who served the king in the tradition of liege-lordship, a relationship based on a sense of personal honour, not of national obligation. In the same spirit nobles used their powers of patronage to recruit their own kinsmen and clients, so that the army, representing a mosaic of interests, could prove unreliable if the king and his grandees fell out. The civil administration was similarly held together by noble ties, again reflecting the sovereign's relationship with his former great vassals. The association of master and *fidèle* bound together the representatives of greater and lesser noble houses, securing for the junior partner a promising career or a suitable marriage, as well as a guarantee of protection even against the king himself. By the same token, the senior partner's demand for unequivocal loyalty against all parties including the king, might ultimately require the *fidèle* to sacrifice his life for his master.[4]

The contract between the nobility and the crown, like that between nobles and clients, remained highly personal and took no account of the king's wider obligations to the totality of his subjects. Even as late as the eighteenth century only about 1 per cent of the population were nobles, yet they owned almost a third of the land and possessed rights of a kind that made it difficult for them to empathize with the vast mass of the population. Their one-sided deal with the crown entitled them to serve in the highest civil and military offices in the state in return for exemption from direct taxation, special juridical status and a host of honorific privileges. Neither the ferment of new ideas concerning the nature of royal authority which erupted during the Wars of Religion, nor Henry IV's efforts to exploit them, had persuaded the ruling class as a whole to view the crown as a national office. Yet, as in all human history, putting the clock back was not an option. Provided that he could control events the force lay with the young king.

Louis XIII's minority ended officially in October 1614 shortly after his thirteenth birthday, but it continued in reality until mid-1617, when his mother's favourite, Concini, was assassinated. The Bourbons were inclined to mistime their successions, so that three out of the four monarchs following Henry IV began their reign with a regency. Regencies tended to encourage a kind of state recidivism as those whose credit was failing saw their opportunity for a come-back. Louis and his mother did not have long to wait before this phenomenon revealed itself. The leader of the discontented was the prince of Condé, Louis' cousin and second in line to the throne after the king and his younger brother, Gaston. This was the same Condé whose wife had caught the dimming but still lecherous gaze of Henry IV in the year before his death, adding personal animosity to princely ambition. He was joined by Louis' half-brother, César, duke of Vendôme, the son of Gabrielle d'Estrées, with whom the king had unwillingly shared his childhood. Their supporters included Henri de la Tour, the duke of Bouillon, linked by marriage to the princes of Nassau and the Elector Palatine, who from his power base in the Auvergne held land across France and the Holy Roman Empire; and the duke of Nevers, whose family name of Gonzague revealed his relationship with the ruling house of Mantua. In the minds of all these men high nobility could not be confined by narrow interests of state. Their revolt, such as it was, for no battles were fought before the treaty of Sainte-Ménehould was signed in May 1614, involved a number of inconsequential troop movements centred on the region of Champagne. Their demands, couched in the obsequious language of support for the king's best interests, were for a summoning of the estates general and for the replacement of the existing royal councillors by others such as themselves.

The most influential figure at court, and a natural enemy of the grandees, was the upstart Italian favourite, Concini, who by this time had collected a field-marshal's baton and the marquisate of Ancre. More directly in the rebels' sights, because of the significance of their long-term threat, were the three chief office-holders upon whom Marie depended for the effective running of her government. These men represented an alternative high nobility, serving the king's state as trained professionals, not the king as his liegemen. They were headed by Nicolas de Neufville, seigneur of Villeroy, who was the regent's secretary of state for foreign affairs. From very humble origins Villeroy's family had reached this position in three generations by providing part of the civil service needed by the crown to support its increasingly complex role. Villeroy's grandfather had been a royal secretary at the beginning of the previous century and a member of Henry II's exclusive *conseil des affaires*. His father was a royal *secrétaire des finances*, an office which Villeroy himself acquired in 1559. From the end of the fifteenth century these secretarial offices bestowed nobility on the holder. As valuable property they were customarily passed on within the family. So too were the personal records from each generation, which were considered to be family documents not state papers, a reminder of the fact that true state bureaucracy was still a distance away. Nevertheless, such transmission helped successive generations of *robe* noblemen to acquire the expertise necessary to realize their vocation of royal service. The other two members of the triumvirate, the chancellor, Brûlart de Sillery, and the superintendent of finance, Pierre Jeannin, shared Villeroy's background of service nobility. Sillery made his reputation as a judge in the parlement of Paris, while Jeannin had been the chief magistrate, or first president, in the parlement of Dijon.[5]

Although it would be simplistic to represent the events of Louis XIII's minority as a clear-cut conflict to redefine the role of the nobility and therefore of French kingship, at a more inchoate level that struggle was already under way. In 1611 Villeroy himself accepted that, though France was still a personal rather than a bureaucratic monarchy, it was necessary to neutralize the power of the grandees in a variety of ways. These included keeping a watchful eye on their activities, isolating them from potential allies and, most importantly, widening the network of royal patronage in order to weaken the hold of the great magnates on their own clients.[6]

Marie de' Medici, who was shrewder than she has been painted (notably by Rubens), was already taking her own measures to tranquillize the country during her son's minority. Much of the treasure painstakingly accrued by Sully was converted into noble pensions, and with an eye to the wider picture Marie republished the edict of Nantes four times between 1610 and 1615.[7] To protect the country from external threat she also reversed her late husband's anti-Spanish policy by signing a marriage alliance with Habsburg Spain, by which Louis XIII was betrothed to the infanta, Anne, and his sister, Elizabeth, to the prince of the Asturias, the future Philip IV. Marie was even willing to accede to Condé's demand for a meeting of the estates general, confident of her ability to influence the elections in her own favour.

These were all short-term, pragmatic responses to a potentially critical situation, an attempt to forestall problems while the kingdom was being governed by proxy. But like all such acts they risked having unforeseen consequences. The opening of the estates general of 1614–15 took place on 27 October, less than a month after the formal ending of Louis XIII's minority, though it would be a further two and a half years before the young man grasped the reins of power for himself. The meeting of the estates produced no dramatic results. But it did offer some encouragement to the young man impatient to make his royal mark sooner rather than later. The famous first article of the Third Estate's *cahier*, subsequently finessed into a legal vacuum in order to placate the sensitivities of the First Estate of the Clergy, read as follows:

> the king shall be asked to declare in the assembly of his estates *as a Fundamental Law of the Kingdom, which shall be inviolable and known to all*: that since he is known to be sovereign in his state, holding his crown from God alone, that there is no power on earth whatever, spiritual or temporal, which has any authority over his kingdom, to take away the sacred nature of our kings, to dispense (or absolve) their subjects of the fidelity and obedience which they owe them for any cause or pretext whatsoever.[8]

The reasons for this powerful restatement of a long-held Gallican position were of course the murder of Henry IV and the proliferation of ultramontane ideas justifying the pope's right to remove ideologically unsuitable kings. The religion of the monarchy, supported by the tradition of Gallican independence, lay at the root of French national identity. There could be no more constructive way to avenge his father's murder than for Louis XIII to impose his sovereignty on behalf of the French nation on all his challengers, within the country as well as outside, in the process restoring to the crown its lost reverential aura.

The *cahiers* of the nobility offered some further hope that such royal ambitions might be fulfilled. The lesser nobility, who dominated the deputation of the Second Estate, showed themselves hostile to the patron–client relationship which gave the grandees a degree of independence. They petitioned 'that no pensions, offices, or other gifts be given in the future through the intercession of the princes and seigneurs of your kingdom so that those who have them will be bound entirely to your majesty'.[9] In other words, if all patronage lay directly with the king then in return he would command universal loyalty, and there would be less room for private enterprise among the king's over-mighty subjects.

But the regent was showing no sign of willingness to give up the exercise of royal power on her son's behalf. This was a matter of growing resentment on Louis' part since her chief purpose was to maintain a regime which furthered the parasitic career of the marquis of Ancre, first gentleman of the king's chamber, marshal of France, lieutenant general of Normandy, alias her old favourite, Concini. Though the young king was in awe of his mother he believed that the security of the state would ultimately require him to exercise in person his God-given authority. For, as well as the corruption of the Italianate court and the chronic rebelliousness of Condé, there were other elements at work in the kingdom which threatened to destabilize it. The most formidable and disquieting source of opposition remained that of the Huguenots.

Henry IV's edict of Nantes had recognized the ecclesiastical organization of the Protestant Church in France and allowed the Huguenots to keep possession of some 150 fortified strongholds, the most significant being La Rochelle. It had banned the holding of political assemblies, but before the end of the reign these too were being permitted at both provincial and national level. The Huguenots were understandably anxious to have a means of confirming and consolidating what they had achieved at Nantes, but there was a danger that in the process they would antagonize the government by drawing further attention to their anomalous status. They certainly alarmed Marie de' Medici in the autumn of 1615 when both the Protestant National Assembly and the town of La Rochelle allied themselves with the rebellious Condé. The prince had no ideological commitment to the Huguenot cause, but the alliance allowed him to pressurize the queen mother's government for his own purposes. By the treaty of Loudon in May 1616 he was made head of a number of royal councils, and his Huguenot allies were given reassurances relating to the edict of Nantes. Conversely, the government took the opportunity to reiterate a longstanding complaint against the Protestants, that the church lands in Henry IV's homeland of Béarn, which had been handed over to the Huguenots by his mother, Jeanne d'Albret, had still not been returned to the established church.

Despite the settlement of Loudon, it was clear that the Huguenots' relationship with government remained highly unstable and capable of deteriorating rapidly. Two additional factors added to the risk of further conflict. The first was the effect on the Protestant cause of the appearance of a charismatic leader in the person of Henri, duke of Rohan, governor of Saint-Jean d'Angély, a Huguenot stronghold close to La Rochelle. Marie de' Medici made the mistake of trying and failing to remove him from his governorship in 1612. The effect of her failure was the recruitment of a formidable adversary to the list of disaffected noblemen. Breton in origin, the Rohan were one of the great noble families of Europe. Prince of Leon in northern Spain, Henri de Rohan had a claim through his d'Albret family connections to Henry IV's kingdom of Navarre. It was unlikely that this upright and principled member of the French 'super-elite' would submit to orders from Paris any more unquestioningly than the prince of Condé himself.[10]

The second destabilizing factor was the militant counter-offensive of the Catholic Reformation. Since the publication of the decrees of the council of Trent in 1564, the Catholic Church had been revitalized both in its spiritual commitment and in its organization. The church in France had serious misgivings about the latter, with its renewed emphasis upon the power of the pope, and the prominence given to his shock troops, the Society of Jesus. The Jesuits had been wrongly accused of involvement in the murder of Henry IV; but their close links with the papacy continued to worry supporters of the traditionally independent Gallican Church. So when this fresh wave of religious fervour threatened a renewed call to arms, it was likely that the battle lines would be more subtly drawn than during the Wars of Religion. For there were Catholic zealots or *dévots*, who supported papal authority and admired Spain for leading the crusade against Protestantism: they identified with their religion, not with their nationality. There were Gallicans, who recognized that French statehood was inextricably bound up with the king's independence, spiritual as well as temporal. There were patriots too, *bons français*, who feared the growth of Habsburg power at the expense of France more than they approved of the religious fervour of His Catholic Majesty. The Huguenots were naturally concerned about the impact of the new Catholicism, and were particularly anxious about the implications of the young king's marriage, in November 1615, to a Spanish infanta. Nevertheless, fortified by the edict of Nantes, which provided them with assurances still unique in the post-Reformation world, they saw themselves as loyal subjects of the crown. When a delegation of leading Protestants came to Paris in the aftermath of Henry IV's assassination, to swear allegiance to his successor, they averred that in accordance with God's word no power could dispense them from their obligation of obedience to their sovereign. This declaration reveals how far their loyalty was reinforced by self-interest, for they had no external power to appeal to, as the ultramontane party could to the pope. They depended for their security upon the power of the French state, manifested in the authority of the king.[11] It remained to be seen how Louis XIII would deal with these complexities when he finally got his hands on the levers of power.

For a biographer of Louis XIII, the period between the accession in 1610 and the spring of 1617 has an air of unreality about it. The king was scarcely a participant in the action and, because there was no dynamic force driving events, there is not much of a story to be told. There was, however, a growing atmosphere of menace compounded of mistrust and disquiet, a brooding sense that the era of political savagery had not yet run its course. This mood was made manifest in a murderous *coup de théâtre* characteristic of the form of political dialogue established in the course of the previous half century. Upon his arrival on 24 April 1617 in the outer courtyard of the Louvre, the queen mother's favourite, Concini, was ambushed and killed by members of the royal guard. Having sanctioned the assassination Louis waited in another part of the palace, pretending to concentrate on a game of billiards. When news of Concini's death reached him he exclaimed triumphantly, 'Now I am king.'

In this way Louis XIII made his effective debut upon the political stage. It was a revealing first appearance. The fifteen-year-old youth was already clearly set on recouping the full cost of his unhappy apprenticeship by asserting the plenitude of his royal power. The maintenance of that authority against all comers, including his mother, would become the *Leitmotiv* of a reign destined to be a largely painful and joyless odyssey. Louis' view of his role was shaped by the fact that he was the successor to two murdered kings – one an admired, vulnerable father – and had therefore to fight to restore the monarchy's fractured reputation. He never believed that he had many dependable allies in that battle: his default mode was to mistrust everybody. He always lacked the self-assurance of his pragmatic father, who dealt easily in shades of grey. For Louis there was only black and white, but in his ruthless determination to fulfil the role that fate had dealt him he added definition to Henry's tentative endorsement of the French state.

The parlement of Paris validated the murder of Concini as a legitimate legal process against a notorious criminal and set about trying his widow for sorcery. She was beheaded in the place de Grève ten weeks after her husband's death. A new favourite now moved to centre stage. This was Charles d'Albert, duke of Luynes, who had played a leading part in the conspiracy to oust Concini. Louis XIII's emotional attachments over the course of his life make it clear that he was bisexual, but his fondness for Luynes, who was over twenty years older than the king, was as a surrogate father figure. One of the complexities of Louis' character was the coexistence of a constant need for moral support with a determination to pursue his own agenda. Predictably, he came to regret the influence which he allowed Luynes to wield, though the favourite, who possessed great personal charm, was never a hate figure like Concini. Nevertheless, the king made it clear on the morrow of Luynes's unexpected death in December 1621 that he welcomed his new freedom of action and would not be contemplating a replacement.[1]

Although Louis heaped favours and titles on Luynes – at the time of his death he was constable of France, the king's deputy in charge of the country's military forces – Luynes was not a policy maker. In important matters of state policy about which the king felt strongly, Luynes's influence was largely benign but not decisive. Only two months after the 1617 coup Louis gave the first indication of what his own priorities were to be. Returning to the matter of the church property in his father's old stamping ground of Béarn which was still in Protestant hands, he signed an edict requiring its restoration to the Catholic Church. Although this longstanding issue would not be settled for several years to come, Louis had laid down a marker for future action that would have weighty consequences. In the meantime he had to deal with the troublesome and embarrassing problem of what to do with his mother, Marie de' Medici, who had grown too used to power to go quietly.

Initially, Marie was forced to submit to a comfortable exile in Blois, but was soon the centre of political intrigue. Among the *grands* who came to her aid, as he had done on the day of her husband's assassination, was the duke of Epernon, governor of Saintonge and Aunis on the west coast and military commander of the key north-eastern frontier post of Metz. Between them an escape plot was hatched, and before first light on the morning of 22 February 1619 the queen mother, in an incongruously undignified exit, climbed out of an upstairs window and by means of a rope ladder lowered herself to the ground. Epernon and his carriage were waiting, and the two set off for Angoulême, a safe town within the boundaries of Epernon's western stronghold.

This was a challenge to his newly won authority which the king could not ignore. He found it emotionally difficult to condemn his mother's conduct as treasonable, though he had no such reservations about Epernon who had compounded his offence by disobeying Louis' order to remain in Metz. The king was determined to put an end to this spirit of noble independence which challenged his sovereignty as head of the French state. His ambivalent feelings towards the queen mother led him, however, to seek a compromise. A royal army was despatched in the direction of Angoulême while at the same time negotiations, which were intended to pre-empt any military operations, were begun. The result, the treaty of Angoulême, demonstrated the continuing correctness of the king's relationship with his mother. She was named as the new governor of Anjou and, at her behest, Epernon received a full pardon and the restoration of all his offices. Neither side viewed this accommodation with any enthusiasm, and just over a year later Louis found himself at the head of another royal army, marching into Normandy. There were now two rival courts, the king's in Paris and his mother's in Angers, and a classic *casus belli* had presented itself in the great nobility's hostility towards the king's favourite, Luynes. Among the disaffected on this occasion were Louis' childhood rival, his half-brother Vendôme, the governors of Normandy and Languedoc, respectively the dukes of Longueville and Montmorency, and the perennial rebel Epernon.

The young king's courageous reaction wrong-footed Marie de' Medici and her grandee supporters. Louis had developed an early liking for the simple rigours of the military life. Like his father he was an unpretentious figure, happier mixing informally with his fellow countrymen than preening himself at court. Indeed, he was to travel more extensively through his country and meet more of his countrymen than any other Bourbon ruler. Now he seized the opportunity presented to him and, rejecting the cautionary advice of Luynes, decided to tackle the opposition head on. At a meeting of his council in July 1620 he announced his intention to begin his campaign in Normandy, where the danger was most pressing, and made a rallying cry for support. He concluded with the call, 'Par conséquent, allons.'[13]

On 7 July Louis left Paris at the head of eight thousand troops. Three days later he was in Rouen and a week after that he had occupied Caen. Rapidly turning south in the direction of Marie de' Medici's stronghold in Anjou, he reached the River Loire where on 7 August he defeated his mother's troops at Ponts-de-Cé. The hapless commander of the queen mother's forces, César de Vendôme, made an ignominious escape by swimming across the river. The king's victory had been swift and comprehensive. What had been demonstrated by the *drôlerie* of Ponts-de-Cé, as the skirmish came to be known, was the fact that the kingdom could no longer be held to ransom by a group of grandees, however ancient their lineage or secure their territorial base. Representing only their own sectional interests they could not compete with the inclusive vision offered to the citizenry by the crowned head of the French state. By the treaty of Angers in August 1620 Louis once more made peace with his mother, who this time was forced to swear that she would join no more conspiracies against the crown. He was now in a strong position to reinforce his authority yet, significantly, within months of his victory, Louis bestowed the governorship of Guyenne upon the staunchly unreliable duke of Epernon. Universal obedience to the sovereign as the representative of the state was not yet an irresistible idea even to the king. By then, however, Louis had another target in his sights, the Protestant regime in Béarn where his 1617 edict of Restitution, intended to restore both the Catholic faith and the Church's lands, was still being ignored.

Buoyed by the success of his campaign against his mother, and finding himself at the head of a royal army in the field, a situation in which he felt completely at ease, he decided to continue south to his kingdom of Navarre. Two aspects of this decision need to be understood. First, it was wholly the king's, taken against the advice of his counsellors, including Luynes. Secondly, Louis did not believe that he was embarking upon a crusade to rid the land of Huguenotism. It is alleged that on one occasion he commented that he did not like Protestants.[14] That certainly wasn't true of individual members of the Reformed faith whom he had known since childhood. Though it reflected Louis' religious convictions in general, it did not indicate a desire on the king's part to reignite religious war. His intention, as he marched south to Béarn, was to compel obedience, and dispel the idea that on account of their religion his Protestant subjects were justified in maintaining a different relationship with the king from that enjoyed by his Catholic subjects. He was reaching for the modern concept of equality of the citizenry, though only in the limited area of religious belief. It was a clear-sighted vision, and one which, with experience, he would use to strengthen the authority of his state.

He progressed rapidly through western France, from Poitiers to Angoulême, reaching Bordeaux by mid-September and Pau, the capital of Béarn, a month later. There he declared the formal annexation of Béarn and the rest of Navarre to the kingdom of France, and ordered the restoration of sequestered church property and the re-establishment of Catholic worship. Indicative of the fact that Louis was not proselytizing during this campaign was his decision to grant pensions to the dispossessed Protestant pastors. All went smoothly and the triumphant king was back home in Paris for Christmas.

The Huguenots, on the other hand, were thrown into panic by the Béarn campaign, believing that it signalled the start of a new era of persecution. The edict of Nantes suddenly seemed a thin guarantee of their security. Consequently, they over-reacted. A national assembly was convened in the west coast port of La Rochelle, the most impregnable Protestant stronghold in the country. In the spring of 1621 that body crossed the Rubicon by adopting a proposal for the defence of the Reformed church which divided the country into eight military departments. Louis responded to the challenge by leading his army southwards into Protestant France. He took the fortified town of Saint-Jean d'Angély after a month's siege, but that was as close as he went to La Rochelle. Instead, he marched into the Midi and laid siege to the next most secure Huguenot place, the walled city of Montauban. But this time the royal army had met its match, and after six weeks the siege had to be lifted. In a gloomier mood Louis returned to his capital.

By April 1622 the king was again on the move at the head of his troops, following the now familiar route to the south, finally swinging east through Languedoc to the Protestant stronghold of Montpellier. Here for a time the history of the previous year seemed likely to repeat itself as the royal army squared up to the troops of the formidable duke of Rohan. Both sides had their reasons for wanting to end the war, however, and the treaty of Montpellier was signed in October. By its terms Louis advanced his ambition to impose his authority uniformly upon his state. The Protestants lost most of their fortified *places de sûreté*, the great exception being La Rochelle: 'the Huguenot South had been conquered by the government.'[15] In return, the edict of Nantes was confirmed.

The crucial factor in these campaigns was a fundamental divergence of outlook between the two sides. Only fifty years had elapsed since the massacre of Saint Bartholomew's Day, and the Huguenots believed that they were still locked in a struggle for survival. Such a view was in step with contemporary attitudes. As the Thirty Years War began, religious toleration was not seriously discussed in the council chambers of Europe. The attitude of Louis XIII, however, was exceptional. He was determined that his Protestant subjects should become indistinguishable from his Catholic ones, except in the private matter of their religious persuasion. In 1621 he assured the duke of Lesdiguières, a leading Huguenot nobleman soon to become constable of France, that 'nothing should be freer than one's conscience ... It is also in His holy care that I leave the secret of your [religious] vocation and that of each and all of my subjects of the *religion prétendue [réformée]*.'[16] This was a view bequeathed by Catherine de' Medici's chancellor, Michel de l'Hôpital, who had warned that insistence upon religious purity would destroy the state. Guaranteeing the state's integrity would require the exercise of royal authority unconstrained by considerations of dynastic ownership. That was what Louis was in the process of undertaking.

In his view of kingship as a God-given office by which to regulate the national interest Louis was assisted by several shifts in opinion provoked by the religious fault line running through the kingdom. Many of the urban Catholic populations wanted an end to the Huguenots' political and economic privileges, with all towns put on an equal footing. More significant was the defection of the grandees from the Protestant cause after 1620. Only Rohan and his brother, the duke of Soubise, were prepared unequivocally to accept the offer of military governorships made by the Protestant Assembly meeting in La Rochelle in 1621. The remaining six all found ways of deserting the Huguenot cause. The reasons for their defection were complex, including an innate hostility to popular rebellion. Even the duke of Rohan allowed his guard to slip when negotiating with a group of Calvinist pastors in 1621: 'I would rather lead a pack of wolves than a troop of ministers.'[17] However, most of the representatives of the great Protestant houses, Sully, Lesdiguières, La Trémoïlle, Bouillon, La Force, appeared to accept l'Hôpital's opinion that allegiance to the crown must ultimately supersede confessional loyalty.

The peace of Montpellier provided no more than a breathing space on the road on which Louis had set out. In the west, between land and sea, the greatest obstacle to a permanent settlement, La Rochelle, remained stubbornly impregnable. Before hostilities were resumed Louis took the momentous decision, in 1624, to admit to his council Armand-Jean du Plessis, who two years earlier had become the cardinal of Richelieu.

Richelieu was no stranger to high office. In 1615 as bishop of Luçon he had delivered the closing speech on behalf of the clergy at the meeting of the estates general. Then, with unfortunate timing, he was appointed a secretary of state just months before the murder of Concini. On that fateful day Louis XIII demanded that Richelieu remove himself from the court, on the assumption that the queen mother's friends were his enemies. Later he changed his mind, aware of the fact that the bishop of Luçon might have a useful part to play in the negotiations with his mother. Richelieu eventually accompanied Marie de' Medici on her journey into political exile in Blois, but was then himself exiled, first to the priory of Coussay close to his family estates in Poitou, then further west to his diocese of Luçon, where he had to make do in a borrowed house next door to the cathedral chapter's bakery.[18] Finally, in the spring of 1618 he was banished to the papal enclave of Avignon, far removed from the levers of political influence.

He was rescued by the queen mother's escape from Blois. A fortnight after that drama he was ordered by the king to join Marie de' Medici at Angoulême.

Louis and his favourite, Luynes, again decided, as they had done after the Concini assassination, that among the queen mother's circle of advisers Luçon was the one most likely to persuade her into an accommodation with the government. Sure enough Richelieu played a key role in the negotiations leading to the signing of the treaty of Angoulême in May 1619. He had to go through similar parleys the following year after the king's triumph at Ponts-de-Cé. The treaty of Angers, however, provided Louis with a more comprehensive victory than Angoulême, and he was prepared to be magnanimous, promising to sponsor the bishop of Luçon for a cardinal's hat. That it was magnanimity expressed through gritted teeth was indicated by the subsequent two-year wait before the red hat arrived. As far as Louis XIII was concerned, Richelieu's incontrovertible skills as a diplomat and political operator had to be weighed against the fact that they had been acquired in the service of the opposition. True to character the king viewed the cardinal with deep suspicion.

Richelieu's readmission to the king's council in April 1624 came therefore as something of a surprise. The reasons for Louis' change of heart were both personal and professional. In December 1621 his friend, the duke of Luynes, had died unexpectedly. Although before his death the king was showing signs of regretting his emotional dependence upon his favourite, there could be no doubting the void left by Luynes' disappearance. Temperamentally the king needed a close adviser with whom to discuss political matters and test his own preferred solutions. For this reason he remained reliant upon his mother's advice, despite her indifferent track record. Indeed, his decision to promote Richelieu was in part in order to demonstrate the renewed rapport between mother and son, though in her case support for the cardinal was part of a tireless campaign to regain the power she had lost on the morning of Concini's assassination. Louis also foresaw how beneficial the expertise of this formidable personality could be if employed in the service of the crown. In particular, he calculated that the cardinal's knowledge of international affairs might be employed to offset France's increasing vulnerability in Europe as the conflict which would later be known as the Thirty Years War gathered pace. During his first, brief spell as a secretary of state, in 1616–17, Richelieu had acted as foreign minister, an experience which taught him that domestic and foreign policies had to be viewed in the round.[19] By 1624 the extent of their interrelationship was posing difficult analogous questions. Were the Huguenots a threat to the French nation, and did considerations of national security require France to enter alliances with Protestant powers? Fortunately, Richelieu's view of the conduct of foreign policy corresponded well with his royal master's opinion of how best to neutralize the role of religion in political affairs.

For both of them loyalty to a particular religious confession came second to the security of the French state. Richelieu did not share the view of his patron,

Marie de' Medici, and the *dévot* party that an alliance with His Catholic Majesty of Spain was in France's best interests because it was in the best interests of the Catholic Church. That policy was already failing on a personal level: Louis XIII's relationship with his bride, the Spanish infanta Anne of Austria, was showing every sign of adding to his abysmal record of family disharmony.

When Richelieu rejoined the king's council in 1624 military conflicts across Europe had reached critical proportions, with inevitable repercussions for France's security. War had first broken out in Bohemia in 1618, taking the form of a Protestant revolt against the Habsburg Archduke Ferdinand, who was shortly to become the Holy Roman Emperor. In 1621 this conflict merged with the renewal, after a twelve-year truce, of the Dutch struggle for independence from Spain. In that struggle the maintenance of Spanish supply routes through the north Italian Alps and the Rhineland was essential if the rebellious provinces were to be regained. Henry IV had earlier set about disrupting this Spanish Road, and his success had caused Spain to open up an important detour through the Valtelline, a river valley linking Lombardy with the Tyrol. Louis XIII was well aware of the strategic importance of this corridor and was prepared to counter the Spanish occupation by force. To this end in 1623 he signed an offensive alliance with Savoy and Venice, France's sole supporter in Italy. In addition to the threat levelled against the Spanish Habsburgs, the treaty aimed a blow at their Austrian cousins by encouraging the German princes to carry on their fight against the emperor. By now thoroughly anti-Habsburg, the king also ostentatiously stationed French troops on the frontier with the Spanish Netherlands.

The king's assessment of what France's European strategy should be was not, therefore, transformed by Richelieu's arrival on the scene. By 1624 the situation had marginally changed, to the extent that papal troops had replaced the Spanish forces controlling the Valtelline forts, though the Spaniards remained the dominant power there. In the first months after Richelieu's entry to the royal council the cardinal was careful to play a secondary role to the marquis of La Vieuville, the *surintendant des finances*, who was its effective head. During that time France signed a subsidy treaty with the Dutch, and sent agents to the Swiss cantons, in the hope of persuading them to take up arms against the imperial and Spanish forces. In August 1624 La Vieuville was dismissed and Richelieu began his long reign as the king's chief minister.

He was now free to pursue more vigorously the policy of separating the encircling Habsburg powers. In November 1624 a combined French-Swiss army expelled the papal troops from the Valtelline, and in the following spring a Franco-Savoyard force attacked the Spanish dependency of Genoa to disrupt traffic on the Spanish Road. By the treaty of Monzon in March 1626 France agreed to withdraw her troops from the Valtelline, and Spain accepted the restoration of the Protestant Grisons as overlords of its Catholic inhabitants. Just under a year earlier Richelieu had overseen the marriage of the king's sister, Henrietta Maria, to Charles I, the new king of England. The fact that many of these allies were Protestant states was a matter of relative indifference to the cardinal. When the pope's representative, Cardinal Barberini, came to Paris to intercede on behalf of the Valtelline Catholics, Richelieu responded, in Louis' presence, that the Grisons were the legal lords of the Valtelline and the king would not permit any diminution of his allies' rights.[20]

The clear subordination of religion to politics in foreign policy was reflected in the attitude already adopted by Louis XIII towards his Huguenot subjects. In both instances the goal was the security of the realm, for which in extreme circumstances everything had to be sacrificed, and that objective had nothing to do with personal morality. Only the ruler, acting as the state's chief officer and not as heir to the Bourbon family fortune, could pursue such a policy. The need to do so, and the need to separate private morality from public necessity, provides the key to an appreciation of the enduring legacy of king and cardinal.

The concept of reason of state was not of course revealed as a new idea: its novelty lay concealed behind the traditional divinely ordained character of French kingship. There was nothing of the revolutionary about Cardinal Richelieu – except in one respect. He understood that whereas before the Wars of Religion the king's authority had derived from his person, afterwards it depended ultimately upon the exercise of a public office. The two concepts had been vying with each other for some time, but it was Louis XIII and his cardinal-minister who finally and unequivocally gave primacy to the office-holder. Even in the world of feudal hierarchies, the crown had succeeded in distancing itself from its subjects, but that personal mystique could not survive the assassinations of Henry III and Henry IV. A new level of authority was needed to allow the crown once more to guarantee the integrity of the French state. That level could be reached without undermining the old social and political order for, as God's consecrated agents, French kings were expected to deploy their sovereign power in defence of a regime of Christian justice, paying due respect to their subjects' rights and privileges; but at the margin, when the state's security was at risk, they were justified in taking whatever action was necessary to redeem the situation.

Richelieu's views on this subject were first voiced by one of his agents, writing in 1625 about the renewed outbreak of Huguenot violence:

An individual is bound promptly to carry out what he promises; the king is bound to do so only if it pleases him, and it should please him only when it can be done without harming his state. The justice of sovereignty places it above ordinary justice in such matters ... We must remember that the promise made by the sovereign to the state when he assumed direction of it limits all promises that he may subsequently make. When the interest of the state is involved, we must return to first principles and recall that the law of the state compels him to prize it above all his individual acts.[21]

In other words, when acting as the custodian of the state no law, either divine or human, should inhibit the king's decisions.

The final battle for La Rochelle provides a perfect illustration of these ideas in action. For La Rochelle stood at that dangerous crossroads where national security was most vulnerable to international assault. The fact that it was the last surviving and most defiant stronghold of French Protestantism was threat enough, though by the 1620s it was clear that national interests were superseding confessional crusades. But La Rochelle was dangerously independent in other areas too. Its economic privileges, based originally upon wine and salt, had made the town largely autonomous, unaffected by the government's inefficient and inadequate tax regime. Finally, and most significant of all was the town's maritime setting. With its back turned on Paris it had long sought to use its dominating position on France's Atlantic coast to make its fortune in the wider world.[22]

At the beginning of 1625, when Richelieu was still in the process of establishing his authority, the Rohan brothers again raised the flag of rebellion at La Rochelle. The younger brother, Soubise, at the head of the Rochelais naval forces, took the lead. Richelieu for his part was forced to temporize, being seriously short of funds and lacking a navy. Not that Soubise's headstrong actions were a prerequisite to persuading the cardinal that France's lack of a royal navy made it vulnerable. He understood perfectly well that state security was increasingly bound up with wider economic issues, potentially global in scale, which governments would ignore at their peril.

European statesmen were being forced to this conclusion by the conduct of the Dutch. Their successful revolt against Spain was consolidated not by military might, which they did not possess, but by an aggressive and expansionist trading policy aimed initially at their erstwhile Protestant sympathizers in England. The logic of the situation was clear. The new Dutch merchant fleet, intent on taking over England's import trade, would have to be supported by a strong navy. The English navy would have to respond to that threat, and did indeed, by waging three trade wars against the United Provinces in the course of the seventeenth century. London's celebrated merchant philosopher, Thomas Mun, expressed the matter thus in 1628:

> ... many well-governed states highly countenance the profession, and carefully cherish the action of foreign trade not only with Policy to increase but also with power to protect it from all foreign injuries: because they know it is a Principle in reason of state to maintain and defend that which doth support them.

This new mercantilist doctrine was not unknown in France. In the year before Richelieu first became a secretary of state Antoine de Montchrétien published his *Traité de l'économie politique*, which he dedicated to Marie de' Medici. In it he pointed out that whatever trading rights individuals might have, the ruler had an overriding authority for reasons of state to control the country's trade as he saw fit. Richelieu was sympathetic to this point of view and, as soon as he regained his membership of the royal council, moved towards the establishment of a French battle fleet.[23] Progress was slow, however, for there was a lack of skilled native shipbuilders. The decisive naval battle of 1625 in which the Rochelais fleet was destroyed, ensuring the eventual surrender of La Rochelle, was a triumph of *Realpolitik* over religion since the victorious French fleet was made up exclusively of borrowed Dutch and English vessels.[24]

Almost at once the English realized their mistake in supporting the emergence of a new naval power capable of threatening their own security. In October 1626 Louis appointed Richelieu as superintendent of navigation and commerce, and the cardinal began to talk of constructing an Atlantic fleet of some forty-five warships to protect French interests. 'On the power of the sea', thundered the archbishop of Bordeaux, 'depends the lowering of the pride of England, Holland, Spain ... and the ruin of the Huguenots', in that order.[25] In July 1627 the English made one last attempt to restore the situation by dispatching a naval expedition to La Rochelle under the command of the duke of Buckingham. After his retreat Louis was free to concentrate on blockading the town and reducing it to obedience. Over a year later, on 1 November 1628, La Rochelle was at last triumphantly reintegrated into the kingdom of France.

The results of this epic struggle were entirely in keeping with the king's view of what essentially had been at stake, namely the security and integrity of the state. Thus the religious settlement, the Grace of Alais, so-called because it was not a treaty but a royal act of pardon, reaffirmed that touchstone of toleration, the edict of Nantes, but significantly only its basic text and not the additional clauses which had guaranteed the Huguenots political and military rights. Gone therefore were the fortified places and the political assemblies which had threatened the unity of the state. In return, French Protestants became legally indistinguishable from the rest of the king's subjects. Gone too were the fiscal privileges which had made La Rochelle a semi-independent city republic. Import and export duties and revenues from shipping now flowed into the crown's coffers. To preserve their exemption from the *taille* the Rochelais were forced to pay an annual subvention, and additional taxes were levied on wine, herrings, sugar and other commodities. Both king and cardinal minister recognized the importance for state security of maximising available financial resources, both from home and overseas. They did not intend this perception to lead to the undermining of the regime of fiscal privilege and exemption which was characteristic of France as a whole, but there could be no doubting the king's determination to make exceptions when necessary.

Even before the dénouement of the long-running Huguenot conflict, the king had become embroiled with another group whose life-style made them a threat to his preferred scheme of things, the high nobility. Louis XIII had no quarrel with the second estate at large. As the chief nobleman in the land he was its natural leader, predisposed therefore to maintain its traditional privileges. But the grandees, headed by the members of the royal family, were a different matter. They remained wedded to a form of unreconstructed feudalism in which the king derived his authority from his headship of the family concern rather than from his wider role as the guarantor of national identity. In the latter capacity his power was absolute, but in the former it was vulnerable to family arguments.

The king's fraught relationship with his mother, for example, became no easier after the defeat of the Huguenots. The nub of the problem was his chief minister and her own former creature, Richelieu, who in Marie's estimation had grown too big for his cardinal's hat. In the queen mother's quasi-feudal view there was no room for a chief minister, particularly one whose career she had been responsible for promoting. Her most prominent supporters in this battle of the old guard against the cardinal were her favourite younger son, Gaston, and her daughter-in-law, Queen Anne. Each was intimately involved in the Bourbon family business, Gaston remaining his brother's heir so long as Anne continued to fail in her pre-eminent task of producing a son. All three resented the redefinition of political priorities being brutally postulated by their son/brother/husband and his unlovable accomplice.

Marie de' Medici's unwillingness to play second fiddle had been well documented since her husband's death, and in 1626 Gaston tried likewise to meddle in high politics. The so-called Chalais conspiracy, named after the unfortunate marquis who found himself caught up with far more dangerous conspirators, was intended to remove Richelieu and possibly the king himself, the latter to be replaced by Gaston, who would in due course marry Louis' queen, Anne. With the exception of the queen mother who inexplicably missed this golden opportunity to indulge in political intrigue, all the usual suspects were present. Besides Gaston they included Louis' half-brothers, César and Alexandre Vendôme, the progeny of Henry IV and Gabrielle d'Estrées, who had been programmed since childhood to torment the unfortunate king; his Bourbon cousins, the prince of Condé and the count of Soissons; and Anne of Austria, who was less a conspirator than a bored and isolated recipient of insider gossip. The queen remained a Spanish infanta at heart, an increasingly uncomfortable stance while her brother, Philip IV, was edging closer to war with her husband. It had also become all too apparent that this attractive and high-spirited young woman was not sexually or temperamentally compatible with a king who was unsure of his own sexuality and morbidly preoccupied with the cares of office.

From the queen's perspective the key figure in the Chalais affair was her bosom friend, the duchess of Chevreuse. Marie de Rohan-Montbazon was a member of the illustrious Rohan family whose most charismatic representative, the Huguenot duke Henri de Rohan, was at the time of the Chalais conspiracy still fighting the king's troops in the battle for La Rochelle. In fact his later career was indicative of the seismic shift in the political landscape which was freeing the crown from the clutches of its extended feudal family. Both Louis and Rohan acted honourably in accordance with the new rules: by the Grace of Alais Rohan was pardoned for his treason, as it had now to be categorized. He responded by committing his military talents to the service of the king.

The career of his kinswoman, Marie, was no less dramatic and colourful, though her loyalties were less clearly defined. Over a long career this celebrated *femme fatale* raised the practice of political intrigue to the level of an art form. Louis himself was one of her early conquests, and his youthful infatuation remained an inhibiting factor in his later dealings with her. In the opinion of the king's most recent biographer Marie de Rohan shared with his wife and mother the responsibility for turning Louis into a misogynist![26] She had made a promising start to her public career by marrying the royal favourite, the duke of Luynes, a match which led to her appointment as head of the queen's household. After the death of Luynes she became duchess of Chevreuse, the title by which she is generally known, following her marriage to a member of the ruling ducal family of Lorraine. The duchess was a survivor of that courtly, irresponsible world gravitating around the collective personalities of great families, which was anathema to state builders like Louis XIII and his cardinal minister.

Their reaction to the challenge posed by the Chalais conspiracy demonstrated their understanding of what was at stake in the high-risk enterprise on which they were embarked. Ruthlessness was to be the chief attribute of state security. The Vendôme brothers went to prison where Alexandre died in 1629; his brother, César, a broken man, was released in the following year. Both Soissons and Chevreuse fled abroad, the former to Italy and the latter to her husband's family base in Lorraine. The prince of Condé made his peace with the king and was readmitted to the court. Louis had no alternative but to patch up relations with his brother, who was still the heir to the throne, and a chastened Gaston was honoured with the title of duke of Orléans. There was no reprieve, however, for the hapless marquis of Chalais, another of Marie de Chevreuse's conquests, who was beheaded at Nantes in 1626. The fact that almost thirty blows were needed to sever the head from the body serves to underline the inhumanity of the new Leviathan towards its enemies as well as the executioner's incompetence.

By its very nature the law of reason of state had to apply equally to all the king's subjects. That lesson was brutally driven home in the following year with the execution of the count of Montmorency-Bouteville. Bouteville was a cousin of the duke of Montmorency, head of the ancient noble family whose representatives had served the crown at a high level for generations. Their semi-independent base was in Languedoc where they monopolized the post of governor; the phrase *primus inter pares* encapsulated their perception of the Bourbon family's relationship with their own.

Bouteville's crime was to flout legislation forbidding duelling, a pastime rich in symbolism for members of the *noblesse d'épée*, who interpreted its prohibition as an affront to their knightly values and a restraint on their freedom of action. From the king's point of view it represented an attempt to impose order on his chief lieutenants, so that they might shed their blood fighting on the state's behalf rather than in support of an outmoded code of honour. This was in no respect an attack upon the honour of the noble estate. But it was a calculated assault upon the *grands*, that small, powerful group of noblemen, estimated by Richelieu to number no more than twenty-five, who had to learn that honour came a poor second to interest of state.[27]

That message was ruthlessly conveyed for the remainder of Louis XIII's reign against conspirators who were increasingly confined to, or certainly inspired by, members of the royal family circle. On the so-called Day of Dupes, 10 November 1630, the queen mother believed that she had at last succeeded in engineering the fall of Richelieu, only to be outwitted by her son, who had no intention of sacrificing his favoured confidant. This was to be her final challenge to Louis' authority: during the summer of the following year she fled to the Spanish Netherlands and would never again set foot on French soil. In 1632 Gaston of Orléans, who had also left the country after the Day of Dupes, returned at the head of a nondescript army, pledged to free the king from the clutches of his evil minister. Gaston's chief supporter in this ill-fated adventure was the duke of Montmorency, the godson of Henry IV and the last representative of a great noble house. Insulated in his southern fiefdom against the demands of the new order, this veritable image of a valorous Christian knight could not grasp the shift in loyalty now being required of him by his friend since childhood, the king. His defeat in battle and subsequent execution brought to an end the House of Montmorency, and perhaps also symbolized the demise of an older *ancien régime*.

Then finally, shortly before his death in 1643, Louis discovered that his latest favourite, the marquis of Cinq-Mars, had entered into a conspiracy with Spain and with Gaston of Orléans. The secondary objective of this plot was to secure peace, but its primary and entirely unoriginal aim was the removal of Richelieu. When it came to reading the new script Gaston was a particularly slow learner, invariably sheltered as he was by his proximity to the throne. Cinq-Mars was an ambitious schemer who mistakenly imagined that his emotional hold over the king would outweigh the latter's commitment to reason of state. In fact, even before proof of Cinq-Mars's treason became available, Louis was prepared to act: 'Having given us ample reason to be suspicious of him, the interest of our state (which we have always held dearer than our life) obliged us to secure his person and those of his accomplices.'[28] The erstwhile favourite was beheaded on 12 September 1642, less than three months before Cardinal Richelieu, the target of so many noble conspiracies, died peacefully in the Palais Cardinal in Paris. One of his last acts was to bequeath that sumptuous residence, henceforth to be known as the Palais Royal, to the king in whose service he had made his fortune.[29]

In the short term, Louis XIII had succeeded in countering the atavistic tendencies of the *grands*. He still, however, had to solve the problem of how to reconcile political and social power and prestige in the governance of France if the established order was not to be undermined. Paradoxically, his strategy was to separate the two. Outside Paris the role of the provincial governor had for a long time epitomized the ethos of the great families. Traditionally the governors represented the king at the highest social and political level. Their duties were diverse but overwhelmingly military, and their provincial network of supporters guaranteed them a quasi-feudal band of loyal dependants. During Louis' reign a number of the most noble names in France were deprived of their regional status. The queen mother, Marie de' Medici, lost the governorship of Anjou, and the duke of Guise lost Provence. Following his part in the Chalais affair César de Vendôme surrendered Brittany, while his legitimate half-brother, the truculent Gaston, was forced to give up both Orléans in 1631, and the Auvergne in 1642. The Montmorency family's governorship of Languedoc, which had endured for over half a century, ended in 1632 with the execution of the last duke.[30] After purging the provinces of unreliable grandees Louis and Richelieu looked for loyal replacements. These might have to be newer men masquerading under inflated titles, or even a trustworthy and socially acceptable lieutenant general taking the place of an absentee incumbent. In that way the potentially dangerous divergence between social influence and political rectitude might be avoided. The best example of reconciliation between old and new is provided by Henri de Condé, a prince of the royal blood who played the *enfant terrible* in his younger years before making a deal with the king and his chief minister in 1626. Thereafter, his exemplary loyalty resulted in his successive acquisition of the governorships of Berry, Burgundy, Guyenne and Languedoc.[31]

The independence of the old-style governors was also threatened by the rise of the provincial intendants, though their emergence as key government officials was not primarily to do with reducing the independence of the regions. During the previous century the crown had regularly dispatched agents to inspect and report on aspects of local government. What dramatically altered their role and status was war, that irresistible engine of change, in which France was directly involved from 1635. The financial demands generated by the Thirty Years War simply could not be met by the age-old, creaking organization aspiring to act as the state's revenue-raising machine. The system was irrational and the methods of collecting taxes grossly incompetent. Besides, assessments were frequently skewed to placate special interest groups, so that the heaviest burden was placed on those least able to pay.

Consequently, the intendants became permanently intrusive figures in the provinces. They were royal commissioners not venal office-holders, and their powers of justice, administration and finance became increasingly flexible and wide-ranging. Not only did they supervise the activities of local financial officials, the *trésoriers* and the *élus*, they also began to intervene to remedy the worst excesses of the tax-gathering regime in order to bolster the king's resources. Like their cousins in central government, the intendants represented a new, professional nobility, of men who for the most part had acquired their social and political status through legal training and state service.[32] Though ideologically very different from the governors, the role of the intendants was not part of a plan to restrict gubernatorial activities. The *ancien régime* did not deal in comprehensive reforms of that kind, preferring ad hoc solutions designed to maintain the status quo as far as possible. In fact, the two offices were expected to work in tandem, and the governors were often consulted about suitable intendant nominees before appointments were made.

In the capital, at the centre of government, the growing influence of the *noblesse de robe*, boosted by Henry IV, continued apace under his son, as it became clearer that the king's state had to be served as well as the king. The office of secretary of state outgrew its humble sixteenth-century origins as its incumbents became essential figures in government. Although Richelieu remained the chief figure in the royal administration, it was the king himself who pushed the new government bureaucracy into the breach between sovereign and subjects. Consequently the secretaries began to receive all the important correspondence from the provinces and abroad, which would previously have gone directly to the king. Embryonic departments of war and foreign affairs developed, where incoming information was processed and made available to the secretary. As the recipient of such knowledge his political influence inevitably grew. So did his authority. The secretary of state for war, for example, was responsible to the king 'for commissioning, mustering and making all other necessary provisions for the chief and principal army which must be commanded by His Majesty or by his lieutenant-general'.[33]

The growing significance of war and foreign policy during the years of Richelieu's ministry also contributed to the growing power of the superintendent of finance at the heart of government. By 1632 these officials (sometimes the post was held jointly) were beginning to draw up annual budget statements of revenue and expenditure, and to earmark sums for particular purposes. Their chief task in this period, however, was to manage the national debt, since the revenue received in direct and indirect taxation, and from the royal domain, was not adequate to meet the demands of war. They had therefore to find extraordinary sources of income from the sale of offices, and from long- and short-term borrowing.[34] It is not surprising that such important administrators should be ex officio members of the king's chief council, the *conseil d'en haut* (as were the leading secretaries of state though in their case still on an *ad hominem* basis). So onerous were their responsibilities that, like the intendants, the superintendents of finance were not allowed to purchase their office; instead they held a royal commission which narrowly limited and defined their powers.

This small group of counsellors gathered around the king was in the process of replacing the *grands*, not on the basis of their personal familiarity with the sovereign but as the chief administrators of his state. The change was a subtle one. In both instances nobility was a *sine qua non*, the fact of noble status remaining more important than its origins. That was why the attempt to reconcile political and social divisions in government was not doomed to failure. Besides, most of the new grandees came from existing noble stock with backgrounds in both robe and sword. Claude le Bouthillier, who was in turn secretary of state and superintendent of finance under Louis XIII, was born an impoverished nobleman, whereas Claude de Bullion, with whom he shared the post of superintendent, had been a councillor in the parlement of Paris, linked through his mother to one of the most influential *robe* families. Like earlier generations of *grands*, the new men had their own lists of clients and supporters, whom they recruited not only as loyal retainers but as reliable subordinates helping to implement the king's policy throughout the provinces. They were also assisted at the centre of government by a number of professional clerks, an embryonic civil service, the most senior amongst whom, the *premier commis*, were themselves elevated to the Second Estate by virtue of their role.[35]

Giving credence to this often ponderous reorganization of government was the image of the sovereign as the source of all justice in the state. There was no perceived separation of powers between the executive and the judiciary at any level, so that it was entirely reasonable, for example, to expect the intendants, who had been commissioned to exercise the king's authority in certain particular respects, to act entirely lawfully as royal judges. Those local officials whose authority was thereby overridden also exercised a judicial role, but justice was *the* royal prerogative and the king remained free to decide how it should be applied. The king's undisputed authority as chief justiciar, however, exemplified in the range of new powers he had bestowed on the intendants, risked provoking potentially dangerous resentments. To suspend the normal exercise of justice through the usual channels smacked of authoritarianism; and a royal administration whose actions did not always reflect a just regime could be accused of despotism.

The body best positioned to express such criticism was the ancient conscience of French kings, the parlement of Paris. Like that of the sovereign, the parlement's political authority ultimately depended upon its judicial role. Supported by the weight of its own forensic evidence, the court maintained that political action, justified in the name of reason of state, risked undermining the king's God-given authority. By the mid-seventeenth century its magistrates were among the capital's social elite, and this new *robe* nobility was intent on reaffirming the old jurisprudential order of which its court was guardian. The argument between the king, his magistrates and his ministers pivoted around the interpretation of the parlement's political role, but although both sides were capable of adopting extreme positions on occasion, neither was comfortable in doing so. The usual outcome of their quarrels was compromise.

Richelieu threw down the gauntlet in 1631 with the establishment of the Chambre de l'Arsenal, an extraordinary commission set up to judge cases in which state security was involved. The parlement protested that such a departure from the legal norm damaged the king's justice, to which Louis famously responded in person: 'You were established only to adjudicate between Master Peter and Master John'.[36] Relations were further damaged by arguments provoked by the government's need for war revenue. In 1641 the king visited the court to hold a *lit de justice*, effectively reclaiming his right to dispense justice in person, where legislation was registered forbidding the parlement to concern itself with affairs of state. Yet the same legislation allowed the magistrates to submit remonstrances on financial issues, more often than not the chief bone of political contention, and to discuss any political matter if invited to do so by the king. In other words, Louis' efforts to reduce the parlement to the level of a purely judicial court were offset by his own recognition that it was far more than that. Shortly before his death he directly acknowledged the parlement's wider significance by requesting it to register two declarations, the first naming Anne of Austria as regent in the event of his early demise, and the second pardoning five of its members who had been exiled from Paris for opposing the political legislation of 1641.

All the existing political uncertainties, affecting the powers of the king and the role of the nobility, were magnified when France found itself embattled in the Thirty Years War. The Second Estate's traditional *raison d'être* was of course personal military service to its lord, the king. Yet, as the king himself began to require a more impersonal kind of service to his state, the essential amateurishness of that role began to be apparent. For warfare waged by the state was becoming ever more large-scale and technical: the noble cavalry charge was yielding before the withering fire of mercenary musketeers. Nevertheless, as Louis XIII and Richelieu committed France to the first Europe-wide conflict of the modern era, they still depended heavily upon the *grands* with their network of clients, to raise and equip a large proportion of the royal army, and upon the assumption of many young noblemen that military service ultimately defined their status.[37]

Although politically overshadowed by the elite group of noble civil servants, the high-born nobility had not left the field. They had suffered further setbacks during the reign, being deprived of their hold over important so-called great offices of the crown. In the 1620s the offices of constable and admiral, chiefs of the king's forces on land and sea, were removed from the high nobility. Both in their time had been among the trophies of the House of Montmorency, but Louis understood perfectly well that such alternative power bases were incompatible with the new political order. In abolishing the office of constable he observed that 'those who hold these positions ... have often used the kingdom's own forces for their personal interests ... to the great detriment of the state'.[38] Only one of the great offices of the crown retained its old authority, that of chancellor, whose incumbent continued to represent the king in the crucial area of royal justice, though by this time, ironically, the route to that summit was through the ranks of the *noblesse de robe*.

The grandees, however, continued to dominate the offices of the royal household, thereby enabling them to retain their proximity to the king's person. The great ceremonial household offices included those of grand master, master of the horse and grand chamberlain. These were invariably set aside for princes of the blood and their natural allies among the higher nobility. The grand mastership was the preserve of the cadet branch of the royal family, notably of the princes of the House of Condé. The offices of grand chamberlain and master of the horse belonged to two semi-independent families, the La Tour d'Auvergne, dukes of Bouillon, who besides their extensive lands in the south west of France were lords of the independent principality of Sedan; and the even more prestigious ducal House of Lorraine.

The foreign policy pursued by the second Bourbon king of France formed part of his vision of kingship. Louis' determination to delimit the freedoms of his most powerful subjects was a reaffirmation of the ruler's ancient obligation to establish a just and secure regime. Why otherwise should his subjects remain loyal? The rise of the Renaissance super-princes had rendered that task more difficult. They represented not European states but European families. Their power, based on dynastic accumulation, spread across the Continent. It produced alliances which challenged the integrity of existing states both by threatening their frontiers and by furnishing disaffected subjects with an alternative focus of loyalty. This destabilizing state of affairs was exacerbated by the splintering of Europe's religious homogeneity, all of which underlined the urgent need for a new-style European order.

Viewed from Paris the threat was too real and immediate not to take action. France was besieged to the south and east by the most predatory of princely families, the Habsburgs. Though the abdication of Charles V had brought about a divided inheritance, the Habsburg rulers who succeeded in Vienna and Madrid nevertheless retained important common interests. The first was their resolute defence of the Catholic cause internationally, the second their joint concern for the security of the Spanish Road, Spain's military lifeline to the Netherlands, and the territories adjacent to it, control of which was a constant threat to France's eastern and south-eastern frontiers. Henry IV had made a start in 1601 when he forced an eastward diversion of the road, through the Valtelline into the Austrian Tyrol and away from the more direct northern route through Savoy. Then in the mid-1620s French troops briefly occupied the Valtelline before combined Habsburg forces reasserted the status quo.

A new opportunity presented itself in 1629 with the disputed succession to the duchy of Mantua. Mantua was strategically situated close to the duchy of Milan, hereditary possession of the kings of Spain and far too close for comfort to the Spanish Road. To complicate matters further, because Mantua was also an imperial fief, the new duke's investiture was subject to the approval of the Habsburg emperor. Finally, the candidate with the best claim to succeed, the duke of Nevers, was a subject of the king of France. In the circumstances of the time an international incident of some significance was bound to follow. First to intervene was the neighbouring Spanish army in Milan, a decision which provoked Louis XIII into military action. Early in 1629 the king crossed the Alps at the head of his troops and forced the Milanese army to withdraw. It was a spectacular military adventure carried out in the depths of winter by a ruler who relished the uncomplicated challenge of battle and felt most at ease amongst the soldiery. After the French withdrawal it was the turn of the emperor to intervene, imperial troops entering Mantua through the Valtelline in the spring of 1629. At the same time Spanish forces reinvaded from Milan. It was clear that, if he intended to maintain his strategic challenge to the power of the Habsburgs, Louis had no alternative but to cross the Alps for a second time and confront the opposition head on. An advance force under Cardinal Richelieu's personal command moved against the duke of Savoy and seized the key fortress of Pinerolo in March 1630. The king himself arrived in time to overrun the rest of Savoy, but another bout of serious illness then threatened to overwhelm him and he was forced to return to France. Efforts to resolve the impasse in Mantua where three large armies, French, imperial and Spanish, were encamped, now passed into the hands of a papal diplomat, Giulio Mazarini, whose meetings with Richelieu made a deep impression on both men. These were the first appearances on the international stage of another of the great servants of the House of Bourbon, Cardinal Mazarin.[39]

What followed highlighted the distinctive path, at home and abroad, on which France was embarked. Religious conflict had so divided Europe for the best part of a century that there was no longer general agreement over what constituted an acceptable political order. France had chosen an inclusive, national approach in its attempts to resolve the Huguenot problem, culminating in the Grace of Alais signed in 1629, in the lull between the two Mantuan campaigns. But the two branches of the Habsburg family viewed matters very differently. Spain's position was encapsulated in a memorandum from the count duke of Olivares, addressed to Philip IV in 1621. 'You are the main support and defence of the Catholic religion', he told the new king; 'for this reason you have renewed the war with the Dutch and with the other enemies of the Church who are their allies.' He also reminded Philip that he was 'the greatest monarch in the world in kingdoms and possessions'.[40] In other words, as ruler of a far-flung empire, Philip IV was bound to look to the universal church as a unifying factor, and beyond the frontiers of Spain for his security. The emperor's position was not very different. The Austrian Habsburgs were the hereditary rulers of lands scattered across central Europe. By virtue of their title of Holy Roman Emperor, to which the family was perennially elected, they also exercised some limited influence among those states which had once formed part of the medieval German empire. In truth that title bestowed more prestige than authority. Nevertheless, along with the restoration of the Catholic faith throughout Germany and the Habsburg lands, it offered the emperor the best means of creating a powerful political organization; though not a unitary state like France.

The Thirty Years War had begun in Germany with the Bohemian revolt, an uprising which had played into Habsburg hands. For the newly elected king of Bohemia, Frederick, the Elector Palatine, was decisively defeated by imperial troops at the battle of the White Mountain in 1620, while Spanish forces occupied the west Rhine area of his Palatinate, thereby adding to the Habsburg pressure on France. This success encouraged the emperor, Ferdinand II, to seek to reinforce his authority in a manner consistent with his imperial role. In March 1629 he issued the Edict of Restitution which attempted to turn the clock back to 1552. All land within the empire that had been taken from the Catholic Church since that date was to be returned, and Calvinism was to be outlawed. This act, promulgated without any reference to the imperial diet or *Reichstag*, was quite reasonably viewed by the German princes as an assault on their independence and a threat to the liberties of the German people.

In the following year the emperor did convene a meeting of the electoral college at Regensburg, where he hoped that the seven electors would agree to elect his eldest son as king of the Romans and therefore heir to the imperial title. French diplomats, headed by the enigmatic Capuchin, *père* Joseph, were well represented there, and nobody doubted whose side they were on. The electors were to be assured that Louis XIII, 'being moved by a very sincere wish to deliver Italy and Germany from the oppression to which they had been reduced by the manifest violence and ambition of the house of Austria', would be offering help 'to re-establish the liberty of Germany, and in particular of the electors, good neighbours and ancient allies'.[41] The reference to Italy was a reminder of the fact that the Mantuan succession had still to be resolved despite the two French military interventions.

From the point of view of French diplomacy, Regensburg was not a success. The French embassy was outmanoeuvred by Emperor Ferdinand's insistence that his investiture of the French candidate in the imperial fief of Mantua would depend on France ceasing to give aid to his enemies in Germany. This proviso formed the basis of the treaty of Regensburg (1630), which, with some reservations, the French diplomats eventually signed. The treaty was never ratified, however, because it flew in the face of the king's and Richelieu's policy of Habsburg containment. In the following year, thanks in large measure to the diplomatic skills of the young Mazarini, Ferdinand agreed to recognize the duke of Nevers as the inheritor of the duchy of Mantua without the reciprocal strings which had been agreed earlier. By this time France had already taken a further step to undermine the emperor's position, by signing the treaty of Bärwalde with the king of Sweden in January 1631, offering Gustavus Adolphus a five-year subsidy to enable him to carry his anti-Habsburg crusade into north Germany. Nothing better illustrates the guiding principle of French foreign policy, that my enemy's enemy is my friend, than this alliance between Protestantism's most formidable champion and His Most Christian Majesty.

In encouraging the 'Lion of the North' to pursue his German adventure Richelieu realized, to mix animal metaphors, that he had a tiger by the tail. His anxiety grew progressively as Gustavus crossed the Elbe into Saxony where in September 1631 he defeated the imperial forces at the battle of Breitenfeld. Before the end of the year he had seized Frankfurt on the Main and by Christmas had reached the Rhine at Mainz. In the following spring he headed south and took control of Bavaria. By this time his forces were overextended and he decided to seek a more secure base in north Germany. In November 1632 at the battle of Lutzen, close to the previous year's battlefield at Breitenfeld, the Swedish army again defeated the imperial troops but on this occasion at the cost of the king's life.

Richelieu had to reassess the situation and advise Louis on where the balance of French interests now lay. Although Sweden's future value as an ally was thrown into question there were nevertheless unilateral actions open to France. The Swedish descent on the Rhine had again underlined French, and Habsburg, vulnerability in the regions surrounding the Spanish Road. Using the excuse furnished by the marriage of the duke of Lorraine's daughter to the rebellious

Gaston of Orléans, the king's brother, French troops invaded the duchy in 1633 and had overrun it by the following year. This success opened the way to Alsace, technically under imperial suzerainty but in fact dominated by France's Swedish ally and Spanish adversary. A number of strategically positioned Alsatian towns placed themselves under French protection, thereby adding to France's defensive ring behind the west bank of the Rhine. One final, and significant, prize was the bridgehead fortress of Phillipsburg on the east bank of the river. It was in the gift of the archbishop-elector of Trier, who sought French protection in the summer of 1632. The importance of these initiatives was dramatically illustrated in September 1634 when the Swedish army was routed at Nordlingen, between the Rhine and the upper Danube, by a combined Habsburg force. The imperial army had joined up with some eight thousand troops en route from Spain to Brussels via the Valtelline, thereby restoring at a stroke the threat of Habsburg hegemony in Europe. Ironically, it had been France's effective blocking of the Spanish Road through Alsace and Lorraine which had forced the Spanish troops to march further east into Germany in order to unite with their Habsburg allies. When Richelieu and his sovereign heard the news of Nordlingen they were forced to acknowledge that France had no alternative left but to enter the war itself.

The *casus belli* was provided by the king of Spain who in March 1635 ordered the invasion of Trier and the capture of the elector. The latter was under the formal protection of the king of France, and Louis was in no doubt that he was honour-bound to respond. Besides, Trier's strategic position on the Rhine made a French response imperative. France duly declared war against Spain in the following May and for some time thereafter maintained the fiction that Spain was the sole enemy. This suited Louis XIII who, notwithstanding his close family links through his wife with the Spanish royal family – perhaps, indeed, because of them – continued to view Madrid as the chief threat to Paris.

For quite predictable reasons the first years of France's direct involvement in the war went badly. French forces had suddenly to fight on many fronts, in Italy, Lorraine and Flanders, yet this leap in military activity was undertaken without any government strategy 'aimed at exercising more effective control over recruitment, supply, payment or discipline'.[42] There was no plan for a new model army, only the old, well-tried expedients.

There were, however, some encouraging signs for the king and the cardinal. In a show of national solidarity Henri de Rohan, the great Protestant hero, led a French army into Italy in 1635 to seize control of the Valtelline; still in the king's service three years later he was mortally wounded further along the Spanish Road at Rheinfelden. In 1636 Spanish troops reached the town of Corbie in Picardy, and were poised to march upon Paris itself. Louis, however, held his nerve. At his most inspirational in the face of physical danger, he courageously took to the streets of the capital without a bodyguard to drum up support for a counter-attack. On this occasion the Parisians rallied patriotically to their king's cause, in contrast to their predecessors during the days of the Catholic League, who had opted to support Spain.[43] Louis moved north at the head of his troops to recapture Corbie and lift the threat to Paris.

Though himself a spirited military leader, the king was not, of course, a professional soldier, and those whom he chose to command his armies had to possess the social cachet to act on his behalf. That convention seriously reduced the likelihood of great soldiers emerging to challenge the incomparable Spanish *tercios*. At a critical moment in its history, however, France was blessed with remarkable good fortune. Not one but two noblemen with the necessary social background emerged to lead the king's armies. Both proved to be outstanding soldiers and one of them, Turenne, under whom Marlborough learnt his craft, became one of the great captains in the history of European warfare. The younger of the two was the duke d'Enghien, son of Henri, prince of Condé, once Henry IV's bitter rival in love but later reconciled to Louis after the Chalais Affair. Condé and his two sons raised five infantry regiments as their contribution to the war effort, with troops recruited from the family governorship of Burgundy.[44] Enghien succeeded to his father's title in 1646 and is better known in history as the Great Condé. Henri de la Tour d'Auvergne, viscount of Turenne, was the younger son of a French Huguenot duke, of Bouillon, and the grandson of William the Silent, the effective founder of the Dutch Republic. Turenne held fast to his Protestant inheritance until near the end of his life.

France's greatest good fortune at this juncture, however, was the series of misfortunes which befell its chief adversary, Spain. For the Spanish kingdom remained essentially a gathering of regions, united only by religion and the Habsburg dynasty, and in 1640 two of those provinces, Catalonia and Portugal, rebelled against Madrid. France in contrast was an increasingly unitary state, where religious divisions mattered less than the overriding quest for national security under the crown.

In the final months of his life Louis XIII witnessed increasing success in the field against both Spain and the emperor (against whom France had belatedly declared war in 1638). One of Cardinal Richelieu's last acts before his death in December 1642 was to recommend to the king that Turenne and Enghien should be given the highest commands in the royal armies. Louis himself died before the impact of that recommendation could be weighed, on 14 May 1643, the thirty-third anniversary of his succession. Five days later the duke d'Enghien routed the once invincible Spanish infantry at the battle of Rocroi.

Louis XIII was a conviction politician whose life was dedicated to the *métier du roi* long before his son coined the phrase. Unlike his son, however, Louis XIII derived little pleasure from the profession of kingship. His often well-grounded mistrust of the *grands* was heightened by an introverted personality which made it difficult for him to maintain good relations with anybody at all. His love affairs with various young men and women of the court – Marie de Hautefort and Louise de La Fayette, François de Barradat and Claude de Saint-Simon – left him emotionally debilitated. All of them ended unsatisfactorily, on the scaffold in the case of Cinq Mars. Rumours of the king's physical ill-health surfaced even before his majority, and chronic illness accompanied him for most of his adult life. Unsurprisingly, Louis' view of the world was habitually tinged with melancholy. His wife's companion, Madame de Motteville, acutely observed in her memoirs that 'that prince was in no way destined to be happy'.[45] He came closest to that state when riding at the head of his troops. Like his father, whose physical courage he inherited, Louis enjoyed the camaraderie of campaigning. It is something of a paradox that Louis was the last of his line to lead his soldiers into battle, a function epitomizing medieval kingship, while intent on changing the perception of the monarchy vis-à-vis the state.

A final judgement on Louis XIII's reign must take into account the part played by his alter ego, the iconic figure of Cardinal Richelieu. Considering Louis' mistrustful personality and his early hostility to the bishop of Luçon, it is a tribute to the cardinal that he kept the king's favour for almost twenty years. He retained that favour without being a favourite for there was never an emotional bond between them. There was simply a growing realization on Louis' part that he had found a dispassionate listener with whom to share his ideas, and an acutely intelligent political operator to help turn them into practice. Richelieu was indeed a formidable presence, strong-minded and ambitious, but also well aware of the potential perils of his position, and of the need to couch his political advice in terms which he knew would be compatible with the royal point of view. There was never any doubt about which of that 'odd couple' held the upper hand.[46]

Crucially, however, on the most fundamental issue confronting them, the two men were in total agreement. Both understood that the security of the state could not be guaranteed so long as the concept of kingship as a family possession continued to impose moral limitations upon the crown's freedom of action. As the state's chief executive, the king had to be able to act in ways which could only be justified by state necessity. This was true in the face of threats posed both externally and internally. It has been observed that reason of state was not a theory put forward by Richelieu and adopted by Louis, but was rather an attitude of mind, a climate of opinion which proved to be irresistible.[47] One of its most significant implications was that subjects' diverse confessional beliefs would be acceptable if the alternative was state insecurity, an idea already implemented by Louis when his future chief minister was still in the service of Marie de' Medici. Throughout his reign Louis strove resolutely to enforce the notion that loyalty to the crown, as chief executive of the state, was the supreme political virtue. In elaborating Henry IV's prototypical design, that achievement promised to build for the Bourbons a powerful, secure state, a model which the rest of Europe would be forced to copy. The king's premature death, however, reopened other possibilities for the shape of France's future development which would not have pleased him.

For most of his married life Louis' relations with his queen, Anne of Austria, were formal and correct but by no means loving, much less passionate. Nevertheless, their recognition of the primary obligation of dynastic marriage – to produce an heir – survived both their relative mutual indifference and over twenty years of failed pregnancies, and miscarriages. Eventually, on 5 September 1638, a son was born to the ill-matched couple. He was formally christened in April 1643, less than a month before his father's death. An amusing if apocryphal story tells how, after the ceremony, the boy visited the dying king and in answer to the question, 'What is your name now?', solemnly replied, 'Louis XIV', thereby revealing at an early age besides an ability to calculate, a burgeoning sense of self-esteem. He would have seventy-two more years in which to work on his image.[48]

5

Apotheosis: the Sun King

Comparisons between the early days of Louis XIV's minority and that of his father are striking and not altogether coincidental. In each instance the chief candidate for the office of regent was the late king's widow, the mother of the new monarch. Both women were viewed with suspicion because of their foreign links – indeed, Anne of Austria inherited a country at war with her native Spain – and therefore needed strong support to establish their authority. Each received the support of the parlement of Paris, and at that point coincidence is superseded by the restatement of an ancient political tradition. The parlement's role as the chief supporter of a lawful regime presided over by the legitimate and divinely approved sovereign had been paramount long before the seventeenth century. So too had been its own assumption that in a state governed by law the supreme court should naturally wield certain political responsibilities. The murder of Henry IV had provided the parlement with an unexpected opportunity to renew that claim, beginning with its judgement that Marie de' Medici should be named as regent. The events which followed in the intervening thirty-three years before the next regency not only disappointed that generation of magistrates but threatened to challenge fundamentally the parlement's view of the properly established order.

For centuries the parlement had defined the French state in terms of the judicial function of its kings. That function, which was ultimately unchallengeable, was intended to preserve the status quo, not to undermine it. Louis XIII and Richelieu had not, however, always found the existing law sacrosanct, being willing on occasion to support an alternative justification for legal enforcement, reasons of state, not to be found in the court's registers. Their approach amounted to what has been called a governmental revolution.[1]

The root of the problem lay in the split nature of the prince's authority, obliging him both to provide a just regime for his subjects and to guarantee their security. Increasingly the latter worked against the former, as dynastic rivalry between Renaissance princes made war and international relations the lodestar for political action. Security on the frontiers required the maintenance of effective armed forces. This in turn depended on additional revenues to support them, however unjustly or illegally exacted. Traditional rights and freedoms could no longer be allowed to hinder the implementation of necessary royal policies. In the final analysis therefore, and this was a royal perception that had been growing for some time, the king's authority depended upon his role of custodian rather than of inherited owner of the French state. The crucial difference between the two roles was that, whereas in the latter capacity the ruler was bound by the same moral rules as his subjects, in the former he was required only to be successful. One of the supreme critics of political hypocrisy, Niccolò Machiavelli, who had observed the rise of the prince at close hand, understood his need 'in order to maintain the state, to act contrary to fidelity, friendship, humanity and religion', secure in the knowledge that 'the means will always be considered honest, and he will be praised by everybody', if he achieves a successful outcome.[2]

The parlement was able to reassert its political influence because Anne of Austria needed its support in overthrowing the late king's will, establishing his widow as regent with only limited powers. The parlement's constitutional position was that the regent, in representing the king as a minor, should possess the same sovereign authority as Louis XIV himself would wield after his majority. Therefore, at the first *lit de justice* of the new reign in May 1643, the court was pleased to amend Louis XIII's will and allow the queen mother to become regent with full authority. It was even more delighted to receive her assurances that henceforth she would welcome its political advice.

Both the naivety and the indignation of the magistrates quickly became apparent as Anne moved enthusiastically from being head of her own household to becoming head of state. One of her first decisions was to recruit as her first minister Richelieu's former protégé, the Roman Giulio Mazarini, now naturalized as Jules Mazarin. Like his former mentor a prince of the church, Cardinal Mazarin seemed intent on emulating his predecessor's policies too. This was a particularly unwelcome development for the judges of the parlement of Paris who, with their advocacy of a legally ordered state, had long viewed Cardinal Richelieu as their enemy in chief.

The questionable legality of the government's desperate search for financial resources under Richelieu's leadership was certain to raise *parlementaire* hackles. In 1635, however, matters became personal with the introduction of a number of edicts creating new offices, including twenty-four in the parlement itself. Offices were family investments and an inflation in their number was likely to undermine their value. Louis XIII added insult to injury by refusing to allow a debate on the legislation, insisting that the edicts concerned be registered in a *lit de justice* and denying the magistrates any subsequent opportunity to discuss the issue. Their protests were met with the summary arrest of the most outspoken judges and their temporary exile from Paris. A judicial strike then ensued before peace was finally re-established between king and court.

This pattern recurred in the early years of the regency. Anne of Austria may have taken the place of Louis XIII, and her favourite, Mazarin, assumed the mantle of Richelieu, but the new executive faced exactly the same old problem of where to find extra revenue. Their inheritance was a mixture of money-raising expedients whose delivery in many instances depended upon a cavalier attitude to established judicial forms. Nobody disputed the fact that the king's role of chief justiciar entitled him both to delegate his authority and to reclaim it. The aura of a just regime could, however, only be sustained if established legal conventions were adhered to and arbitrary interventions reduced to a minimum. That was by no means the case. One leading magistrate complained bitterly that 'there are more affairs in petty justice decided by commissions than by ordinary judges', while the parlement as a whole had reminded Louis XIII that 'great kings ... gladly leave their subjects the liberty and security which is most commonly found before ordinary justices'.[3] The court's quarrels with the king encompassed a number of examples of *justice retenue*, from the use of the *lit de justice* and evocations to other courts or provincial parlements, to the establishment of commissioners whose powers under the royal seal were extensive and subject only to review by the king's council.

Most prominent among this new breed of government officials were the intendants. What distinguished the commissioners from the majority of government officials was the fact that they had not purchased their office. Commissions were temporary and could be revoked at any moment by the sovereign. Commissioners could therefore be employed as shock troops to enforce policies which permanent local officials might have reason to oppose. The *officiers* on the other hand could not be dismissed, since their office was part of their property. It represented a serious financial investment, was a source of great social status, and enabled government servants to resist government pressure. These officeholders existed at a number of levels, ranging from the *élus* and treasurers who acted as the crown's financial agents in the regions to the sovereign court judges in the parlements of France. Collectively they represented the normal processes underpinning the conduct of public affairs. Unsurprisingly their champion was the parlement of Paris, whose history enshrined those processes and whose members owned some of the most prestigious and highly priced offices in the land.

Its opposition to government policies escalated from the beginning of 1648, though its skilful, legalistically turned arguments were not intended to challenge the status quo, much less provoke the dénouement of civil war. The trouble was that by this time the issue of state necessity was forcing both crown and parlement to define their respective positions in a mutually unhelpful way. In calmer moments both sides knew that a degree of constructive ambiguity had long characterized their relationship. From January 1648, however, that relationship was put under serious threat.

On the 15th of that month the young king, who was not yet ten, came to the great chamber in the parlement to preside over a *lit de justice*. He was accompanied by his mother and by his godfather, Cardinal Mazarin. The object of the visit was to force through the registration of further revenue-raising measures, including the creation of twelve new legal offices which would be made available for purchase. In offering his opinion the advocate general, Omer Talon, made a justly celebrated speech, in which he initiated the dangerous process of trying to bring the parlement's constitutional role into sharper definition. He challenged the recent use of *lits de justice* to stifle discussion, maintaining that:

> it is a kind of illusion in morals and a contradiction in politics to believe that edicts, which by the laws of the kingdom are not susceptible of execution until they have been brought to the sovereign companies and there debated, shall pass for verified when Your Majesty has had them read and published in his presence ... it concerns your glory that we be free men and not slaves; the grandeur of your state and the dignity of your crown are measured by the quality of those who obey you.[4]

This was stirring oratory, and all the more dangerous coming from the lips of one of the crown's own officials in the parlement. The formal registration which followed was the harbinger of months of skirmishing between the court of law and the regent.

A few days later the parlement began to review this legislation, even though it had already been registered by the king's express command, and within the month it was seeking to introduce its own modifications. This provoked Anne into calling the magistrates' bluff by demanding to know whether the court was now asserting the right to alter edicts already verified in the king's presence. By further reducing both sides' room for manoeuvre the regent was risking a constitutional crisis, but the royal judges in the parlement were not to be compared to the revolutionary parliamentarians across the Channel. Talon duly reported to the queen mother that they 'confess that they neither can nor should decide a question of this sort which could involve them in piercing the ultimate mystery of government'. This view was reiterated by the archbishop of Paris, who later as Cardinal de Retz would play a leading role in the civil wars of the Fronde. He warned against tearing aside the veil which shielded the mystery of state, thereby exposing the kingdom to anarchy.[5]

Having rescued a victory of sorts from her clumsy dealings with the parlement, the regent trumped her political naivety by mishandling an issue close to the hearts, and pockets, of all the office-holders in the Parisian sovereign courts: the *paulette*. This annual tax, which since 1604 had guaranteed full ownership of office, came up for renewal every nine years and was invariably the cause of unseemly wrangling between the crown and the office-holders, as the former attempted to extract a financial quid pro quo. In April 1648 Anne offered to renew the annual tax for members of the parlement of Paris but not for members of the provincial parlements or of the other sovereign courts in Paris, the *cour des aides*, the *grand conseil*, and the *chambre des comptes*. To gain the security of office provided by the *paulette* these office-holders would have to contribute the equivalent of four years' salary to the needy government. This transparent attempt to buy the support of the parlement was a gamble on the evident self-interest of its members. Instead, the self-confidence derived from recent skirmishes with the government encouraged them to lead the opposition rather than side with the regent.

Consequently, in May 1648, the parlement authorized its deputies to meet representatives of the other three Parisian courts in the Chambre Saint Louis, part of the complex of the Palais de Justice, in order to pursue a common course of action against this latest financial threat. Although the magistrates had not become revolutionaries overnight, an air of crisis began to grip Paris as the weakness of the regent's authority became ever more apparent. In the course of a few weeks government actions had ranged from arresting a number of the more outspoken judges, and forbidding any further meetings in the Chambre Saint Louis, to offering to restore the *paulette* without strings, releasing the prisoners and permitting the assemblies to continue. In the face of such vacillation the parlement felt emboldened to raise the level of its demands.

The parlement took aim at two of its most hated targets, intendants and tax-farmers. They were easy and obvious targets for the court, which viewed them as responsible for a combination of financial and judicial malpractice. The financial demands of the Thirty Years War had ushered in a golden age for the *traitants*, those financiers who signed treaties with the government allowing them, in return for lump sum payments, to farm taxes for their own benefit. This practice was universally unpopular, both because the methods employed were extortionate and because the money was seen to go straight into the pockets of the tax-farmers rather than into the king's coffers. To add insult to injury, the king's own commissioners, the intendants, colluded with the *traitants*, using force to ensure the collection of taxes and to prevent the local tax officials from functioning normally. This was classic ground for the parlement to exploit. In condemning the extra-legal nature of these activities, and in questioning the legality of the intendants' commissions because they lacked verification in a sovereign court, the judges were not seeking to lead a revolution. On the contrary they were demanding that the clock be put back to a time before reason of state overrode each and every law enshrined in their company's registers. The danger for the crown, especially while effective power lay in the hands of an unpopular regent and an even more hated first minister, was of a descent into anarchy. By this time the word *Fronde* was becoming part of the argot of the capital. It meant a catapult of the kind wielded by mischievous children, an odd word to stand for the civil upheaval which would afflict France for four years. Yet at its end it might well be argued that those who participated in the Fronde were indeed playing games, serious games intended to test the limitations of the new order, but not to challenge the ultimate authority of the young man who had inherited the crown of Saint Louis. That interpretation is not inconsistent with the fact that, as the greatest corporation in France acting in a 'corporation ridden society', the parlement had its own axe to grind, the dispensation of justice providing its members with their income and prestige.[6]

By mid-July 1648 it appeared that Queen Anne and Cardinal Mazarin had decided that it was possible to buy off the parlement without compromising the authority of the crown. On 18 July Mazarin persuaded the court to accept a royal declaration abolishing the commission of intendant except in those frontier areas where military needs dictated its survival. Then, on the last day of the month, the queen mother returned with her son to the Palais de Justice to hold a *lit de justice* at which another conciliatory declaration was registered. The *taille* was to be reduced by a quarter, no new taxes were to be imposed except by edicts 'well and duly registered', the *paulette* was to be unconditionally restored to the members of the sovereign courts, and the king's council was not to flout the authority of the established courts. In his politic response Talon succeeded in encapsulating in one sentence, admittedly a lengthy one, the parlement's political theory:

> The opposition of our votes, the respectful resistance which we bring to bear in public affairs must not be interpreted as disobedience but rather as a necessary result of the exercise of our office and of the fulfilling of our obligations, and certainly the king's majesty is not diminished by his having to respect the decrees of his kingdom; by so doing he governs, in the words of the Scriptures, a lawful kingdom.[7]

The government could live with that thesis. Unfortunately for the tranquillity of the kingdom the magistrates' momentum was already sweeping them beyond the middle ground towards further confrontation.

The court renewed its attack upon the tax-farmers and challenged the validity of existing financial legislation which had not been registered by the parlement. The government's riposte was to arrest two of the most belligerent judges, including a senior magistrate, Pierre Broussel, who by this time had become a folk hero among the Parisian poor. The latter's reaction was to riot and set up barricades in the streets, an ominous sign which immediately persuaded the frightened regent to release the two men. Broussel's proposal, immediately after his release, that the parlement should order the barricades to be removed, provides a telling insight into the court's true position.[8]

The final days of the judges' revolt became something of a personal confrontation between the parlement and the new *éminence grise*, Cardinal Mazarin. In September 1648 the young king, his mother, and Mazarin left Paris, apparently as a preliminary to launching a military attack on the parlement, to be led by

Condé. The court's response was to invoke the 1617 decree which forbade foreigners to play any part in governing France.

This was a crucial moment in the history of Bourbon kingship. Henceforth, until the dying days of the monarchy, the crown would have to demonstrate, paradoxically, that it still exercised the fullness of power, preferably with the support of its traditional advisers. The king's historic mission was to govern in person, not to allow others to govern in his name. The impact of Richelieu's ministry had been traumatic for the sovereign's natural allies, and now his protégé, Mazarin, was threatening to turn precedent into routine. For his part Mazarin chose to interpret the parlement's assault on him as a direct challenge to the authority of the crown, the mirror image of the magistrates' point of view. Accordingly, he gambled on a military victory. Once more, this time on 5 January 1649, the royal party slipped out of Paris to the château of Saint-Germain and preparations were put in train to besiege the capital and crush the parlement's revolt. Neither side, however, had the stomach to pursue extreme measures with unknowable consequences; especially after news reached France that the king of England had been found guilty of committing treason against his subjects and executed on 30th January, less than a month after the French royal court had made its clandestine exit from Paris.[9] In the spring of 1649 the treaty of Rueil was signed between the regent and the parlement, which effectively preserved the status quo. The reforms of 1648 survived, but so did the cardinal-minister.

This increasingly bitter conflict between the regent and the judges had encouraged that other group of frustrated and disillusioned royal advisers, the *grands*, the great noblemen of the realm who still clung to the notion of the king as *primus inter pares*, to enter the lists. Their chief was the enigmatic Louis de Bourbon, the Great Condé, premier prince of the blood, whose crusade to replace the usurper Mazarin at the king's right hand turned him in the end from fealty to treason. For Monsieur le Prince and his supporters, governing France remained an extended family enterprise, and being *primus inter pares* meant having a fair share of the family silver. From this point of view the career of Mazarin represented an unacceptable intrusion. Not only was he a foreigner of low birth – portrayed in the vitriolic Parisian propaganda pamphlets of the time, the Mazarinades, as the son of a Sicilian oyster-seller – but he had added insult to injury by accumulating a vast fortune.[10] Few considered this wealth to have been legitimately acquired, and Condé and his supporters wanted it confiscated.[11] In the autumn of 1649 Monsieur le Prince demanded a veto over the appointment of provincial governorships, a profitable source of income for the cardinal, and over senior positions in the army and royal household. Mazarin was forced to agree but struck back in the following January by having Condé arrested, together with his younger brother, the prince of Conti, and the governor of Normandy, the duke of Longueville, who was a member of the house of Orléans and the husband of Condé's sister, Anne-Geneviève de Bourbon. This sister was no less formidable than her famous brother. Attractive, intelligent, conspiratorial, she brought to mind the heyday of Marie, duchess of Chevreuse, who herself was still very much alive and enjoying something of a comeback at the side of the cardinal. Madame de Longueville's chief contribution to her brother's cause was to capture the affections of the greatest soldier of the age, Henri de la Tour d'Auvergne, viscount of Turenne, who with his elder brother, the duke of Bouillon, and the king's uncle, Gaston, duke of Orléans, joined the revolt of the princes.

The subsequent civil war reflected the powerful provincial base of the *grands*, and the deep-seated, quasi-feudal loyalty of their clients. It also sparked off more radical movements, such as the Ormée in Bordeaux, but essentially this was an attempt by the displaced political establishment to regain its authority at the centre of government. The great noble families around the throne, who had once been the king's natural councillors, demanded that that relationship should be restored while the king remained a minor and a regency was in place. What that boiled down to was one overriding war aim: Mazarin had to go. The cardinal, however, played his usual astute hand, aided by the unrealistic and anachronistic outlook of the opposition. By this time the real power of the *grands* lay outside the capital. These people were amateurs in the art of governing the country, and as a consequence were preoccupied with status and riven with faction. Mazarin's policy of divide and rule further weakened noble resistance, as did bribery on a massive scale, often involving the reward of provincial governorships to those opting for loyalty to the crown. The most significant turncoat was Turenne, whose decision to place his formidable military talents at the king's service was probably influenced by the offer of staggering, and backdated, compensation for his family's loss of the principality of Sedan, together with the title of sovereign prince and, from 1653, the governorship of the Limousin.[12] With the exception of Condé the rest of the *grands* made their peace with the crown, more easily and willingly after 7 September 1651 when the king's majority was proclaimed, just two days after his thirteenth birthday. For his part Condé redeployed his considerable fighting qualities in the service of King Philip IV of Spain, who was still engaged in war against France. His reconciliation with Louis XIV, and with Mazarin, was deferred until after the cessation of hostilities in 1659.

In September 1651, as Louis XIV took nominal control of his own and his country's fortunes, his reign had over sixty years to run. By its end he would have acquired an enduring reputation far beyond the boundaries of his country and of his time. He would be famous for many things but mainly for being famous. The character of his reign was a calculated response to the political questions posed by the traumatic events of his childhood. By the time of his majority that childhood was passing, and the thirteen-year-old was already capable of acting the king. Physically he was well suited for the part. Fit, extremely athletic and an accomplished dancer, he excelled in the traditional royal pursuits of hunting and horsemanship. He appeared to be a confident, gracious young man, exhibiting early that innate sense of dignity which by extension would eventually characterise his whole world. He did not enjoy academic study, though he coped well enough with the teaching programme devised for him. Intellectual debate was not his métier, and he viewed the world in conventional terms. Nevertheless, Louis XIV was no fool and Saint-Simon's characterization of the king as of below average intelligence says more about the great memorialist's prejudices than about the Sun King's intellectual capacity. Yet, despite the inherent partiality of that work and its author's outrageous vanity, the *Mémoires* of the duke of Saint-Simon still offer a unique insight into the public-private world of the *grand monarque.*[13]

It gradually became clear that the new king had his own way of dealing with the fundamental question posed so dramatically during the time of the Frondes, namely whether the proto-bureaucratic form of government favoured by Richelieu and Mazarin should finally replace the highly personalized style of dynastic kingship with its strong emphasis on the support of the royal family and its time-honoured allies. Louis XIV's response was to refuse to contemplate an answer in those terms. Rather he would attempt to reconcile what contemporaries were minded to view as irreconcilable.

His affection and admiration for Mazarin was unwavering, and during the 1650s he was eager to learn from his practised chief minister the skills needed to govern his country well.[14] Serious minded and self-confident about his royal vocation, he was still only in his twenties when he composed one of the most premature of political memoirs for the benefit of his son, the dauphin. In it he made clear both his debt to the cardinal, 'who loved me and whom I loved', and his resolve after Mazarin's death to continue to rely on the professionalism of the new elite to inform his own decision making. The great civil service families of seventeenth-century France, the Colbert, the Le Tellier, the Phélypeaux, made their appearance in the king's memoirs. Their qualifications were duly noted: they were intelligent, informed and committed. They were also, despite all the honours bestowed upon them, simply the king's creatures. In a most revealing passage Louis XIV acknowledged that he could have chosen as his ministers less well qualified persons of higher social standing. But it was his intention to govern in person, and to be observed at all times as the embodiment of sovereign authority. In that respect he agreed with the position taken by the parlement of Paris during the heady days of its opposition to Mazarin. He famously confirmed his intentions at a council meeting on the morrow of the cardinal's death in March 1661. Addressing his chancellor, he announced,

> Monsieur, I have called you, together with my secretaries and ministers of state, to tell you that up to this moment I have been pleased to entrust the government of my affairs to the late Cardinal. It is now time that I govern them myself. You will assist me with your counsels when I ask for them.[15]

Both in satisfying the demands of the Fronde rebels that France should not be governed by a chief minister, and in exploiting the revolution in government over which the hated cardinals had presided, Louis was adroitly repositioning the authority of the crown on a new and elevated level. He was particularly determined once and for all to refute the threadbare doctrine of *primus inter pares* which had sustained the Princes' Fronde. He elaborated on the thinking behind his decision not to choose eminent individuals as his ministers:

> It was above all necessary to establish my own reputation and to make the public realize, by the very rank of those whom I selected, that it was not my intention to share my authority with them. It was important for they themselves not to conceive any greater hopes than I would please to give them, which is difficult for persons of high birth.[16]

It would be a mistake, however, to assume that Louis XIV's relations with the *grands*, and with his own family, were permanently soured by the experiences of his youth. Indeed, he never lost that sense of pride of ownership which had originally made government a family concern. But in inheriting the kingdom as head of the ruling dynasty Louis also understood that he had become its chief administrator, and in that capacity he required the help of officials not family. In every other respect, however, as the greatest nobleman in the realm, he believed that the bearers of great names should retain their traditional prestige. How this was to be accomplished when the essential constituent of that prestige, political influence at the highest level, was being removed, was far from clear as the young king was composing his memoirs for the instruction of the dauphin. Yet these same memoirs provide an early clue to the metamorphosis to come.

Under the year 1662 Louis related to his son the story of the great tournament, *le grand carrousel*, held in June in a specially prepared arena between the Louvre and Tuileries, a spot still identifiable in Paris as the Place du Carrousel. The whole event was a pastiche harking back to medieval models of chivalry and derring-do. The king's athleticism and horsemanship would have made him a star performer without the added symbolism of the occasion, but that symbolism in fact transformed a spectacular public performance into a political allegory for the whole of Louis' reign. From this moment date the king's choice of his motto, *nec pluribus impar* (not unequal to many), and of his emblem, the sun. Surrounding the sun king in their own starring roles were other members of the royal House of Bourbon as well as representatives of distinguished noble families such as the Guise. The king's brother, Philippe, duke of Orléans, was present and so was the prince of Bourbon-Condé, the Great Condé himself, now rehabilitated after his defection to Spain. In an earlier period, when the *carrousel* authentically reflected the spirit of the age, such a group might have viewed the king as simply first among equals; Louis' achievement in 1662 was to evoke that ethos in an environment which honoured the participants but posed no threat to the crown. He explained his reasoning to his son, setting it against the backdrop of the Fronde:

> But the more necessary it was to find some acceptable remedies to this excess, the more I was obliged to preserve and cultivate carefully whatever, without diminishing my authority and the respect that was due me, bound my people, and especially persons of quality, to me by affection, so as to show them thereby that it was neither aversion for them, nor affected severity, nor rudeness of manners, but simply reason and duty that rendered me more reserved and more strict toward them in other things. This community of pleasures that produces a courteous familiarity between our courtiers and ourselves strikes them and charms them beyond words.[17]

During the remainder of this long reign much effort and expense would be deployed both in the service of that 'courteous familiarity' and to add lustre to the sun king's image.

Initially, the latter task was largely entrusted to Jean-Baptiste Colbert whom Louis had inherited from Mazarin's service. Colbert was the king's chief financial adviser for two decades, his posthumous reputation depending chiefly upon his achievements in macro-economic management. From 1664, however, he was also director-general of buildings, arts, academies and manufactures, and it was arguably in that capacity that he performed the greatest service to his sovereign. Like his master, Colbert understood the importance of royal patronage of the arts as a means to the king's greater glory. From the artists' point of view too the support of wealthy and influential clients was a routine stimulus for the production of great works. There was, however, a fine line to be drawn between a commission pre-eminently reflecting the artist's vision and one intended by the authorities to polish the sun king's image. The line was a thin one. For Louis was not primarily concerned with censorship nor was he a philistine, and in any case great art has a habit of setting its own agenda.

The system developed under Colbert's direction depended upon the work of a number of new academies founded on the model of Richelieu's Académie Française. They included the Petite Académie, which began as a committee dedicated to scrutinizing and approving public texts, and grew into the Académie des Inscriptions et des Belles-Lettres; the Académie Royale de Peinture et de Sculpture; the Académie Royale des Sciences; the Académie Royale de Musique; and the Académie d'Architecture. The members of these societies sought directly or by means of patronage to produce art, literature and music which would honour the king. They were supported by other intellectual and artistic enterprises with the same objective. The Gobelins factory, officially the Manufacture royal des meubles de la Couronne, produced a dazzling array of furnishings and tapestries. Its director from 1663 was Charles Le Brun, who also enjoyed the title of the king's first painter. Le Brun provided the designs and supervised a team of high-quality craftsmen including painters, sculptors, cabinet-makers, engravers, gold and silversmiths, weavers and dyers, charged with producing the luxury furnishings intended to decorate the royal palaces. Most famous among them was the series of tapestries depicting the life of King Louis. Finally, the king was associated with the world of learning through the *Journal des Savants*, printed on the royal press from 1665.

A word of explanation is needed about the nature of this exercise in image building. The emphasis throughout was upon the king as the head of the ruling line rather than as the administrator of the state. Although the lengthy progression of the French monarchy from proprietary to office-holding kingship had become irreversible, Louis appeared to recognize intuitively from early in his reign the need to blur the two concepts in the interests of political stability. There would be countless examples of this tendency, a point made by the historian who has devoted a whole study to this theme: 'There can be no question that the king sometimes did distinguish between himself and the state; but on other occasions his intense personalism washed that difference away.'[18]

That Colbert's marketing of the king was not primarily an attempt to inflate the grandeur of France is evidenced by the number of foreigners invited to make a contribution. The Italian astronomer Cassini and the Dutch mathematician Huygens led the way, together with Swiss, Flemish and Danish practitioners of the arts and sciences. But the most famous visitor came from Rome. The great Baroque architect and sculptor Gianlorenzo Bernini had already transformed the image of the Eternal City when, in 1665, he set out for Paris. Colbert, who hoped to persuade the king to keep his headquarters in the capital, commissioned Bernini to produce a design which would complete the Louvre along its eastern front. His first offering was too Baroque for the minister's taste, though its swirling lines would have provided a counterpoint to the new left-bank building facing the palace across the river. This was the Collège des Quatre-Nations, now the Institut de France, designed by Le Vau and heavily influenced by Bernini's Roman contemporary, Borromini. In fact, none of Bernini's three proposals proved acceptable. In the end the great eastern colonnade of the Louvre was designed by a three-man committee consisting of the first architect, Le Vau, the first painter, Le Brun, and Claude Perrault, brother of Charles, who was a founder member of the Petite Académie. Committees are not normally the inspiration for great architecture, but the long, classical façade still conveys an impressive sense of order and power, an effect which the political architect, Colbert, was certainly seeking to create.[19] As for Bernini, his visit had one tangible outcome: a Baroque masterpiece in marble, the magnificent and true to life bust of the twenty-two-year-old king. Fittingly, that work resides not in the Louvre but in the palace of Versailles, which was already Louis' chief domestic preoccupation by the time Bernini left Paris to return to Rome.[20]

The Versailles project was the *leitmotiv* of Louis XIV's reign. It describes an idea as well as a royal residence. The king's objective was to dazzle his subjects and the world with his magnificence, but also to accommodate that 'courteous familiarity' which he knew the great men of his kingdom had always expected. He had long favoured the rose brick hunting lodge built by his father near the village of Versailles, some fifteen miles to the south west of Paris. Under his guiding hand it became the symbol of Bourbon power, and it remains one of the wonders of the modern world. The transformation began in the 1660s and took the rest of Louis' reign to complete.

The first sign of the coming metamorphosis occurred in 1664, before the vast building programme had begun. This was a week-long festival organized at the king's behest, and attended by some six hundred guests representing the apex of courtly society. The entertainment was entitled Les plaisirs de l'île enchantée. It was part tournament and part theatre, a spectacle of performance – plays, music and ballet – with fireworks and feasting, and, during the mid-May evenings, gardens transformed into a candlelit, romantic world. The inspiration for the Enchanted Isle was Ariosto's sixteenth-century epic poem, *Orlando furioso*, but there was also a contemporary meaning behind this rejection of the mundane in favour of the exotic. Louis was intent on redefining his authority in an environment calculated to work entirely in his favour.

An essential element in the creation of this environment was provided by the artists whose accomplishments there were intended to reflect the king's own civility. Much of the incidental music played on the Enchanted Isle was by the master of the royal music, Jean-Baptiste Lully, while the climax of the entertainment was the first performance of a new play, *Tartuffe*, by the king's *valet de chambre*. His name was Jean-Baptiste Poquelin; as Molière he would come to be recognized as the greatest comic writer in the French language. His reputation was established early, unlike that of the herald of arms, Charles d'Artagnan, who also played a role in the festival. He would only become famous two centuries later through the pages of Alexandre Dumas.

Having established his *mise en scène*, Louis proceeded apace with the task of enlarging and embellishing his theatre. The first extension of Louis XIII's château was entrusted to the king's leading architect, Louis le Vau. His design wrapped the new building around the existing one. The effect from the village side was of an elegantly balanced façade focused on the original courtyard, and from the garden side of an imposing classical-Baroque construction worthy of Bernini, with its recessed central terrace.[21]

Le Vau died in 1670, and responsibility for the present appearance of the palace of Versailles rests largely with his successor, Jules Hardouin Mansart. Mansart sacrificed the delicate symmetry of Le Vau's concept by adding two wings on the garden side, thereby more than trebling the length of the façade while retaining the same elevation. He also filled in the recessed terrace at the centre of Le Vau's garden front. The result was a monumental building, a statement of royal magnificence rather than a prize-winning architectural design. Although Mansart deprived visitors of the opportunity to admire the proportions of Le Vau's palace, he added an interior feature along the closed off terrace which would provide a metaphor for all the glories of the sun king's reign. Flanked at either end by the salons of War and Peace, the Great Gallery, the Hall of Mirrors, measured some 75 by 10 metres, its seventeen full-length windows exactly matching the seventeen facing mirrors of Venetian glass. The walls were richly panelled with the finest multi-coloured marble from the Pyrenees, the furniture – tables, candelabra, chandeliers – was solid silver, and Le Brun's ceiling painting, *The King Governs Alone*, reminded the world that Louis was the master of his own destiny. The whole of this extension, overlooking the gardens, was linked to the king's apartment, a magnificent suite of six state rooms built by Le Vau and decorated by Le Brun. The last of them, the sumptuous salon of Apollo with its silver throne, led into the equally spectacular Salon of War. From there a right angle turn revealed the dramatic and unexpected vista of the Grand Gallery stretching away along the garden front.

The gardens themselves also formed part of Louis' grand design for his Enchanted Island. The realization of his vision depended first upon the decorative plans of Le Brun but ultimately upon the ability of André Le Nôtre, heir to a gardening dynasty whose grandfather had been gardener to Catherine de' Medici. Once again Louis was fortunate to be able to call upon a servant of exceptional artistry to make manifest his ideas, and the gardens at Versailles continue to bear witness to Le Nôtre's talent. The whole Versailles project was rich in the iconography of the king's alter ego, Apollo, the sun god, and nowhere was that relationship more dramatically proclaimed than along the east-west axis of Le Nôtre's great formal garden. As the sun rose it first illuminated the marble court and the king's bedroom which was precisely placed at the centre of the building. Rising above roof level its rays caught Tuby's breathtaking sculpture of the gilded figure of Apollo driving his team of horses out of the deep and in the direction of the awakening palace. From the middle of the raised terrace in front of the Garden facade the straight-line view carried the eye over the Apollo basin to the mile-long Grand Canal beyond, and further into the middle distance. Below the terrace and separated from the basin of Apollo by a tree-lined avenue, stood the Fountain of Latona, the most explicitly political of all the iconographical allusions to be found at Versailles. Latona was the mother of Apollo, and both are depicted in this sculptural ensemble by the brothers Balthasar and Gaspard Marsy, acting out a legend related in Ovid's *Metamorphoses*. According to this account the goddess wreaked vengeance on a group of peasants who were intent on depriving her and her children of water, by having them turned into frogs. It is not fanciful to see in these marble and leaden figures an allegory of the Fronde, a time when the king's mother, Anne of Austria, sheltered her young son from the menace of rebellious subjects and ultimately triumphed over them. The brief guide to the gardens at Versailles which Louis himself composed includes the pointed instruction to pause at the fountain in order to reflect on Latona and the lizards.[22]

This then was the place from which, permanently after 1682, Louis XIV chose to govern his kingdom. The problems of the real world had still to be tackled, but the elaborate ritual and ceremonial which dominated life at Versailles subtly shifted the balance in favour of the untrammelled exercise of royal power. In particular, Versailles offered the prospect of a new alliance between the king and his great subjects, thereby bringing to an end the mutual hostility of their post-feudal relationship.

In Louis XIV's time there were twenty-two departments in the king's household, and all the senior positions were reserved exclusively for members of the royal family and of illustrious noble houses. The grandmastership of France was still in the hands of the Condé family in 1789. Between the reign of Louis XIV and the Revolution the title of grandmaster of ceremonies remained with successive marquises of Brézé, descendants of the Great Condé's wife, Claire Clémence de Brézé, who also happened to be Cardinal Richelieu's niece. The offices of grand chamberlain and master of the horse continued in the possession of the ducal Houses of Bouillon and Lorraine. The first gentleman of the bedchamber was a scion of a thirteenth-century noble family, the duke of Aumont, who also held the strategically sensitive governorship of Boulogne. Another governor, of Poitou, and holder of one of the most prestigious names in the ranks of the French nobility, the duke of La Rochefoucauld, was the recipient of a new office, grandmaster of the wardrobe (1669), and later of that of *grand veneur*, one of the oldest household appointments with responsibility for organizing the king's hunts.[23]

None of these offices was directly concerned with the business of administration and government. That was the responsibility of the 'new men', headed by the secretaries of state and the controller general of finance, who were also routinely present to carry out their duties. But the court nobility played a crucial role in the elaborate ritual and ceremonial which characterized life at Versailles, from participation in the royal *lever* and *coucher* to privileged access to the king at mass, at his dining table and out hunting. Louis was in a position therefore, informally and off the record, to enlist the opinions of those courtiers whose political judgement he trusted, without undermining the authority of his professional administrators. Indeed, he went further in seeking to reconcile the two groups by encouraging some carefully selected marriages between robe and sword. What the king would have abhorred in the wider social milieu he found acceptable in the 'other' world of Versailles.

Both the dukes of Chevreuse and Beauvillier, the former a direct descendant of Louis XIII's favourite, Luynes, the latter a gentleman of the bedchamber and also a member of the government, married daughters of Louis' powerful minister, Colbert; while La Rochefoucauld's son became the son-in-law of the marquis of Louvois, the formidable secretary of state for war and a member of the Le Tellier family, one of the leading civil service dynasties of the age. In the closed world of Versailles some surprising social gulfs could be bridged. Michel Chamillart, who became Louis XIV's controller general of finance and then his secretary of state for war, had both robe and sword credentials. His father had been governor of Caen and Chamillart himself a councillor in the parlement of Paris. It was not his forensic gifts, however, which attracted the king's attention but his skill at billiards. Louis was a very keen exponent of the game and played in what might be termed a regular foursome. This consisted of the duke of Vendôme, a great-grandson of Henry IV and Gabrielle d'Estrées; the master of the horse, Count d'Armagnac, a member of the house of Lorraine; and either Marshal Villeroy, who commanded the French army at the battle of Ramillies, or the duke of Gramont, governor in Henry IV's old stamping ground of Béarn, who according to Saint-Simon's poison pen, 'had in his favour name, rank, and an impressive appearance, but nothing else'.[24] The *parlementaire* was welcomed into this august company with enthusiasm even though he could outplay them all. In due course Chamillart was given lodgings at Versailles, became the governor of Rouen, and finally achieved high ministerial office.

The saga ended disappointingly in the course of the War of the Spanish Succession, the last and most traumatic conflict of Louis' reign, with first his resignation as controller general and then his dismissal from the war ministry. In truth Chamillart possessed few talents beyond an impressive hand-eye coordination, as Saint-Simon testified. The splenetic duke, who eyed the world of Versailles with a rare mixture of honesty and prejudice, was indeed a close friend. But his subtly modulated assessment of Chamillart, with its sting in the tail, would have given a modicum of satisfaction to his enemies too:

> agreeable, straightforward, obliging, genuine, upright, hardworking, as dedicated to the state and the king as to a mistress, devoted to his friends but grievously misjudging them, neither suspicious nor full of hatred, doing what he believed to be best with limited understanding, excessively opinionated, incapable of admitting to mistakes.

Saint-Simon added for good measure that Chamillart had the misfortune to be surrounded by people who were entirely lacking in common sense.[25]

Chamillart was succeeded as secretary of state for war by Daniel Voysin, another former magistrate in the parlement of Paris. Like his father before him Voysin had risen in the king's service as an intendant, one of that new breed of royal officials operating in the provinces on the government's behalf. Needless to say Saint-Simon took a dim view of such an *arriviste* joining the government elite at Versailles. His verdict was cutting and dismissive:

> Voysin possessed in abundance the most essential quality without which no man could, nor ever did, enter the council of Louis XIV during his entire reign, with the single exception of the duke de Beauvilliers, namely a complete lack of breeding ... Voysin was the grandson of the chief clerk in the Parlement's criminal office and died in that position. There is clearly no need to go back any further.[26]

Saint-Simon's protestations missed the point. Versailles was a club with its own set of rules to which all the members subscribed: nobles of robe and sword, descendants of ancient noble houses and distinguished public servants, governors of the old style and intendants of the new. The purpose of the rules quite simply was to safeguard the king's authority. The imagery of Apollo, first adopted by Louis in 1662, had played its part in the creation of a formidable power base.[27]

By the late 1650s Louis XIV was becoming impatient to govern. For several decades to come this grandson of Henry IV would exude the circumspect self-confidence of a privileged young man powerful and charismatic enough to make his name in the world, and to attract the attentions of countless female admirers. One who scarcely fits that bill, except in an ex officio capacity, was his first wife, the infanta Maria Teresa.

In 1648 the peace of Westphalia brought an end to the Thirty Years War for most of the combatants, but not for France and Spain, whose mutual hostility was further fuelled by Condé's defection after the Fronde. During the 1650s, however, the pendulum of war swung decisively against Spain, and the treaty of the Pyrenees (1659), Mazarin's final service to his adopted country, established France as the dominant force in Europe. It also marked the ascendancy of the House of Bourbon over the Spanish Habsburgs. For this treaty was as much a settlement between dynastic rivals as between states. That was why it contained clauses relating to the restoration of Condé's possessions and his status as the premier prince of the blood, and why it included the marriage contract between Louis and Maria Teresa, the elder daughter of Philip IV, the king of Spain. The contract also included Maria Teresa's renunciation of her rights, and those of her children yet unborn, to succeed to the Spanish throne. For generation after generation, marriage alliances between Europe's ruling families had remained at the heart of international relations. Paradoxically the stability they provided was regularly offset by the family quarrels which they were all too capable of generating. Both Louis XIV and Maria Teresa were great-grandchildren of King Philip II, the first Habsburg to rule in Spain but not in the family's traditional central European strongholds. This latest union of Bourbon and Spanish Habsburg merely marked the end of one cycle of conflict. The issue of the Spanish Succession, apparently resolved in the treaty of the Pyrenees, was still being disputed fifty years later on the bloody field of Malplaquet.

Louis accepted the fact that his marriage had to reflect the interests of his House, not his personal preference, and treated his queen with consideration and respect until her premature death in 1683. There was never much likelihood of his falling in love with her, however, an emotion he had already experienced at least once before his wedding. Falling in love did not of course equate with acquiring sexual experience, which, aided by an obliging lady of the court, Louis had already achieved as a teenager. More seriously for the marriage brokers he began to take a keen interest in Mazarin's five nieces, the Mancini sisters, who were known collectively by the title of the Mazarinettes. His preference was for the second sister, Olympe, who had to be hastily married off to the count of Soissons. Undeterred, Louis turned his attentions to her younger sister, Marie, and for a time it appeared that the king's determination to marry her would jeopardise the dynastic master plan. Marie certainly wanted to be queen, and Mazarin had to work hard to persuade Louis that such an eventuality was unacceptable: 'It is not a question of your desires ... your subjects' welfare and your kingdom are at stake.'[28]

The first genuine love of his life, Marie Mancini, was a spirited, highly intelligent young woman who shared the king's interests in music and sporting activities, and fired his enthusiasm for French literature. Maria Teresa, on the other hand, was by temperament more submissive and unquestioning, had no interest in hunting or the outdoor life, and spoke French with difficulty. On a personal level, she was no match for Marie nor for the women who succeeded her. That list began with Henrietta Stuart, daughter of the executed Charles I, who had recently married Louis' younger brother, Philippe. Minette, as she was called within the family, was in the Mancini mould: a vibrant, puckish personality, a keen horsewoman, and a devotee of song and dance. Her liaison with the king seriously embarrassed the queen mother, Anne of Austria, whose influence over her son remained strong. To outflank her, the young couple hit on a deception: Louis would invent an interest in one of Henrietta's ladies-in-waiting whom he would affect to visit when actually calling on his sister-in-law. The name of the seventeen-year-old chosen as the royal decoy was Louise de la Vallière.

Thus began in 1661 in a web of deceit one of the great *affaires* of the reign. In the course of the following six years Louise bore the king four children, only one of whom lived beyond childhood. It was not immediately apparent why the pale young blonde from Tours should have triggered such a grand passion. Though she shared Louis' love of music and was a brilliant horsewoman, she was far less dynamic than Marie or Henrietta, and was intellectually undistinguished. But she was pretty and uncomplicated, and Louis found her irresistible. It was with Louise in mind that he orchestrated Les plaisirs de l'île enchantée at Versailles in 1664; two years later he acknowledged her official status as *maîtresse en titre*. These were heady days, the early summer of Louis' reign, when the blossoming world of Versailles with its pleasures and pomp, intoxicated him and made everything he desired seem possible to achieve. What he most desired by 1667, however, was a change of mistress, from the increasingly guilt-ridden duchess of La Vallière to her friend and confidante, Françoise-Athénaïs, the marquise of Montespan.

Montespan's combination of wit and beauty, allied to her lineage – she belonged to one of France's most ancient families, the Rochechouart-Mortemart – and her single-minded determination, rendered her a formidable presence in the royal court. She was not, however, simply a gold-digger; indeed, there was nothing at all about her that could be characterized as simple. Certainly she aspired to a more comfortable and exciting lifestyle than that offered by her indigent and somewhat eccentric husband, but once established as La Vallière's successor she revealed a commanding personality capable, as her predecessor had never been, of dominating the court by her presence and by her *bons mots*. Her sense of humour was irrepressible and infectious. She loved life and its pleasures yet managed unexpectedly to combine her hedonism with what appeared to be a genuine spirituality, which was evident long before she finally left the sun king's court in 1691. Because both partners were married, the doubly adulterous union between the king and Montespan was a cause of considerable scandal. The marquis and his wife were not legally separated until 1673, so before that date Louis fell back on a proven strategy. Louise de la Vallière had acted once before as a decoy in order to mask the king's complicated love life. Now she was asked to repeat the performance by remaining *maîtresse en titre* though nobody at court had any doubts about the identity of the real mistress. The mutterings grew after La Vallière's conspicuous decision to become a Carmelite nun in April 1674. The opposition was led by the powerful, orthodox figure of Bishop Bossuet, court preacher and tutor to the young dauphin. It culminated in the spring of 1675 with the refusal of Montespan's local curé at Versailles to grant her absolution. Louis had no choice but to ask her to leave his court, and both king and mistress appeared conscience-stricken. The power of their mutual attraction caused them to defer any spiritual reckoning, however, and the two remained lovers until 1679. After her final departure from court Montespan lived for a further sixteen years, her zest for living scarcely diminished by her growing religious enthusiasm.[29]

Montespan gave Louis seven children, of whom three survived the hazards of a seventeenth-century childhood. All were legitimized, and would play a part in the events of the Regency following the king's death, as would her legitimate son, the duke of Antin. She herself was not interested in politics: apart from her obvious allure, her hold over the king was based on a shared enthusiasm for art and literature. The two of them enjoyed chatting together either in the 'Porcelain Trianon', Le Vau's exquisite mini-palace built for Montespan in the gardens of Versailles, and decorated inside and out in the fashionable blue and white of Delft; or in her famous bathroom apartment on the ground floor of the main palace, surrounded by works of art including paintings by Le Brun and sculptures by Tuby, Girardon and Le Hongre. As a cultivated patron of the arts Athénaïs de Montespan prefigures Madame de Pompadour.[30]

For some time before the official end of her reign, Louis' hitherto sunny world had begun to darken. His personal life began to spin out of control as one affair followed another, culminating in the short-lived liaison with Mlle de Fontanges, 'beautiful as an angel, stupid as a mule'.[31] It was as if Louis was resisting taking stock of his life and reign while sensing that the time to do so had arrived. The public criticism of his relationship with Montespan had affected him, and his earlier attitude of joyous certitude was beginning to give way to more sombre considerations, both personal and political. This change of mood was, however, less the result of his confessor's admonitions than of another's quiet persistence.

When Athénaïs was looking for a sympathetic and reliable foster-mother for Louis-Auguste, duke du Maine, her eldest child by the king, her choice fell upon a noble lady in straitened circumstances who was both the widow and granddaughter of poets. Françoise d'Aubigné, whose grandfather had been a close companion of King Henry IV, was known as Madame Scarron when she entered the household of Athénaïs de Montespan. From this influential vantage point she began to attract the king's attention, not as a siren figure, but quite on the contrary, as a devout and devoted admirer of the king, concerned for his eternal salvation. She had no scruples therefore about urging Louis to mend his moral ways, despite the fact that in so doing she was betraying Athénaïs, her friend. Indeed, hers was an important contribution to his deepening crisis of conscience. Eventually, by the kind of musical chairs process which seemed to govern the succession of the king's principal female favourites, Montespan was removed, the mother of the king's son being replaced by his governess. Louis' last and most enigmatic mistress would later become his wife, with influence far greater than that of any of her predecessors. Her understated presence at the king's side set the tone for the final, sombre decades of the reign. By then of course she was no longer the widow Scarron. In 1674, possibly with the encouragement of Madame de Montespan, the king provided her with the funds to purchase an estate south west of Versailles on the road to Chartres. Thereafter she would be known at court and in history as the marquise of Maintenon.

For all the carefully choreographed magnificence of his domestic lifestyle, Louis XIV believed that in the long term his reputation would depend upon his success as an international statesman. From its beginnings therefore, Louis' foreign policy was governed by the need for glory. That word, in French *gloire*, had a very precise meaning in its seventeenth-century context. For a dynastic ruler it meant renown, not only among contemporaries but, crucially, in the eyes of posterity too. Effectively it meant success in war, for war remained the profession of kings, even though kings were ceasing to be warriors themselves. The concept of *gloire* underlines the continuing relevance of the dynastic in French politics despite the ineluctable development of state power. One distinguished commentator on the wars of Louis XIV has recently observed that 'Louis employed the term [*gloire*] much as a modern statesman speaks of national prestige or national interest. And these are regarded as reasonable motivations today.'[32] Indeed, European conflicts at this time frequently had the appearance of family quarrels. Not until late in his reign, when the final climactic struggle for the Spanish Succession was beginning, did this great-grandson of Philip II begin to modify his views about how international disputes should be settled.

As a young man he had no inhibitions about seeking *gloire* through the agency of military conquest in accordance with the well-established dynastic tenets he had inherited. His first conflict, the so-called War of Devolution of 1667–8, was a classic example of the genre. The French invasion of the Spanish Netherlands was justified on the grounds that Louis' wife, Maria Teresa, the elder half-sister of Charles II, the king of Spain (their father, Philip IV, having married twice), had been denied the right, according to the family law of Brabant, to succeed her father in that region. A detailed manifesto drawn up by the king's lawyers was political dynamite, though it made reasonable forensic sense. It concluded:

> To propose that a male child born of a second marriage can exclude a female of a first marriage is to be ignorant of the nature and effects of the law of devolution. For by devolution the children of a first marriage inherit, from the very moment of one of their parent's death, the fiefs of the surviving parent. How then could a male child born of a second marriage possibly deprive them of ownership rightly acquired by law?[33]

By the treaty of Aix-la-Chapelle, which ended the war in 1668, most of the Spanish Netherlands remained part of Charles II's empire, but France did strengthen its north-eastern frontier through the acquisition of a number of strategic fortresses, including most notably Lille, which protected Paris from attack. In other words, recourse to family law, the dynast's natural approach to foreign policy issues, was ultimately subordinate to the only law which was non-negotiable, his obligation to maintain the security of his state.

That obligation was again momentarily submerged at the beginning of the following conflict, the long-planned sequel to the War of Devolution, against the Dutch Republic. Louis' decision to invade the United Provinces in 1672 was driven by hubris rather than by security considerations or legal arguments. There *was* an underlying security issue – the abiding vulnerability of France's north-eastern frontier – but the uncompromising nature of the assault and of the king's subsequent demands suggest a different scenario. The young king was seeking a triumph to match his own propaganda, and what more fitting victim could he find than the thrice-hated Dutch: Calvinists, republicans and traders.

Consequently, when the king declared war on the United Provinces in April 1672, he had one eye on immortality. The Dutch were defeated within three weeks and Amsterdam itself awaited French occupation. As was the rule in seventeenth-century warfare, peace negotiations began shortly after the outbreak of military hostilities, and from the middle of June the Dutch ambassador in France was shuttling between the warring parties in an effort to broker a peace agreement. By the end of the month a generous offer was on the table. It included the cession of territory in the south of the country (the so-called Generality Lands), and of the key strategic fortress of Maastricht, together with a sizeable war indemnity. That wasn't enough for Louis and his bellicose war minister, Le Tellier's son Louvois, who demanded terms which were quite unacceptable, indeed indistinguishable from unconditional surrender. That was not how conflicts were traditionally resolved in Europe. Negotiations usually produced a moderate victory or defeat, certainly not a knockout blow. In his dash for glory the young king gave his adversaries a propaganda coup which they exploited relentlessly during the rest of his reign, assisted on occasion, it must be said, by his own willingness to act according to their script.

Quite suddenly the military situation became less one-sided. The French forces were increasingly frustrated by the Dutch tactic of opening the dykes and flooding parts of their country. Their English allies took fright over Louis' religious intentions, and Charles II decided to make peace. Most menacing of all was the appearance of Louis XIV's nemesis in the shape of William of Orange, who in the aftermath of the French rejection of the peace offer, became stadtholder of the republic and the sun king's sworn enemy. He would occupy both positions for the rest of his life. His diplomatic endeavours resulted in the Grand Alliance of the Hague (1673), uniting the Dutch Republic with Spain, the Emperor, Brandenburg and Lorraine. Then two years later Louis suffered a double blow. The defeat of his ally, Sweden, by the Great Elector's Brandenberger forces was a setback, but much more devastating in terms of military morale was the death in battle of France's and Europe's greatest commander, Marshal Turenne.

Although French arms continued to hold the upper hand, Louis was ready for peace. Negotiations commenced at Nijmegen in 1676, and were concluded there over the autumn and winter of 1678/9. Like all international settlements of the age, the peace of Nijmegen was a compromise. France returned the fortress of Maastricht to the Dutch but acquired from Spain the region of Franche-Comté on its vulnerable eastern frontier, and more strongholds further north, including Ypres and Cambrai, protecting it from attack from the Spanish Netherlands. Despite the setbacks of the preceding years, Louis' position after Nijmegen was unquestionably that of head of the dominant power in Europe, and in 1680 the city of Paris bestowed upon him the title of 'the Great'.

Yet at this moment, when the king's foreign adventures appeared to depend upon the unbridled pursuit of *gloire*, Louis was aware of another dimension which he sensed he would do well to heed. The almost instant victory which in 1672 had appeared to be within his grasp had given way to a much longer war of attrition. This had forced him to confront the old issue facing all French kings at war, namely how to afford the necessary military expenditure from the relatively modest resources available to a dynastic ruler. By the second half of the seventeenth century armies were mushrooming in size; at the end of the Dutch war France could call upon a quarter of a million troops. Yet financial support for such unprecedented numbers continued to depend on the antediluvian tax system which belonged to a different age. The conventionally minded Louis may not have instantly appreciated the implications of that fact, but there is evidence from the 1670s that the scale of his ambitions drove him to exercise a degree of authoritarianism at odds with his dynastic powers.

In 1675 Bordeaux and Brittany erupted in one of the most serious rebellions of the reign, in opposition to the imposition of financial expedients designed to support the war effort. In particular, widespread rioting in the towns against a new stamp tax spread to the Breton countryside where it mutated into peasant attacks upon their landlords. The revolts were savagely put down by royal troops, ten thousand of whom were quartered in Brittany until the following year. The whole episode underlined the king's understanding that in wartime the nation's security overrode the norms of political behaviour. He pursued the issue with his old antagonists in the parlements. Both the parlements of Bordeaux and Brittany were exiled to small provincial towns within their area of jurisdiction where they remained until 1690, as a punishment for their less than supportive attitude to the new taxes.[34] In fact all the parlements had been antagonized by a declaration of 1673 which limited the courts' traditional right to remonstrate against royal legislation. For the first time, this right was prohibited until after registration. The government's clear intention was to ensure that financial legislation designed to support the war effort should not be held up by constitutional lawyers. The king's justification was state necessity, but for the magistrates the new law signalled a descent into despotism. Louis did not, however, set out to flout his traditional obligations. He was not prepared to waive altogether the ancient right of remonstrance, nor did he intend his declaration to be permanent. It was meant to be a wartime expedient; but, because France remained at war or on a war footing until 1715, the veto on remonstrances before registration eventually appeared to be the rule rather than the exception.[35]

By the mid-1670s Louis' self-absorbed, hedonistic outlook on the world was being challenged on a number of levels, including the highly personal. Montespan still reigned officially at Versailles but her star was in decline. By 1679, in the aftermath of the Dutch War, the growing influence of Madame de Maintenon was one of the factors beginning to change the mood of the king and his court. After Nijmegen, Louis' pursuit of *gloire* in Europe became less flamboyant, his policy more defensive, his method ever more legalistic. He established a series of reunion courts to discover whether any of his recently acquired territories had jurisdiction over other areas, which should therefore also belong to France. If such areas occupied important strategic positions in vulnerable frontier regions so much the better. Unsurprisingly some of them did. In fact most of the cities of Alsace and much of the duchy of Luxembourg qualified for a French takeover. And after the lawyers had deliberated and pronounced, troops would be made available to enforce their judgements. The king's intention may have been to secure more defensible frontiers but his methods persuaded his former enemies that he was as dangerous as ever. That perception was reinforced in September 1681 when Louis seized the free imperial city of Strasbourg, which commanded the key crossing of the Rhine between Alsace and the Empire. On this occasion he did not rely on the legalistic opportunism of the reunion policy that did indeed reflect the manner in which great ruling families traditionally sought to maintain and justify their inheritance. Instead, he invoked unequivocally the extra-legal doctrine of reason of state: Strasbourg's pro-German stance posed an unacceptable threat to French security.[36] The belligerence and brutality of the French approach, culminating in 1684 in the near destruction of the free city of Genoa by naval bombardment as a punishment for siding with the Spanish enemy, had two outcomes. The first, short-term one was to persuade the emperor and Spain to sign the twenty-year truce of Ratisbon with the French king, confirming Louis' possession of territory acquired since Nijmegen, including Luxembourg and Strasbourg. The second, fateful consequence was to convince his European rivals that sooner or later they would have to stand up to French aggression.

Before that moment could arrive, Louis XIV took an historic decision which reinforced all the fears of his enemies abroad and terrorized a number of his own subjects: in October 1685 he revoked the edict of Nantes which for almost a century had sheltered French Protestants from persecution. Louis' motives were complex. It would be wrong to depict his action as simply that of a religious

1. Bronze Head of Henry IV, Mathieu Jacquet (c. 1545–1611). Henry IV was the first and most charismatic of the Bourbon kings. *(Musée du Louvre/Bridgeman Art Library.)*

2. Anne of Austria with her son, Louis XIV. French School (Seventeenth Century). Queen, Queen-Mother, Regent. Anne's Spanish background underlined the potential for conflict between dynastic and national interest. *(Château de Versailles/Bridgeman Art Library.)*

3. Madame de Pompadour, François Boucher (1703–70). One of the most elegant and influential of royal mistresses, Pompadour was painted by Boucher on a number of occasions. This portrait, standing at a clavichord, probably dates from 1750. *(Musée du Louvre/Bridgeman Art Library.)*

4. Marie-Antoinette with a rose, Elizabeth Vigée-Lebrun (1755–1842). This portrait was painted in the same year, 1783, as her more controversial representation of the queen 'en chemise'. *(Château de Versailles/ Bridgeman Art Library.)*

5. The Execution of Louis XVI, 21 January 1793. Contemporary faïence from Nevers, France. The savage denouement of the Old Regime. *(Bowes Museum.)*

fanatic, though the accompanying brutality of the *dragonnades*, the billeting of soldiers on Protestant families to 'encourage' conversion, added to that impression. But the reception of the Revocation in France was overwhelmingly favourable. By restoring unity of faith His Most Christian Majesty was adding to the glory of his name, becoming worthy to be acclaimed, in Bishop Bossuet's phrase, as 'this new Charlemagne'.[37] More personally, his decision also reflected a greater, more middle-aged concern for his immortal soul than the brash young king had ever exhibited. Sometime in 1683 after the death of his wife, Maria Teresa, the king secretly married Françoise de Maintenon. She exercised considerable influence over the king's lifestyle and undoubtedly approved of his decision over the edict, though she was not its principal advocate, the Huguenots having already been subjected to reforming pressures for some time.[38] Her role was to encourage the king to set a new devotional tone at court, a challenge to which he responded with a convert's zeal.

There were other pressures at work, more political than religious, more international than national, which contributed to the Revocation. Particularly in his new devotional mode Louis did not enjoy being portrayed as a less resolute supporter of the church than the Habsburg emperor. His relations with the papacy had been poor since the mid-1670s, when his attempts to extend the traditional right of *régale*, which allowed him to administer vacant bishoprics in France as well as to draw revenue from them, culminated in the publication in 1682 of the Gallican Articles as a law of the French state. This legislation was thoroughly in line with the Gallican tradition of independence from Rome, limiting papal authority over both the king and the French bishops. Unfortunately, His Most Christian Majesty found himself thus embattled against the spiritual head of the church at the precise moment that the traditional scourge of Christendom, the Ottoman Turks, were threatening to capture Vienna. Louis turned down the pope's efforts to enlist his engagement in a new crusade, so that when Vienna was relieved in 1683 all the plaudits as champion of Christendom went to his rival, Emperor Leopold I. The opportunity to match the Habsburg credentials as defender of the faith by excluding the Huguenots was too good to miss. Following the death in 1683 of his most influential and moderate minister, Colbert, the king was encouraged in that judgement by the newly dominant advice of the rival Le Tellier family, increasingly led by the formidable though unsubtle marquis of Louvois.

By this time Louis XIV had become so preoccupied with the rightness of his cause, both in pursuing measures to defend his frontiers and in the exercise of his domestic authority, that he failed to recognize the dangers inherent in the image he was projecting. For its part the rest of Europe was beginning to seek safety in numbers. Shortly before the Revocation, Frederick William, the Great Elector of Brandenburg, entered into an alliance with Louis' mortal enemy, Prince William of Orange. In the following year he signed a treaty with the emperor, and later in the same year the League of Augsburg came into existence. All these treaties were essentially defensive alliances against the perceived excessive ambitions of the French king. The League of Augsburg included the emperor, Spain, Sweden, Bavaria, the Palatinate and Savoy. All its members were also allied with England, the Dutch Republic and Brandenburg. By 1686 therefore France faced a veritable European League, one established to avoid war rather than to ignite it.

The latter task could safely be left to Louis, though his intent too was defensive. What worried him more than increasing diplomatic isolation was the change in the balance of power in eastern Europe. The emperor was clearly on the brink of a decisive victory over the Ottoman Turks, that would free him to transfer his forces westwards and threaten the frontiers of France established at the truce of Ratisbon. A pre-emptive strike was called for, and in September 1688 French troops invaded the Palatinate. As in the case of the War of Devolution, Louis justified his assault on the grounds of family rights, arguing that his sister-in law, the late elector's sister, had a claim to the Palatine inheritance. His real objective was to defend Alsace against possible imperial attack, chiefly by capturing the key fortress of Phillipsburg, situated beyond the Palatinate on the right bank of the Rhine: the last open gateway into France on its eastern frontier. Initially the military campaign went well. After a month's siege Phillipsburg surrendered on 29 October 1688 to the most brilliant military engineer of the age, Vauban. Then within a few days events far from the Rhineland transformed Versailles's view of Europe: on 15 November William of Orange landed at Torbay on his way to becoming king of England.

Louis XIV was fifty. The old vigour had left him, and the proud boast of *nec pluribus impar* now distorted more than emboldened his judgements. Under the austere regime of his second wife, Versailles had ceased to be a pleasure palace though as both royal residence and seat of government it remained an object of awe. Its trappings, and the power of his armies, encouraged him to underestimate his enemies, who in their turn were reinforced in their opposition by his overweening conduct. Symptomatic of this propensity to make matters unnecessarily worse was Louis' considered response to the news that his unforgiving enemy had acquired the English crown. As he withdrew his forces to more defensible positions, his devastation of the Palatinate outraged European opinion and permanently compromised his quest for *gloire*. It also provided his enemies with further propaganda material. One medal of the period proclaims that 'Whatever atrocities may have been committed by the Turks in 1683 [before Vienna], those committed by the French in 1689 were far worse'; another appealed to the people of Germany to rally to the emperor's cause.[39] France now found itself at war against a Grand Alliance, whose signatories at Vienna in 1689 included the emperor, Spain, England, the Dutch Republic, Savoy, Brandenburg and Bavaria. This war is sometimes called after the earlier League of Augsburg because most of the allies had also joined that federation. Usually, however it is known as the Nine Years War. Its outbreak marked the beginning of a quarter of a century of anguish for the French state, and of personal tragedy for its king.

The decline in French power was relative and limited, but as it gathered pace and momentum the king seemed increasingly incapable of reversing it. Finally, in old age, his enemies had cornered him like a stag at bay, and he would be forced to make desperate choices between the claims of his Bourbon dynasty and the security of his state. Until then he would continue to deploy the traditional language of the civil lawyer, maintaining the illusion that matters of state were decided by the same rules as those governing private possession.

The story in full was revealed at Versailles. There the king's country house was also the seat of government. There the head of the Bourbon family metamorphosed into the head of state. As the former, he acted the country gentleman. He busied himself in the gardens cultivating his favourite flowers, heliotrope and orange blossom, pruning his apple and pear trees, even writing his own guidebook for visitors. Inside the palace the king's bedroom, from 1701 symbolically sited at the very centre of the building, was next door to the council chamber where decisions were taken by the king and his ministers which affected issues of war and peace throughout Europe and overseas. It is true that these 'ministers' only retained that title for as long as Louis chose to summon them to his high council; they were in that regard his creatures as much as they were government servants. Because most of them had bought their high offices or had been allowed by the king to inherit them like any other valuable piece of property, however, they retained a certain independence. Louis was very loyal to his public servants and respected the principle of hereditary, venal service. The inevitable result was that some of his ministers were a good deal less professional than others. The marquis of Barbézieux, for example, who succeeded his father, Louvois, as secretary of state for war, was far less effective in that office than either his father or grandfather.

Yet the king also understood the need for greater professionalism in the conduct of government than the prevailing system guaranteed. The *métier du roi*, the craft of kingship, was Louis' own phrase, suggesting the need for professionalism at the top level. That approach was gradually percolating through his conciliar system which was becoming more specialized and institutionalized. It was apparent too in the dominance of the bureaucrats – secretaries of state and controllers general of finance – at the expense of the king's chief judicial officer, the chancellor. It was physically revealed at Versailles in the shape of the new ministerial wing built to provide offices for civil servants whose job was to translate council decisions into formal policy statements, and to house government records. Another government archive was established at the Louvre in Paris, and before the end of the reign efforts would be made to provide government training and finance for the support of career diplomats.[40]

The fact was that government had become too complex and expensive to operate adequately according to the conventions of dynastic kingship. While taking account of that reality Louis, as a traditionalist, preferred to innovate as little as possible. In the crucial financial sphere he therefore saw no alternative but to plead exceptional circumstances and resort to temporary expedients within the existing framework. By the beginning of the Nine Years War the system was beginning to buckle under the strain, and it is instructive to observe how French efforts to raise money contrasted with their rivals'. Louis made the gesture of selling the family silver; in fact almost 1200 pieces of solid silver furniture were melted down to support the war effort, leaving the grandeur of the Hall of Mirrors permanently diminished. It was a classic dynastic response to a proto-national need, in marked contrast to the establishment in 1694 of the Bank of England, which provided the king's enemies with a firm surety for their military campaigns. In the following year Louis was persuaded to introduce the capitation, a direct tax to be levied proportionately on all his lay subjects. Twenty-two classes of payee were introduced, ranging from the dauphin and the princes of the blood at the top who each paid 2000 livres, to soldiers and day labourers paying one livre each at the bottom. The capitation was potentially a revolutionary departure in the direction of universal taxation, and as an incentive for the emergence of the idea of state sovereignty its potential is obvious. The king, however, made it clear that the capitation was a temporary wartime measure, and true to his word it was suppressed after the Peace of Ryswick.

The financial crisis that had brought the capitation into being was caused not only by the costs of war but by the effect of successive harvest failures between 1691 and 1693. A great famine silenced the countryside as up to a tenth of the population starved to death within a few months.[41] Madame de Maintenon wrote, 'I would give everything for peace', adding that Louis shared her yearning. Her protégé, *abbé* Fénelon, was more sceptical and demanding. He wanted to know how the aims of the ruling family were to be reconciled with the needs of the subjects:

> Your people, Sire, are dying of hunger. For the sake of getting and keeping vain conquests abroad, you have destroyed half the real strength of your own state. All France is now no more than one great hospital, desolate and unprovided … if the king had a father's heart for his people, he would surely think his glory lay rather in giving them bread and a little respite after such tribulations than in keeping hold of a few frontier posts which are a cause of war.[42]

In strictly military and naval terms the Nine Years War was something of a stalemate though French victories – at Fleurus, Beachy Head, Steenkirk and

Marseille – outnumbered those of the allies. When peace was signed at Ryswick in 1697, Louis agreed to withdraw from Lorraine and to give back to Spain most of the fortresses, including Luxembourg, which he had acquired through his reunion policy. Phillipsburg too was returned to the empire. But France retained Alsace, including Strasbourg, as well as its earlier eastern frontier acquisitions of Metz, Toul, Verdun and Franche-Comté. Louis made two further, highly significant, concessions at Ryswick. First, he agreed to recognize William III as the de facto king of England, despite the fact that James II, still the legitimate king in Louis' opinion, was living in exile in France. It was a pragmatic decision and one of a number of straws in the wind suggesting that Louis XIV was seeking to reconcile the need for a stable world order with the rights of his House and the security of his subjects. His second concession was to agree to the establishment of a defensive line of fortresses, manned by the Dutch, on the border between France and the Spanish Netherlands. This so-called barrier was intended to delay an invading army from France long enough to allow the United Provinces to organize their defences. The concept of national security was thus beginning to receive international recognition.

The diplomats at Ryswick did not have to deal with potentially the most explosive and divisive issue facing Europe: the Spanish Succession. Ever since his marriage to Maria Teresa, the question of who should succeed to the throne and empire of Spain had never been far from the mind of Louis XIV. As it became clear that her childless half-brother, Charles II, would not survive for long that concern became a preoccupation. This was the setting for the conflict which provides the supreme example of international relations as dynastic politics, with the two greatest ruling families in Europe seeking to establish their prior claim to this matchless inheritance. The irony was that the prize was too great for either side to win outright, however compelling the legal arguments, if a dangerously unstable international order was to be avoided. Louis understood this, and made an attempt to short-circuit the problem during the Nine Years War. He approached the emperor in secret, offering to renounce all Bourbon claims to the Spanish Succession on condition that Leopold recognize his sovereignty over the eastern frontier including Lorraine, and that the Austrian and Spanish Habsburg lands should not be united under a single ruler. The offer, which the emperor rejected, was indicative of Louis' serious anxiety about his vulnerability in the east.

After Ryswick Louis tried again, this time with a most unlikely partner in the shape of the king of England, William III. In 1698 Louis approached William with the proposition that, together with the Dutch, they should agree a partition of the Spanish Empire to come into effect after the death of Charles II. What made this a revolutionary proposal was the fact that William himself had no claim to the Spanish throne. Louis viewed him as an important power broker, however, an enforcer who could help to impose a settlement. This was not to be a partition treaty strictly speaking, but an attempt to maintain the balance of power in Europe by means of the novel doctrine of collective security. William was willing to enter into discussions and the first partition treaty was duly signed in 1698. By its terms the bulk of the inheritance was assigned to the least powerful candidate, the infant son of the elector of Bavaria whose wife was a daughter of Emperor Leopold. He was to receive Spain, the Spanish Netherlands, Sardinia and the overseas territories. The Spanish lands in Italy were to be divided between the other two candidates: the emperor's younger son would receive Milan, and the dauphin Naples and Sicily.

This was *terra incognita* for Louis XIV, a life-long believer in the laws of hereditary succession. Yet in the course of the negotiations he indicated that he was prepared to go even further. Were the electoral prince to die without heirs, Louis would consider replacing him with his father, the elector, despite the fact that young Joseph Ferdinand's claim was through his mother, Maria Antonia. More striking still was the king's willingness to contemplate ceding parts of the Spanish Empire in the Mediterranean to William, in order to safeguard English and Dutch trade. The treaty also invited other European powers to sign and commit themselves, along with the three original signatories, to enforcing its terms.

In 1699 the electoral prince died and the whole process had to begin again. The second partition treaty, signed by the same parties, was published in 1700. The Spanish Empire was to be divided between the two remaining candidates. The emperor's son, Archduke Charles, was to receive the major share originally intended for the electoral prince, while the dauphin was to add Milan to his earlier Italian acquisitions of Naples and Sicily. The principle of collective security was heavily underlined in this treaty, for Milan was then to be exchanged for Lorraine, thereby firmly bolting France's eastern frontier defences. Indeed, Louis and William also discussed the possibility of a second exchange, Naples and Sicily for Savoy. The treaty also stipulated that the lands allocated to the archduke could never be united to the Austrian domains. Finally, like its predecessor, the second partition treaty envisaged armed intervention by the signatories against any power which flouted its terms.[43] This was a truly remarkable document. In the interests of security, and with that purpose alone in mind, the great powers were willing to reorder the map of Europe. According to the proposed new order the dynastic rights of individual rulers would at best only entitle them to consideration as part of a final settlement; the dukes of Savoy and Lorraine apparently had no rights at all.

While Europe tried to come to terms with this revolutionary doctrine, the king of Spain, Charles II, finally died, having threatened to do so for most of his troubled life. In death he seriously confused the issue by leaving the whole of the

Spanish Empire to Louis XIV's grandson, Philippe, duke of Anjou. This bequest put Louis in an impossible situation. He knew that if he adhered to the partition treaty the Spaniards, determined to avoid the division of their empire, would invite Archduke Charles to succeed. He also knew that the emperor, who had refused to take any part in the partition treaty negotiations, would enthusiastically accept that offer on behalf of his son, and that in that situation the English and the Dutch would be disinclined to go to war to enforce acceptance of the partition treaty. With some reluctance therefore, and after days of reflection, he proclaimed his recognition of his grandson as King Philip V of Spain.

Was Louis naïve or hypocritical in his dealings with William III? The failure of the partition treaties might suggest the former; some of his subsequent actions the latter. In fact he acted pragmatically throughout, anxious not to be wrong-footed by the emperor's Habsburg connections in Madrid. What defeated him in the end was time. Had Charles II lived longer, in particular had the young Joseph Ferdinand of Bavaria survived, the virtues of the new proposals as a means of avoiding a European-wide conflict might have become clearer. As it was, Louis fell back on his belief in hereditary right, maintaining that the legitimacy of his grandson's accession in Spain depended not upon the will of Charles II but upon his descent from Maria Teresa. Then in 1701, when the deposed king of England, James II, died in exile, Louis recognized his son, the Old Pretender, as King James III. In fact he had no intention of challenging William III's tenure of the English throne. He was simply salving his conscience by distinguishing between de facto and de jure kingship.

Once the die was cast Louis appeared to throw caution to the wind and allow old illusions of grandeur to reassert themselves, presumably on the assumption that a large-scale war could not now be averted. Not only was his recognition of the Old Pretender ill-advised. So was his proclamation that his grandson Philippe remained eligible to succeed to the French throne. Again, the evidence suggests that he recognized the practical impossibility of uniting the two crowns of France and Spain, but did not bother to elaborate his preferred alternative, namely the accession of the junior Orléanist branch of the Bourbon family in Spain if the senior line, represented by Philip V, should inherit the French throne.[44] More directly challenging were his decisions to take over the Dutch barrier fortresses, and to give French merchants preferential treatment in Spanish markets, including the *asiento*, the exclusive right to supply slaves to the Spanish colonies. The cumulative effect of all these actions was to persuade most of Europe that the old Louis had reappeared and this time must be brought finally to book. Both England and the United Province had initially recognized Philip V as king of Spain, but Louis' various acts of provocation, whatever their motivation, so antagonized his opponents that for them the ensuing war of the Spanish Succession became a crusade to obtain the sun king's unconditional surrender.

From the beginning France found itself in difficulties against the forces of the emperor and the maritime powers, which had joined together to form the Grand Alliance of the Hague. Louis had to fight on four fronts, in Germany, Spain, the Low Countries and Italy, and support his troops without the sophisticated financial backing available to the allies, of the banks of England and Amsterdam. Once more the king invoked short-term expedients: the sale of offices, manipulations of the currency, forced loans, extensive borrowing. The capitation was reintroduced in 1701 and augmented in 1705. In addition to the inequality of resources flowing into the war effort, the allies were overwhelmingly superior on the battlefield, thanks to the command of their captain-general, John Churchill, duke of Marlborough, who revealed himself as a soldier to be ranked alongside Turenne. The greatest French marshal of his generation, Luxembourg, had died in the course of the Nine Years War, and none of his replacements came close to matching the captain-general. Marlborough established an unusually close relationship with the leader of the imperial troops, Prince Eugene of Savoy, another distinguished soldier, whose mother, by a cruel irony was the countess of Soissons, one of the young king Louis' first loves, Olympe Mancini. Together and separately Marlborough and Eugene inflicted a series of hammer blows on the French troops at Blenheim on the Danube in 1704, at Turin in 1706, at Ramillies and Oudenarde in the Low Countries in 1706 and 1708. Everywhere the war went disastrously for France, except in Spain where the Castillians rallied to the cause of Philip V, primarily because their ancient Catalan rivals were supporting the allies' alternative candidate for king, Archduke Charles.

By 1709 the situation had become critical. One way and another, this was to be the most important year in Louis XIV's long reign. On Twelfth Night the worst winter in living memory began to grip the country, turning the seas around the coast into frozen extensions of the land. After two months a sudden thaw was cut short by a further visitation of extreme weather. Saint-Simon graphically describes the course of events:

> This second frost destroyed everything. Practically all the fruit trees, walnut, olive, apple, and the vines, perished … and all the grain in the ground. The desolation caused by this ruinous situation was beyond comprehension. Everybody hoarded what grain they had, and the price of bread rose as the harvest failed … And what of all the money in the kingdom: nobody could make payments because nobody was being paid … There appeared to be no remedy for a situation in which money had ceased to circulate. The king was no longer able to pay his troops.[45]

In this dire predicament Louis was willing to sue for peace on almost any terms. He was prepared to sanction the loss of key defensive fortresses guarding the Netherlands, including Ypres, Tournai and Lille, as well as the great prize of Strasbourg in Alsace. He was even prepared for the expulsion of his grandson from the Spanish Empire. His plan for secure eastern frontiers and for a Bourbon family bloc to replace the Habsburg Vienna–Madrid axis was in ruins. The glorious reputation that he had once sought before everything else was irrevocably tarnished.

Paradoxically, he was saved at the eleventh hour by the allies' perception of that very reputation. When Louis' foreign minister, the marquis of Torcy, nephew of the great Colbert, returned to Versailles from the Hague on 1 June 1709 bearing the infamous 'Preliminary Articles', it became clear that the members of the Grand Alliance so distrusted Louis that they would settle for nothing less than his unconditional surrender. By that means they would also solve the problem posed by Spain, the one war zone in which they had been unable to achieve a military victory.

The Preliminaries offered a limited, two-month truce to allow time for Philip's removal from Spain, which might even require Louis to take up arms against his own grandson. As a surety he would be required to surrender certain key frontier fortresses which would remain in allied hands if the truce ended without a settlement. The subsequent conquest of France would then be that much easier to achieve. In making such an unreasonable demand of the king as head of the Bourbon family, the Grand Alliance was also challenging his role as the head of state, charged with guaranteeing the security of his subjects. Louis rejected the Preliminaries and took the opportunity to make a unique appeal for popular support in continuing the war. Having already recognized that international problems could not be resolved by dynastic methods alone, he was beginning to comprehend in this critical moment that ensuring the safety of the state, which was an expensive business in men and money, might ultimately need the nation's support as well as the agreement of foreign governments. Had not the English recently demonstrated that fact by removing James II, and were not the Castillians making the same point by their support for Philip V?[46] In his widely circulated letter of 12 June 1709, addressed to the provincial governors, Louis XIV concentrated on the threat to national security:

> In order to re-establish a general peace, I should have accepted terms very much opposite to the security of my frontier provinces ... It is therefore my intention, that all those who for such a series of years have given me proofs of their zeal, in contributing by their labour, their property, and their blood, to support so burdensome a war, should be informed, that the only return the enemy pretended to make to my offers, was a suspension of arms; which being limited to the space of two months, would have procured them much greater advantages, than they can expect from the confidence they put in their troops.[47]

Although it was impossible to know it at the time, a turning point had been reached. Three months later in Flanders, Marlborough and Eugene met the best of the French marshals, the quarrelsome but valiant duke of Villars, near the village of Malplaquet. The outcome was technically an allied victory, since the French left the field; but they left in good order and with only half the casualties suffered by the allies. For the moment at least, the threat of an allied invasion aimed at Paris had been lifted.

Louis' need for peace remained pressing, however, and negotiations were renewed in 1710 at Gertruydenberg in the Dutch Republic. Once again the allies overplayed their hand, this time fatally. They insisted that if Philip refused to leave Spain voluntarily French forces alone would have the responsibility of driving him out, while the allies simply acted as observers. The fact that Louis was willing to provide a sizeable subsidy to help the Grand Alliance powers to remove Philip indicates the scale of their misjudgement of the situation. Louis had no alternative but to fight on. In October 1710 in an increasingly desperate quest for finance, he introduced a new tax, the tenth, to be paid on all sources of income and by all classes of the population. Like the capitation and the king's appeal to his people in 1709, the tenth implied a radical departure, signifying that the nation at large had a stake in its own destiny. But Louis was still not thinking of a fundamental reform of the society of orders which by definition was based on inequality. Consequently, he stipulated that the tax would cease to be levied after the cessation of hostilities.

From the second half of 1710 events moved rapidly in France's favour. The new Tory government in England opposed continuing the war, and unilaterally barred its forces from active campaigning. Archduke Charles, still the allies' candidate for the Spanish crown, succeeded to the imperial title as Charles VI in 1711, and neither England nor the United Provinces looked favourably upon the prospect of the revival of the Habsburg empire of Charles V. Finally, Louis' fortunes took a turn for the better on the battlefield; in 1712 the irrepressible Villars won an important psychological victory at Denain.

The result of this *bouleversement* was that France emerged from the peace of Utrecht (1713–14) with a far more advantageous settlement than had seemed possible in the dark days of 1709. The inner ring of fortresses securing the French frontier with the Netherlands remained French, as did Strasbourg and Alsace. Louis' grandson remained king of Spain and the Indies. Louis' long-term accomplishment was to bequeath to his successors the definitive shape of France with its frontiers secure. Metz, Toul and Verdun, Alsace, Strasbourg and Franche-Comté, and the north-east frontier towns of Lille, Condé and Maubeuge, all lie within the boundaries of modern France. Arguably therefore he deserves what he most sought as a young man in pursuit of *gloire*, a favourable verdict from posterity. Ironically, much of what he finally achieved depended upon his enemies' implacable and misguided response to the litany of his earlier, inglorious excesses.

There was little laughter to be heard in Versailles during the final decade of the sun king's reign. The unexpected reprieve at the close of the Spanish Succession war did nothing to lighten the spirits, for by then the house of Bourbon was facing a new threat to its very survival, and one which it had no way of averting. In April 1711 the king's only legitimate son, the grand dauphin, died of smallpox. The new dauphin was his eldest son, the duke of Burgundy. Burgundy's wife was the fun-loving Marie-Adélaïde of Savoy, who was as devoted to the king and the marquise as they were to her. Both husband and wife died within a week of each other in February 1712, and their eldest son, who briefly became the third dauphin, died a fortnight later. The new heir to the throne was Burgundy's younger son, the duke of Anjou, who was just two years old. To complete the cycle of death visited upon the royal family, Anjou's uncle, the duke of Berry, Burgundy's youngest brother, died following a hunting accident in 1714. Were the duke of Anjou also to succumb, the only remaining legitimate Bourbon heir would have been the grand dauphin's middle son, King Philip V of Spain, who had been forced to renounce his title to the French throne as part of the peace settlement at Utrecht.

These deaths affected the old king profoundly. He viewed the loss of his son, grandsons and great-grandson as divine punishment for his failures as king. The gloom pervading every corner of the once vibrant palace of Versailles deepened by the day as Louis, encouraged by his devout consort, contemplated God's judgement on his performance as Most Christian Majesty. There was more than a whiff of religiosity about the place, and an aura of nemesis which stayed with the king until the end. Less than a week before his death, he warned his successor, 'Do not follow my bad example; I have often started a war rashly and sustained it out of vanity.'[48]

The unhinging effect on Louis of the family tragedy was demonstrated by his decision, in July 1714 after the death of the duke of Berry, to issue an edict permitting his two illegitimate sons by Madame de Montespan, the duke du Maine and the count of Toulouse, to succeed to the throne in the absence of legitimate heirs. No civil or canon law, no precedent of any kind could justify this desperate act by an old *père de famille* who feared that he might be the last of his proud line. His aberration would be given short shrift in the following reign.

Louis XIV's final battle was over the issue of Jansenism. Increasingly preoccupied with his own eternal salvation, he determined to end once and for all the schism which had sullied the Gallican Church since the days of his minority. Because Jansenism was not easily defined it had proved difficult to eradicate, so finally in 1713 Louis requested the pope, Clement XI, to proscribe the movement once and for all. He promised the pope that the condemnation would be enforced in France. The pope duly obliged with the publication of the bull *Unigenitus*. Immediately, however, the king found himself in difficulties, for his assurances to the pope clashed with his own edict of 1682 which spelt out the Gallican tradition of both royal and ecclesiastical independence from the papacy. Despite the opposition of his legal advisers, Louis nevertheless sent the bull to be registered in the parlement of Paris in February 1714. For the first time since 1673 the magistrates demanded the right to draw up prior remonstrances, though in the end they settled for a qualified registration, which preserved the authority of the bishops and the liberties of the Gallican Church.

This was the second example from the year 1714 of the king imprudently seeking a quick solution to a long-term problem by circumventing the established law. He failed in his objective on both occasions. On the subject of *Unigenitus* he succeeded only in recharging the batteries of an old adversary of French kings, the parlement of Paris, whose rediscovered political importance would become instantly clear on the morrow of the king's death. Louis knew that his successor's reign would begin with a regency, as his own and his father's had done. He was anxious to prepare the ground as far as he could, and after more than seventy years as king he was impatient of dissent. This, however, was not typical behaviour. Louis' stance generally was to accept Bishop Bossuet's famous distinction between absolute and arbitrary power; the latter, the exercise of authority without recourse to legal principles, was unacceptable in France though it might pass in Moscow or Constantinople.

When Louis XIV died in the early morning of 1 September 1715, he was just four days short of his seventy-seventh birthday. His long reign had been characterized by a growth of professionalism in all aspects of government. That, as well as the pressures of war and international diplomacy, had contributed to the perception that the king was pre-eminently the nation's chief official rather than its proprietor. The distinction, however, was never clear-cut in the king's mind, which helps to explain why Louis did so little to modernize the country's antique fiscal system, or to loosen the straitjacket of social conservatism. Above all he was a great self-publicist. His true legacy was his reputation, which his successors strove to emulate. Their efforts were in vain but, dazzled by the sun king's image, they saw no alternative but to try.

Losing the Kingdom

6

Louis XV

THE DECLINE OF THE WELL BELOVED

Like his great-grandfather, Louis XV was five years old when he became king of France. For the third consecutive reign therefore the Bourbon dynasty faced a minority and a period of regency. In 1715, unlike 1610 and 1643, there was no queen mother available to play the leading role, and no powerful minister to assist her. Indeed, the leading candidate for the office of regent, Philippe, duke of Orléans, the late king's nephew, was considered by many to be outstandingly unsuitable for the role. This was because his reputation for ungodliness and sexual depravity, which he had cultivated assiduously since his youth, was in such contrast with the ethos of the latter-day Versailles. In fact Orléans was a complex personality, a far more attractive human being than his well-documented public image might suggest. Many of his problems stemmed from a sense of alienation. No member of the collateral royal line could be allowed to compete with, much less outshine, the king's own children and grandchildren. This fact irked Philippe for several reasons. Though he was himself the grandson of Louis XIII, and therefore enjoyed the status of a *petit-fils de France*, he had been forced by Louis XIV to marry the king's illegitimate daughter by Athénaïs de Montespan, Mademoiselle de Blois. He considered this union to be an affront to his family. His resentment was exacerbated by the realization that, whereas he possessed great talents, his Bourbon cousins emphatically did not. Orléans was a distinguished soldier, a highly competent painter and musician, and an art collector of global significance. He also possessed an abundance of intellectual curiosity, not an unmixed blessing in a prince of the blood.

Though his claim to be regent was well founded in law and precedent, he had one very specific problem to overcome. For obvious reasons, the marquise of Maintenon was not one of Orléans's greatest supporters. Having already used her influence with the king to persuade him to legitimize Maine and Toulouse, she then nagged him (Louis' own observations make the nature of her intervention clear) into writing a will which would tie Orléans's hands and give real power to her protégé, the duke du Maine.[1] According to the will, the latter would take charge of the young king's education and of the household troops, while Orléans would merely be the chairman of a regency council. Though Louis XIV knew from his own father's example that no French king could dictate his successor's policy, his bequest of the will certainly added to Philippe's difficulties.

The prospective regent needed supporters and he was hard at work finding them before the old king's death. Louis himself had inadvertently signposted where Orléans's chief ally would be found, by depositing his will in the parlement of Paris. During each of the previous two regencies this court had played a leading political role, and under Philippe of Orléans it was destined to do so again. Its long political tradition continued to be an affirmation of the legitimacy of royal government, and it was in Philippe's interests to build his regime upon such an unimpeachable legal foundation. A deal was therefore done, and on 2 September the parlement annulled the late king's testament and proclaimed the duke as regent with undivided authority. The quid pro quo was provided almost a fortnight later when a royal declaration restored the right of remonstrance to its pre-1673 form, entitling the magistrates to submit their legal complaints before new laws were registered.

Having succeeded impressively in establishing his own authority, the new regent had the unenviable task of transforming the sun king's legacy into an inheritance suitable for an eighteenth-century monarch. The state of France in 1715 suggested that significant changes were needed if the old order was to regain its vigour; merely reacting to emergencies would not suffice. On the face of it there appeared to be no better candidate to stage-manage such a transformation than the free-thinking intellectual now in charge of government. With hindsight that may well have been the case, and Orléans's regency may indeed have presented the last opportunity for reinvigorating the body politic. But that is not to tell the whole story, for Orléans was determined to remain entirely loyal to the interests of the young man in his charge, and to hand on to Louis XV at his majority the fullness of power which his great-grandfather had enjoyed at his death. Consequently, his radical policies were invariably hedged about with caution. Besides, he was not a disinterested servant of the regime, but a *petit-fils de France*. Indeed, provided that Philip V's renunciation at Utrecht was respected, he was next in line of succession to the throne.

Nevertheless, Orléans understood that a basic disparity did exist between the needs of a modern state and the rights of a society of privileged orders. France's financial plight in particular was grim. A contemporary account relates a story of uncultivated land, impoverished peasants in debt to the king, to their local seigneur and to the village usurers, manufacturing at a halt, merchants bankrupt and troops on the verge of mutiny.[2] The new regent had to tread carefully. He decided against declaring the state bankrupt, accepting that such a move would simply add to the widespread mood of despair and alienation.

Instead, he concentrated initially on paying the troops and doing what he could to appease his allies in the parlement. To assist the late war effort, the judges as office-holders had been forced to contribute substantial loans which were speciously characterized as increases in salary, the 'increase' being no more than the interest paid on the loan. To mitigate the government's financial problems Orléans reduced the interest rate from 5 per cent to 4 per cent early in the regency, but went to great lengths to assure the magistrates that he accepted the moral validity of their financial claims, and that money would be found for them.[3] More generally, Orléans endeavoured to improve existing financial machinery, as Colbert had done in the previous century, updating accounting procedures to get a clearer picture of tax arrears and of the monies accruing from different taxes.

The regent did support two genuinely reforming measures before John Law's system took over the running of the French economy. In 1716 the *taille tarifé* or *proportionelle* was introduced, a graduated tax on all non-privileged subjects. Although it did not directly challenge the exemptions of the various privileged groups, its principle of payment according to means had radical implications. Then in 1718 Orléans approved the introduction of a *dîme royal*. This was a watered-down version of Marshal Vauban's famous project of the same title, which had been a bold proposal for a single tax to be paid by privileged and non-privileged alike. It was an attempt to tax the produce of all land, whether in noble or non-noble ownership. Neither of these initiatives was successful. By 1718, however, the experiment offering the best chance of restoring and revolutionizing French public finances was well under way. It had begun in May 1716 with the setting up of John Law's *banque générale*.

A Scot from Edinburgh's financial circles, Law had first settled in London, where he witnessed the establishment of the Bank of England in 1694. His life became nomadic after killing an opponent in a duel, and in the late 1690s he had his first meeting with the future regent in Paris. His economic ideas were based on the use of bank notes, whose value would be reflected in the amount of the country's bullion reserves, topped up by foreign trade, and whose circulation would enrich all parts of the body politic. Despite his rakish reputation, Law's economics deserve to be taken seriously. So do the political implications flowing from them, whose radical nature he certainly acknowledged. Indeed, Law's system presupposed a serious reappraisal of the relationship between king, subjects and state.

In particular, his ideas implied a significant increase both in the state's right to intervene in the lives of the subjects, and in their reciprocal obligations. Law's objective was national prosperity, which he maintained could only be achieved if all the subjects made a contribution. One of the heretical political implications flowing from that doctrine was that nobles should be allowed to take part in trade. Equally, Law defended the state's right to 'resort to sanctions in order to persuade people to contribute to their own happiness', a phrase reminiscent of the later eighteenth-century political doctrine of enlightened absolutism.[4] His proposed political reforms proceeded logically from his economic vision, and represented nothing less than the dismantling of the old regime:

> Immunities, privileges and exemptions must be regarded as abuses which cannot be abolished too soon. Clergymen, nobles or commoners, we are all equally the subjects of the same king; it is against the essence of being a subject to claim to be distinguished from the rest by the privilege of not paying tribute to the prince ... in particular the clergy and nobility, as the two premier orders of the kingdom, must seek to distinguish themselves by their eagerness to contribute to the expenses of the state rather than by immunities and exemptions. Nothing is more important for the good order of a kingdom than uniformity and it is to be wished that it may reign in the law and in taxation.[5]

Here was an end to the regime of estates presided over by a sovereign obliged to preserve the distinguishing legal characteristics of each. Instead, Law was conjuring up a vision of the corporate state in which all the subjects, without discrimination, would obey the dictates of its chief executive, the king.

The regent was attracted by Law's bold ideas, and as soon as he felt his own position to be secure he began to implement the Scotsman's proposals. In 1716 the *banque générale* was established to help create confidence among the public in the use of paper money. In the following year the Mississippi Company was founded to exploit the commercial possibilities of the French colony of Louisiana. In 1718 Law's general bank became the royal bank of France, and eventually, having taken over the other trading companies, the Mississippi Company became the Compagnie des Indes. By February 1720 the bank and the company had been merged into a single, massive organization, a commercial company with a monopoly of maritime and colonial trade which was also a monopoly bank of issue empowered to raise taxes, to coin and print money.

At the very moment of Law's public triumph, however, his appointment as controller general of finance early in the new year of 1720, his system was beginning to crumple. Inflation rocketed as the number and cost of company shares rose and more and more banknotes were printed to help speculators purchase them. But confidence in paper holdings was fragile, and when the dam burst there was nothing the hapless controller general could do to deflect the frenzy of abuse which overwhelmed him. In May 1720 he made a despairing effort to save the system by devaluing both the shares and the bank notes by 50 per cent. He succeeded only in provoking serious public disorder. Saint-Simon records that 'There was a most violent disturbance. Every rich man thought himself irretrievably ruined, either immediately or in the not so distant future; every poor man saw himself beggared.'[6] Orléans was forced to dismiss Law, and to provide an armed guard for his protection. While the former controller general took refuge in the regent's home, the Palais-Royal, the regent himself was presiding over the official repudiation of his friend's scheme. From 1 November 1720 it was decreed that bank notes could not be given or received as part of any financial transaction. Paper money, as the young Voltaire sarcastically remarked, was being reduced to its intrinsic value.[7]

In view of this débâcle it is tempting to dismiss John Law's schemes as a charlatan's deceit. This would be an unjust judgement on a man of vision and originality, and incidentally an unmerited slur on the regent, who was far too sharp to be taken in by a mountebank. In fact, the system did produce an economic boom. More land was cleared and cultivated, enabling more owners to pay off their mortgages; rural wages doubled and so did the consumption of meat. The western ports of Lorient and Nantes prospered as the Compagnie des Indes prepared to cash in on its colonial opportunities. But John Law made serious miscalculations at both the macro- and micro-economic levels. He failed to anticipate that the perceived benefits of overseas trade might lag behind the erosion of confidence in the system, and when the situation became critical his corrective measures simply reinforced the investors' anxiety. There were twenty-six changes in the value of the coinage in 1720 alone, and his disastrous devaluation decree in May of that year finally annihilated public confidence. It was also a fundamental intellectual weakness of Law that, as one of his contemporary admirers reflected, 'He could not dwell on small matters and consequently was a little remiss in providing the details of how his schemes were to be executed, merely sketching the broad strategy and leaving the precise management to others.'[8]

The most daunting obstacle faced by Law was, however, one beyond his control. To support his system a new political and social order would have had to evolve, uniting the king's interests with those of his people in such a way that every subject would wish to contribute to the enrichment of the state. At the heart of that grand design lurked a fundamental weakness, which Law himself identified before the regency began. In July 1715 he remarked that 'Constraint is contrary to the principles upon which credit must be built'.[9] Absolute power was a very blunt instrument when it came to rallying the subjects' confidence.

Had Orléans been king and not regent his unconventional thinking might have persuaded him to push John Law's ideas further. But he was not prepared to risk Louis XV reaching his majority with his traditional royal authority compromised in any way. So, having with characteristic loyalty assisted his friend to flee the country, Philippe turned his back on the Scotsman's schemes and settled for the restoration of an ultimately unsustainable status quo.

In the area of foreign affairs the regent pursued the somewhat ambiguous policies favoured by the late king. By the peace of Utrecht, which Louis XIV and his grandson, Philip V of Spain, had grudgingly signed, the latter renounced his right to succeed to the French throne if the young king Louis XV died without heirs. The successor in that event would be the regent, whose foreign policy has sometimes been interpreted as favouring the interests of the House of Orléans. Philippe was indeed a dynast, but he was also a pragmatist who recognized that the interests of the child-king under his protection were best served by safeguarding the peace in Europe. He therefore adopted a policy of collective security based on mutual guarantees, which was reminiscent of the two partition treaties negotiated by Louis XIV and William III in 1698 and 1700. In January 1717 he joined the old enemies, Britain and the Dutch Republic, in the Triple Alliance of the Hague. The three signatories confirmed their support for the French and British successions as established at Utrecht (the Stuarts to be replaced in Britain by the Hanoverians), and guaranteed reciprocal military, naval or financial help if either were subjected to challenge.

The Triple Alliance was an important plank in the building of a collective security platform in Europe. But so long as the original rival candidates for the Spanish Succession, Emperor Charles VI and Philip V, refused to abide by the terms of the Utrecht settlement for Spain, war was never far away, and it broke out later in 1717 when Spanish forces invaded the island of Sardinia, which was part of the Habsburg Empire. The proposed resolution of the conflict dictated by the Triple Alliance powers under Anglo-French leadership heralded the triumph of *force majeure* over dynasticism: the emperor to renounce his claim to Spain and add his guarantee of the French and British successions as laid down at Utrecht; Philip V to return Sardinia to the emperor, who would in turn hand it over to the duke of Savoy, Victor Amadeus, in return for Sicily; Philip V's children to inherit Parma and Tuscany. The emperor and the king of Spain were given three months in which to concur, failing which France and Britain would enforce their solution. Charles VI accepted the terms, and the Quadruple Alliance was signed in August 1718 (in the event the signatories were France, Britain, the emperor and Savoy, the Dutch having opted out at the last minute). Philip V chose to fight his cousin and rival for the French throne, but was speedily crushed by an unholy alliance of French troops and the British navy. In February 1720 Spain was forced to join the Quadruple Alliance.

Orléans's final contribution to securing a peaceful Europe was to sign a defensive alliance with Philip V in March 1721, by which both powers guaranteed to uphold the settlement agreed at Utrecht. By the end of the regency therefore Europe was coming to terms with the idea, already broached by Louis XIV in the partition treaties, that collective security, based on powerful persuasion and a series of mutual guarantees, would govern the conduct of international relations in the future. Ironically, shortly after the signing of the Franco-Spanish convention Philip V suggested a double marriage alliance to celebrate the

Bourbons' reconciliation: his daughter would be betrothed to the king of France, and the regent's daughter would marry the heir to the Spanish crown. Dynastic motivation remained a powerful factor in international relations, too powerful in fact for its own good, since it threatened to compromise attempts to establish a balance of power. As such attempts became more commonplace, the image of Europe as the hunting ground of great families continued to fade. It was becoming instead a collection of states whose *raison d'être*, though still ill-defined, clearly amounted to more than being part of a prince's inheritance.[10]

Finally, in the matter of governing the country Orléans subtly adapted Louis XIV's approach to ensure the old king's successor a tranquil passage through his minority. The Bourbons were unfortunate in having to cope with three successive regencies; the late king and the regent deserve equal credit for preserving Louis XV's minority from the internecine turmoil that marred the first two. In the elaborately organized world of Versailles, where old and new nobility, gentle- men and players, fulfilled their respective roles without threatening the other, Louis XIV had succeeded in reconciling the *grands* to a more professional style of kingship. In 1715, recognizing the potential weakness of his own position, the new regent took steps to maintain the *Louisquatorzian* balance by other means. He sensed that for the moment it would be politically prudent to reduce the influence of the late king's ministers and to broaden the administrative base. He observed that people were tired of seeing whole sections of the government under the control of a single individual, and that a new form of administration was required to restore confidence. He therefore instituted a conciliar system, headed by a regency council supported by seven specialized satellite bodies. This was the so-called *polysynodie* which appeared to bring an end to the predominance in government of the secretaries of state and the controller general of finance. The four secretaryships were reduced to three, and only one of the survivors, La Vrillière, a member of the Phélypeaux family, had a place on the regency council and that only to take the minutes. The controller general, Desmaretz, was dismissed and not replaced. The work of these once all-powerful officials was taken over by the members of the seven supporting councils, for foreign affairs, war, the marine, finance, the interior, religion and commerce.

The membership of these new bodies reflected the regent's need to keep the 'old court' onside. Louis XIV's two newly legitimated sons, Maine and Toulouse, became members of the regency council along with the duke of Bourbon, great- grandson of the Great Condé. Indeed, other princes of the royal family were admitted as they came of age, including Orléans's own son, the duke of Chartres. All the satellite councils were headed by a great nobleman rather than by a representative of the *noblesse de robe*, and other *grands seigneurs* were included in their membership. It appeared therefore that the king's natural advisers were regaining their place in the sun at the expense of the proto-civil servants. But behind the façade the regent was working to a different agenda.

In January 1716 La Vrillière was made a full member of the regency council. Already enjoying that status was the marquis of Torcy, the nephew of Colbert, who had been Louis XIV's foreign secretary during the later years of the reign and was by far the most experienced and professional of the old king's administrators. Both of these men exercised a good deal of independent authority within the structure of the *polysynodie*. Torcy in particular became a key adviser to the regent, who authorized him to receive and respond to messages from French agents abroad without reference to the council for foreign affairs. A relatively unknown member of the *polysynodie*, Claude le Blanc, a former intendant of Rouen and a member of the council for war, was also a confidential adviser to Orléans from the early days of the regency. Most significant of all was the fact that the two men on whom the regent leant most heavily for support, the abbé Dubois, his lifelong friend and foreign policy adviser, and the financier John Law, had no official role in government at all during the period of the *polysynodie*.

In the autumn of 1718, when the political climate allowed Orléans to breathe more easily, he decided to reform the conciliar system. Out went four of the councils, for religion, foreign affairs, the interior and war, in came Dubois and Le Blanc as secretaries of state respectively for foreign affairs and war. They were joined by the three existing secretaries of state, who suddenly found themselves reinstated as the holders of high political office. Two of them were members of the Phélypeaux family, the cousins La Vrillière and Maurepas, who had inherited their secretaryships. The third, Fleuriau d'Armenonville, a former intendant of finance and a future keeper of the seals, was related to the Phélypeaux by marriage. He had had the prescience, and the money, to purchase Torcy's office of secretary when the latter resigned it three weeks after Louis XIV's death. In January 1720, after a five year vacancy, the office of controller general of finance was restored and given to John Law; two years later the offices of intendant of finance were similarly resurrected. As the king approached his majority therefore, normal administrative services were being resumed at the centre of government, while in the provinces they had never been disturbed. The intendants continued to implement government policy as best they could, and provide intelligence on affairs within their *généralité*. Orléans made no attempt to change the personnel, and most of Louis XIV's intendants were still in post when his successor reached his majority.[11]

That event took place when Louis XV reached his thirteenth birthday, in February 1723. Six months earlier, in August 1722, the regent began the task of formally instructing the shy young man in the political arts. The two held a series of private meetings which clearly went well. Orléans's approach to the king was invariably light-hearted yet respectful; Louis called him 'uncle' and trusted him. When the minority came to an end the king asked the former regent to remain at his side, and appointed Orléans's old friend, by this time Cardinal Dubois, to take over as first minister. By the end of the year both men were dead, leaving the young Louis XV with the daunting task of stepping into his great-grandfather's shoes with only his aged tutor, the abbé Fleury, to guide him.

Louis was a handsome youth with a broad forehead, regular features and wide brown eyes. Early portraits suggest that he bore a striking resemblance to his great uncle, the duke du Maine. His open countenance was a misleading guide to his personality, however, for he was secretive, timid and introspective, and inclined to melancholia. It appears that this last trait was inherited from his paternal grandmother, Marie-Anne of Bavaria, the wife of the grand dauphin. But in truth the experiences of his early life were sufficient to induce a despondent and morbid view of the world without the additional handicap of the Wittelsbach genes.[12] By the age of two Louis had lost his grandfather, mother, father and elder brother. Before the king's death in 1715 one of his two surviving uncles, the duke of Berry, had died, and the other, Philip V of Spain, had departed France forever. Then, as he was struggling to come to terms with the nature of his authority as king, he lost the service of an astute minister who might have become his Cardinal Mazarin, and the loyal support of his worldly-wise kinsman.

The inner loneliness and sense of personal inadequacy which dogged him for life were not characteristics likely to assist him in emulating the *grand monarque*. Yet that was what he set out to do, with a degree of conscientiousness not always acknowledged by historians. The first step was to return to the theatre where the sun king had played the greatest leading role in Europe. Since 1715 Louis' home had been in Paris, at the Tuileries palace, but in 1722, much to his delight, the royal court went back to Versailles. The king was so excited by his return that he lay on the floor in the Hall of Mirrors in order to admire Le Brun's magnificent ceiling. Thereafter he resumed the rituals established by his great-grandfather. Each day was framed by the *lever* and *coucher*. In the morning the king received a succession of visitors arriving in strict order of precedence while he was getting washed, shaved, dressed, and having his breakfast. Most of the same personnel reappeared, in reverse order, for the evening *coucher*. After morning mass Louis met his ministers and dealt with the routine political issues of the day. Specific times were set aside for council meetings: the high council on Sundays and Wednesdays, the council for finance on Tuesdays, the council for religion on Thursdays, and the council for the interior on Saturdays. The king attended to his political responsibilities as assiduously as he danced to the ceremonial steps of his great-grandfather, the old puppet-master.

In the decades immediately following his majority Louis XV's peace of mind was eased by two relationships, with his queen and with his chief minister. Whatever Bavarian genes he may have possessed, Louis XV certainly inherited his predecessor's liking for the opposite sex. This was the cause of an early diplomatic incident, for Louis was promised in marriage to the three-year-old daughter of Philip V of Spain, Maria Anna, who was already living in Paris. The marriage was not to take place for ten years and nobody at the court of Versailles imagined that the king would remain celibate for that length of time. Besides, France was in desperate need of an heir if Europe was to avoid another round of succession crises. The duke of Bourbon, who had taken over as first minister after the death of Orléans, lacked the latter's political astuteness, but even he recognized the logic of the situation. The infanta was duly packed off to Madrid and the search for a new queen began. The choice eventually fell on Maria Lesczinska, the daughter of the exiled king of Poland, and not therefore a brilliant match for the great house of Bourbon. But she was strong, attractive without being a beauty, a devout Catholic, and most important of all, eighteen years older than the unfortunate Maria Anna. Louis fell in love with her at once, and a dauphin was born in 1729. Between 1727 and 1737 the couple had two sons and eight daughters, of whom one son and six daughters reached adulthood.

In this early, uncharacteristically uxorious period of his life, Louis was also able to rely on the support of his former tutor, the remarkable Cardinal Fleury, who became his chief minister in 1726 at the age of seventy-three. The cardinal minister remained in charge of government until his death in 1743. Throughout most of that period Louis gave Fleury his unstinting support, the *sine qua non* of effective authority in *ancien régime* France. With this royal backing Fleury's ministry provided a period of relative stability after the stormy last decades of Louis XIV's reign and the unquiet days of the regency. The cardinal, in consultation with the ministers, took the decisions which the king ratified. That procedure was not simply a product of royal laziness, though Louis' timidity and innate sense of insecurity made him a less than dynamic figure; it was the necessary result of an increasingly bureaucratic system. The king's theoretical powers remained immense but the administration for which he was nominally responsible was becoming too vast and complex for him to cope with. It has been truly observed that by this time, 'a king had no independent access to information'.[13] For all his efforts to honour his predecessor's concept of the *métier du roi*, Louis XV was an amateur in politics. The real professionals were the chancellor, the secretaries of state, the controller general of finance, and principally Cardinal Fleury, who moderated all the discussions between the king and his ministers.

Despite his intellectual inhibitions, Louis XV was an intelligent man and with the passage of time he became disillusioned with his role. For increasingly he recognized that the part he was playing was a pale imitation of the sun king's original performance. That fact is aptly demonstrated by reference to some of the changes he introduced at Versailles. Upon his return to the palace in 1722 Louis had inherited his great-grandfather's bedroom, symbolically situated at the centre of the building and providing the focal point for the main rituals of the day. Unfortunately the great-grandson, like Madame de Maintenon, found it too cold and was not enamoured of its monumental proportions. In search of greater privacy and of accommodation on a more intimate scale, he looked to his architect, Jacques-Ange Gabriel, to plan a new set of royal apartments close to the old. Gabriel ranks alongside Le Vau and Mansart in defining the great palace for posterity. He enjoyed a close, relaxed relationship with the king, comparable to that of his predecessors, Mansart and Le Nôtre, with the *grand monarque*. The essential difference in this regard between great-grandfather and great-grandson was that Louis XV knew that he was presiding over, and patronizing, a rare artistic moment.[14]

Gabriel's new apartments at Versailles began to take shape in 1735 in what originally had been the northern wing of Louis XIII's old hunting lodge. Ultimately they consisted of a small suite of rooms centred on the king's new bedchamber, the *Petite Chambre*. Next door was the Clock Room, named after its astronomic centrepiece, a gift from the Académie des Sciences. Then came the king's study situated on the angle of the Marble and Royal Courts with its balcony facing the road to Paris. The following room, once occupied by Athénaïs de Montespan, was given by the king to his favourite daughter, Madame Adélaïde. It was there in 1763 that the royal family gathered to listen to a clavichord recital by the Austrian *Wunderkind*, Wolfgang Amadeus Mozart. Above the first-floor suite were scores of smaller rooms, the *petits appartements*, which offered even more privacy and seclusion to a monarch desperate to offset the stresses induced by his public persona. The increasing falsity of that persona was symbolized by the king's adaptation of the *lever* and *coucher* after taking possession of his new private apartments in 1738. It was still considered necessary for the king to retire formally in Louis XIV's bedroom, to go through the motions of getting into bed while the courtiers hovered and then withdrew, according to the proper procedure. Under the new regime, however, as soon as the courtiers had retired, Louis got out of bed and made his way to his own room, or even left the palace altogether in search of entertainment. Indeed, after a while he ceased to take off his clothes during the *coucher* so that he could make a speedy exit. Similarly with the *lever*, the king would come from his *Petite Chambre* to his official bedroom in order to get out of bed again under the ceremonial eye of the court. It was a ridiculous performance, reducing the king and his courtiers to the level of players acting out an old and meaningless ritual: Louis XV playing at being Louis XIV.[15]

Yet the private world created for Louis XV also represented the apogee of a new decorative style. During the regency *le goût moderne* in the contemporary phrase,

Rococo as it came to be known much later, began to dominate the French artistic scene. It was primarily an ornamental style associated with interior decoration, and with embroidery, painting and furniture, but it defies precise definition. Most suggestive is the analogy with the crest of a wave caught at the moment of its unfurling. Characteristically mobile and exuberant, its curved lines represent subjects largely abstracted from nature, a cascading profusion of shells, vines, foliage and flowers. By a reduction of scale to more intimate proportions, and by the use of mirrors, of pastel colours, white and gold, it introduced into great houses and palaces a sense of lightness and elegance.[16] Its artistic achievement was to elevate the name of Louis Quinze above that of his illustrious predecessor. For the creation of his own secret world in Versailles Louis was indebted to his architect and designer, Gabriel, and to two sculptors of rare quality, Verberckt and Rousseau, who were responsible for the delicately carved wainscoting in the Rococo style.

Louis' desire to shun the public world which his predecessor had embraced with such enthusiasm was quickened by another shift in his lifestyle. He was becoming tired of playing the role of faithful husband. Having produced ten children in twelve years, Maria Lesczinska was showing understandable signs of diminishing interest in sexual relations. Instead, her attentions were increasingly directed towards ensuring her own eternal salvation, an objective which of course the king also desired for himself, though at this stage of his life more in theory than in practice. Finding himself excluded from the queen's bed whenever an important feast day occurred – and the number of significant saints in her liturgical calendar tended to grow year by year – Louis may have felt that he had met his Madame de Maintenon at the wrong end of his life. The *petits appartements* therefore provided him with the opportunity to install a series of royal mistresses out of the sight of his lugubrious queen.

Like the young Louis XIV, Louis XV chose his first mistresses from a single family. On the Mancini model he moved from the eldest daughter of the marquis of Nesle, the countess of Mailly, to her younger sister, the marquise of Vintimille, who died in childbirth in 1741. There were still two sisters available, one of whom, the voluptuous and prematurely widowed marquise of La Tournelle, drove a hard bargain with the besotted king. Formally admitted to the court, she became Louis' first *maîtresse en titre*, acquiring in the process the title of duchess of Châteauroux together with a large personal allowance. She was an ambitious woman and her influence with the king was rising at precisely the time that the apparently indestructible Cardinal Fleury was at last beginning to lose his grip on affairs.

Fleury died in January 1743 while France was engaged in the War of the Austrian Succession. Although the king maintained that he intended to take over himself as first minister after his old tutor had gone, it was clear that he was incapable of doing so. Instead, faction reigned as rival groups and individuals sought to capture the king's support. One such aspirant was the duke of Richelieu, who was closely linked with the Nesle family and therefore hoped for preferment through the good offices of the king's mistress. For her part Châteauroux was keen to persuade Louis to seize the initiative by joining his troops on campaign in the Austrian Netherlands. She accompanied him as far as Metz where suddenly, as if by an act of God, she lost her powerful hold over the king's will. Taken dangerously ill, Louis decided that his eternal salvation outranked the allures of the marquise. She was dismissed and he received the last sacraments. However, he quickly recovered and set about reversing his premature decision to turn his back on worldly pleasures. This morality play had a predictable ending: Châteauroux was recalled to Versailles but, before she could make the short journey from Paris, she too was struck down by serious illness, from which she quickly died at the age of twenty-seven.

The months before and after the death of the marquise of Châteauroux formed in retrospect the turning point of Louis' reign. The dependable Fleury was dead and, particularly since it was a time of war, the political nation looked to the king to take control of the government. Louis' stock had never been so high: following his dramatic recovery from life-threatening illness at Metz he was embraced by his people with the title of Bien-Aimé, Louis the Well-Beloved. Yet, for all his new-found popularity in the wider world, this diffident man felt more isolated, more vulnerable than ever, without a soul-mate in whom to confide. At court, speculation about a new mistress began to grow early in 1745, the year of the morale-raising French victory at Fontenoy. On 25 February a grand fancy dress ball was held in the Hall of Mirrors at Versailles to celebrate the dauphin's marriage to a Spanish infanta. The king attended in the bizarre uniform of a clipped yew tree, inspired by the topiary of the palace gardens. This glittering occasion marks the moment when a successor to Châteauroux did indeed appear on the scene, but the new favourite was destined to occupy a place far beyond the dreams of the Nesle sisters. Louis was about to enter the most deeply felt and permanent relationship of his life with the captivating young Madame d'Etiolles.

Jeanne-Antoinette Poisson was of a very different stamp from her predecessors as royal mistresses. The daughter of a notorious beauty and a failed financier, she profited immensely as a child and young woman from the patronage of Le Normant de Tournehem, an exceedingly wealthy tax-farmer, who was one of her mother's many lovers. His money provided Jeanne with an exclusive education that enabled her to acquire all the social arts and graces as she grew up. She showed early signs of becoming an accomplished actress. She learnt to play the clavichord, to sing and act and dance, to paint and ride. She was invited to mix with the intellectual and artistic elite of Parisian *salon* society, and in due course she was betrothed to Le Normant's nephew, Charles-Guillaume d'Etiolles. Her new husband's grandfather and father had acquired personal noble status by virtue of their venal office, thereby entitling the grandson to full hereditary nobility. Thus Madame d'Etiolles scraped into the second estate with no quarters of nobility to spare, but that fact, together with her background in new money and new ideas, did not endear her to the court establishment. She possessed, however, qualities which Louis XV found quite irresistible.[17]

First and foremost Jeanne-Antoinette d'Etiolles was a very beautiful woman. It is possible that some of her portraits, including Boucher's spectacular painting of 1756, ignore the inevitable inroads of time, but others, notably by the pastelist, Quentin de La Tour, portray breathtaking images of serene beauty which defy artifice. The Parisian judge and man about town, President Hénault, described her as 'one of the prettiest women I have ever seen', an observation made before the king had met her and not therefore to be construed as flattery.[18] She exuded charm and sexual allure, but she was also *sympathique*, a quality which enabled her to establish a *modus vivendi* with her chief enemy at court, Queen Maria Lesczinska. In the early summer of 1745 the king left the court to join the military campaign which was to culminate in the victory at Fontenoy. His new mistress also withdrew from Versailles to her husband's château d'Etiolles near Choisy. She was in residence there when the news reached her that the king had revived an extinct title in her favour: henceforth she was to be the marquise of Pompadour.

Madame de Pompadour dominated the king's court from 1745 until her premature death in 1764. She provided Louis with emotional support long after 1752, when their physical relationship ended. It was a measure of her importance to the king that for a further decade she continued to dominate his world, shrugging off the opposition of ministers and would-be favourites, increasingly influencing Louis' political judgements, especially in the field of foreign policy, and stamping her taste indelibly on the Louis Quinze style.

She brought her love of the theatre to Versailles, and in 1746 Louis had built for her the Théâtre des Petits Cabinets, which opened in 1747 with a performance of *Tartuffe*. The theatre was decorated by the artist François Boucher, who also designed some of the costumes. In fact, he became Pompadour's chief artistic collaborator. Besides painting a famous series of portraits of the marquise, he played a leading role in decorating her new château at Bellevue, on the Seine between Meudon and Sèvres. The destruction of Bellevue during the French Revolution deprived posterity of countless works of art, including wood-panelling by Verberckt and sculptures by Pigalle and Falconet. There could, however, be no denying the extravagance and exclusivity of her patronage. Among unprivileged Parisians living down the road from Versailles, she came to personify the feckless indulgence of a tiny, aristocratic and increasingly irrelevant world. She collected houses as the poor garnered their loaves: the hôtel d'Evreux, now the Elysée Palace, two châteaux, one on the Loire at Menars, and one east of Paris at Champs, whose previous owner, the duke of La Vallière, was a descendant of an earlier royal mistress, as well as houses at Saint Ouen and Crécy, and hermitages at Versailles, Fontainebleau and Compiègne. All were lavishly built or rebuilt, and sumptuously decorated.

Yet on the credit side there is some evidence that the marquise appreciated that state-sponsored art needed to attract a wider clientele than the court set. This was the case with her patronage of Sèvres porcelain. A soft-paste porcelain factory had been established with royal backing at Vincennes in 1738. With Pompadour's support it was transferred to Sèvres, close to Bellevue, in 1756. Boucher and Falconet were both engaged in this enterprise too, helping Sèvres to rival Meissen as Europe's porcelain capital. The colours of royal blue and Pompadour rose are a permanent reminder of the powerful patronage enjoyed by the Manufacture royale de Sèvres from the time of its foundation. Both the king and the marquise spent heavily each year on the firm's products, and a shop was opened off the rue Saint-Honoré to allow Parisians to invest too. A contemporary diarist recorded Pompadour's assertion that 'not to buy as much of this porcelain as one can afford is simply not to be a good citizen'.[19]

Louis XV depended on Madame la Marquise, not only to invest his world with affection, entertainment and style, but also to advise him on affairs of state. After Fleury's death, for both temperamental and practical reasons, the king found it impossible to run the country himself; nor was he willing to appoint another chief minister to act on his behalf. The result was government by faction as rival groups vied with each other to catch the king's eye and gain his approval for their strategies. Louis' perennial vacillation threatened to reduce government policy to the whims of intriguers. In this situation Pompadour had a significant role to play, both as political patron and adviser. She was a supporter of Machault d'Arnouville, who became controller general of finance, keeper of the seals and secretary of state for the navy; and of the count of Stainville, later duke of Choiseul, who profited from the marquise's patronage to become successively ambassador in Rome and Vienna, secretary of state for foreign affairs, war and the navy. Conversely, she was resolutely hostile to one of Choiseul's predecessors as secretary of state for war, Count d'Argenson, in part at least because of the enmity between himself and Machault; and she bore a special grudge against the able secretary of state for the navy, the count of Maurepas, who was dismissed for his association with a lubricious anti-Pompadour street song.[20] D'Argenson reflected in 1751 that 'The mistress is prime minister and is becoming more and more despotic, such as no favourite has ever been in France'. The future duke of Choiseul predictably took a more sympathetic line:

Madame de Pompadour wanted the king at least to be able to pronounce in the council an opinion which would appear to be his own. In consequence she had the courage to take a part in business matters and was soon up in them because she had a lively and accurate mind. She gave the king advice and it was rare that it was not judicious. Louis XV acquired the habit of letting himself be guided by her advice, and she became the arbitress of the destinies of the kingdom.[21]

Pompadour did indeed influence government policy, particularly foreign policy, with her concern for a *rapprochement* between old adversaries, the Bourbons and the Habsburgs. She was the intermediary approached in 1755 by the Austrian chancellor, Count Kaunitz, the chief architect of the so-called Diplomatic Revolution, with a note to the king from the empress, Maria Teresa. Subsequently she was present at Brimborion, her retreat in the gardens of Bellevue, for the key meeting between the Austrian envoy, Count Stahremberg, and the *abbé* Bernis, another of her protégés, which led in 1756 to the signing of the treaty of Versailles between France and Austria. Three years later a grateful Maria Teresa presented the marquise with a writing desk inlaid with the empress's portrait in precious stones. Nevertheless the Seven Years War ended disastrously for France in 1763 with the treaty of Paris. Canada was lost to Britain and so were a string of West Indian islands. In India Britain's control of Bengal and Madras allowed it to dominate the subcontinent's trade; in Africa France ceded Senegal to Britain, and in America Louisiana to Spain. The British Empire was well on the way to achieving a decisive victory over France in the struggle for global commercial hegemony. This setback was the result in part of French preoccupation with continental military security. Louis XIV to some degree, and Orléans and Dubois in particular, failed to pay the necessary attention to the implications of Great Britain's developing worldwide role. Choiseul, on the other hand, understood very well the nature of the threat being posed to France's prosperity and status as a great power, and the need to continue challenging Britain's imperial might. That was why his old adversary, the earl of Chatham, remarked in parliament that 'since the late Cardinal de Richelieu France has not had so great a minister as the Duke de Choiseul'.[22]

The humiliation of the peace of Paris was no more the responsibility of Madame de Pompadour than it was of Choiseul. But it marked the end of the marquise's public career. She died just over a year later, on the evening of 15 April 1764, Palm Sunday, in her apartment at Versailles. She was forty-two years old. Her death closed a brilliant but fateful chapter in the long reign of the once-loved king. She left a superb library, a magnificent collection of engravings in precious stone, and a wealth of furniture and crystal. Her patronage inspired works of great beauty in Gobelins tapestry and Sèvres porcelain. She employed the greatest decorative artists of the age and her name remains synonymous with 'a moment of perfection in French art'.[23] Pompadour's collaboration with Gabriel contributed to the construction of the Ecole Militaire in Paris, where twenty years after her death the young Napoleon would complete his military training; to the architectural masterpiece in the grounds of Versailles, the Petit Trianon; and to Gabriel's first venture into town planning, the elegant place Louis XV (now the place de la Concorde), where the next king would face the guillotine.

The very brilliance of the Pompadour years highlights the surrounding darkness. For in fashioning an inner world into which this diffident and insecure king could escape, she inadvertently helped to diminish the monarchy's role in the people's eyes. It appeared that the *métier du roi* was being replaced by a preoccupation with self-indulgence on a mammoth scale; and this at a time when more enlightened public opinion was beginning to question the established order. Ironically, Pompadour herself was not hostile to new ideas. She had been exposed to them in the *salon* during her formative years, and Dr Quesnay, leader of the physiocrats, was her personal physician. But all that was beside the point to the forlorn man left quite alone in 1764. The most compelling image of the reign dates from the day of her funeral, which protocol forbade the king to attend. As the cortège made its slow way through the rain and the gathering gloom along the Paris road, Louis stepped onto the balcony of his study at the corner of the marble court to watch in silence as it disappeared from view. Then the tearful sovereign turned to his *valet de chambre* and remarked bitterly, 'This is the sum of the respect I am allowed to pay to my friend of twenty years.'[24]

Louis' failure either to govern France in person as the inheritor of his Bourbon patrimony, or through a professional cadre of administrators as the chief executive of his state, had profound consequences for the French monarchy. His great-grandfather's policy of separating government officials, *noblesse de robe*, from the old nobility, a strategy also followed by the regent with his *polysynodie*, had confirmed the principle that in inheriting the French state the ruling house acquired, besides its own proprietorial rights, a territorial community whose security and well being it was obliged to safeguard. Louis' collapse in the face of faction meant that the ancient image of kingship, personal leadership at the head of his followers, *primus inter pares*, was lost. The alternative concept, of the king and his government officials working together to ensure the effective running of the state, also fell foul of faction. For Louis began to permit members of the court nobility, the *grands seigneurs*, to re-enter the political arena as secretaries of state. For a long time such posts had been reserved for the professional families of the *robe*, men like Maurepas and Saint-Florentin, both members of the Phélypeaux clan and both secretaries of state under Louis. Later in the reign, however, the *grands* began to take over, headed by Choiseul and his cousin, the duke of Praslin, Marshal Belle-Isle and the *abbé* Bernis. It seemed that the old feudal order was seeking to re-establish itself at the heart of government.

By the time of Pompadour's death Louis XV had been king for almost half a century. Without his constant companion and supporter, he was left drifting in whatever direction ministerial faction pointed him. No longer the Well-Beloved, Louis' reputation was irredeemably tarnished. A contemporary chronicler commented on the unenthusiastic reaction from the citizens whenever the king showed his face in Paris, and his personal unpopularity had a corrosive effect upon his kingly role.[25] If it appeared that the business of government was the responsibility either of a strong minister, the regent or Cardinal Fleury, or of a succession of favoured groups, with Louis simply acting the part with diminishing diligence, then there was a danger that the monarchy might seem irrelevant. Serious questions began to be asked about what its role should be.

The chief inquisitor was the parlement of Paris, back to its old adversarial ways following the deal struck with the regent, Philippe of Orléans, in 1715. It had a ready-made cause for opposition in the form of the papal bull, *Unigenitus*, which had not only failed to extirpate Jansenism but actually succeeded in breathing new life into the controversy. Through much of the eighteenth century the bull would continue to be exploited by both government and opposition in quarrels which, though overtly theological, were fundamentally about the nature of the king's authority. During Louis XV's minority the pope raised the stakes by promulgating the letters *Pastoralis officii*, requiring unqualified acceptance of *Unigenitus*. The parlement, mindful of the fact that it had already qualified the bull's acceptance in its 1714 registration, promptly declared the letters invalid. Eventually, in 1720, a compromise was worked out in the form of a royal declaration interpreting how *Unigenitus* should be understood, being registered by the parlement with the customary Gallican provisos.

The controversy erupted again in 1730 when Cardinal Fleury was effectively running the country. Fleury's position was entirely pragmatic: he believed that division within the church threatened to undermine obedience to the authority of the state, and that therefore it was in the national interest to put an end to the dispute, whatever the traditional freedoms of the Gallican Church. An appeal to reasons of state, the very negation of the rule of law, was of course anathema to the chief law court. It was also, potentially, a dangerous line to pursue at a time when the precise nature of the king's function was becoming problematic. In March 1730 Fleury presented a royal declaration to the parlement, requiring *Unigenitus* to be recognized as a law of church and state. It became immediately clear that to have this legislation approved the king would have to hold a *lit de justice*, attending the parlement in person in order to impose the legal authority which the court normally exercised on his behalf. This took place in April and was followed by more than two and a half years of guerrilla and open warfare between crown and parlement. During this period the king's council and the court regularly issued conflicting judgements on matters relating to the bull, magistrates were arrested or exiled, and resigned their offices *en masse*: the normal processes of royal justice came to a halt.

The parlement was incensed by the cavalier treatment meted out to it, but more particularly by the political implications of declaring *Unigenitus* to be an unqualified law of the state. It interpreted that pronouncement as constituting a grave threat to the sovereign's secular authority, from spiritual powers at home and abroad. The Parisian judges maintained that the pope would be entitled to excommunicate the king of France and thereby free his subjects from their allegiance. They also deeply resented Fleury's proscription of the appeal *comme d'abus* in matters involving *Unigenitus*. This legal procedure, stretching back into the fifteenth century, allowed complaints against ecclesiastical judges accused of exceeding their powers, of trespassing on secular jurisdiction, or of contravening the liberties of the Gallican Church, to be heard in the parlement. It appeared that the court was about to lose this key role of arbiter between lay and spiritual jurisdictions, which enabled it to subordinate the church's judicial authority in France to that of the king. The magistrates were playing their traditional political role, that of protecting the king's legitimate authority even when that meant challenging his own measures. For his part, Fleury judged that the greater threat to the crown's authority was posed by the opponents of *Unigenitus*. But by dispensing with time-honoured legal procedures the cardinal gave hard-line Jansenists in the parlement the opportunity to provoke a damaging confrontation with the government, and to demand from an all but invisible king the potent right of free speech. In the end another compromise was agreed. In return for a show of servility, the exiled magistrates were allowed to return to the capital, and the recent draconian legislation levelled against the parlement was suspended though not revoked.[26]

The whole episode had been damaging for the prestige of the law, and therefore for the authority of the king. On the face of it the argument was an old one, but attitudes to kingship were changing with the advance of scepticism, and there was no knowing in 1732 where such an argument might lead. Baron Montesquieu, himself a former magistrate in the parlement of Bordeaux, had already demolished in a single, cutting phrase, the idea that the king could cure his subjects by touching them: 'In France the king is a great magician.'[27] Before the next confrontation took place between crown and parlement over the enforcement of *Unigenitus*, Montesquieu had published his masterpiece, *De l'esprit des lois*, in 1748.

In the second half of the eighteenth century this great work became the magistrates' bible. It translated the periodic, mundane disputes between the government and the parlement into debates about the extent and limitations of political power. Unfortunately for the judges, by starting to express their traditional and innately conservative ideas in the new language of the president from

Bordeaux, they were inadvertently encouraging a fundamental reconsideration of the values of the existing order. The actual disputes in which they were engaged, and the manner in which each side sought to checkmate the other, were to modern minds exercises in mutual futility. Priests who were in favour of *Unigenitus* began to refuse the last sacraments to parishioners who opposed it. The parlement drew up remonstrances which the king refused to receive. Paris was filled with contradictory judgements emanating from the parlement and the king's council, the one prosecuting pro-*Unigenitus* clergy, the other annulling those prosecutions. Pamphlets and printed versions of the court's remonstrances raised the emotional temperature in the capital to dangerous levels. The judges went on strike and were promptly exiled to their own estates or to towns far away from Paris. Finally, a royal declaration of silence was imposed on both sides, and the parlement was reinstated.

By this time France was enmeshed in the Seven Years War, and the parlement predictably was opposing the introduction of emergency financial legislation intended to support the war effort. In the light of previous history Louis had a poor hand to play, but he made matters worse by sacrificing successive controllers general in order to appease the court. Following the dismissal of Henri Bertin after the conclusion of the war in 1763, the king appointed as controller general Clément de Laverdy, a prominent Jansenist member of the parlement. The war had left France submerged in debt, requiring a regime of high taxation in order to service it. Yet traditionally it had been impossible to justify such exceptional tax levels when hostilities had ceased. Louis' appointment of Laverdy underlined the hopelessly reactive nature of government policy by this date, and the fact that, following the collapse of John Law's experiment, there was still no viable financial system capable of sustaining the state through a period of war and its aftermath. The most recent judgement on these events is unsympathetic: 'With the kingdom facing the worst financial crisis since the collapse of Law's system, a completely unsuitable, although personally worthy, candidate was named *contrôleur général*.'[28]

As Louis lost control of the situation his enemies intensified their attack. The remonstrances of the parlement of Paris began to sound like *De l'esprit des lois*. Instead of the subjects' relationship with the king being expressed in terms of estates or orders, as was customary, there was a mysterious intervention of 'society', in which each individual related equally to the crown. The court's remonstrances of 1755, for example, refer to the rights of society, and to man's natural desire to form a society for the common good. Words like 'subjects', 'citizens' and 'people' were increasingly replaced by 'men', meaning humanity: 'without justice, man will face nothing but disorder, strife and anarchy'. Taken to its logical conclusion the language of the parlement risked undermining the juridical basis of the ancien régime. Of course that wasn't the court's intention.

Its true opinion was revealed in its defence of the principle that the king's subjects 'are divided into as many different bodies as there are different estates in the kingdom', and in its condemnation of 'absolute equality'. Yet as early as 1764 it was also proclaiming that 'every citizen born into a monarchy possesses the right to liberty, a heritage more precious than fortune and circumstances, and ordained by natural law'. Though the messages were mixed it is not fanciful to detect the emerging idea of the universal rights of man.[29]

The parlement also sought a more explicitly constitutional role for itself through its advocacy of an historical fiction, the union of classes. It put its argument to the king in 1755: 'the parlement of Paris and the other parlements form a single body and are only different divisions of the royal parlement'. The implications were obvious, and dangerously Anglo-Saxon: not twelve sovereign courts spread across the country but a united magistracy and a nationwide institution to regulate the law. Had not Montesquieu nominated the judges for this intermediary role between king and people in order to eliminate 'a single individual's momentary and capricious actions'?[30] The government reacted to this doctrine by straddling the line between legitimacy and despotism. Thirty members of the parlement of Besançon were exiled to frontier fortresses for three years for upholding the liberties of their province. All the members of the parlement of Toulouse suffered two months' house arrest for their opposition to financial legislation. Members of the parlement of Pau resigned over the issue of free speech and were replaced by judges acceptable to the government. Most dramatically in Brittany, the parlement of Rennes resigned en bloc in protest over an unpopular financial imposition, only for the king to set up a new parlement in its place. This move provoked repeated remonstrances from the Parisian magistrates in favour of their Breton colleagues.

The end product of these politico-legal battles was a definitive statement from an uncharacteristically combative Louis XV which sought once and for all to crush *parlementaire* pretensions. It was delivered in March 1766 at a *lit de justice* in the parlement of Paris, a celebrated occasion known as the *séance de la flagellation*. The king condemned the notion of a union of all the parlements, and the idea that the magistrates possessed any independent authority in the business of lawmaking. Nevertheless the Breton dispute rumbled on, and the Parisian judges continued to show solidarity with their colleagues in Rennes. The climax came in 1770–71 with *lits de justice*, judicial strikes and a thinly disguised campaign of civil disobedience by the members of the Parisian court, who were in turn warned by the chancellor that the king would regard 'all correspondence with the other parlements as a criminal confederation against his authority'. 'This astonishing anarchy cannot last,' commented Voltaire, 'either the crown must reassert its authority or the parlements will gain the upper hand.'[31] The crown in fact reasserted its authority in the most drastic and dramatic fashion.

Its instrument was a poacher turned gamekeeper, René Nicolas de Maupeou, the former first president of the parlement of Paris, who became chancellor in 1768. In late January 1771 the venal offices of all the magistrates, an important element of their wealth, were confiscated and they were exiled to near and distant parts of the kingdom. This time there was no attempt on the government's part to negotiate a compromise; after five hundred years the parlement had ceased to exist.

Maupeou's judicial reform was a belated *coup de force* of which few thought Louis XV capable. Yet it reflected not the strength but the weakness of the king's position. For he was cutting himself adrift from the one body which, for all its illusions of political grandeur, had long guaranteed the legitimacy of his authority and that of his Bourbon predecessors. Neither king nor parlement was willing to contemplate a fundamental reform of the old order of the kind envisaged by John Law. Paradoxically, that fact both bound them together and set them at odds with each other, since the government continually required more financial resources than it could justify raising. The resulting altercations were along well-established and predictable lines, but by the second half of the eighteenth century they were being played out more publicly and were beginning to attract a wider audience. The parlement regularly published its remonstrances, which sometimes ran to several editions, and ministers responded with their version of events in the *Gazette de France*.[32] The more colourful episodes were also reported in French periodical literature and in the foreign press. The parlement never seriously aspired to become an English parliament, but the publicity afforded to its opposition allied with its more outlandish claims, helps to explain the unusual vehemence of the king's antagonism.

That hostility was honed by the most traumatic episode of Louis' whole life. At Versailles on an early January evening in 1757 the king was the victim of an attempted assassination. His attacker, Robert François Damiens, was a deranged victim of the hysterical religious emotions which gripped Paris during the 1750s, whipped up by the activities of the parlement. During this period of frenzy anonymous letters were circulated, some of them threatening the king. Very similar letters appeared some years later when the parlement was becoming involved in the Brittany affair. It is not surprising therefore that after years of near anonymity Louis should belatedly lead the charge in person against those who were slyly but publicly questioning his authority, and provoking others to contemplate regicide.[33]

But it was too late for Louis to redeem his reputation. He had never taken personal control of government, his ministerial teams were not disinterested servants of his state, and he had always avoided the temptation to initiate necessary reform. All he had left was an inherited office whose legitimacy was mirrored in the registers of the ancient court of parlement, to which the crown had long been symbiotically linked. By jettisoning that body Louis risked casting aside his lawful authority, and falling back on despotism.

That is certainly how it seemed on the morrow of the Maupeou revolution to those who formed the Patriot party. The title was significant. The French form, *patriotisme*, had only crossed the Channel from England around the middle of the eighteenth century, at once posing the difficult question of whether patriotism and absolute monarchy could coexist. 'True patriotism', wrote Holbach in 1776, 'is only to be found in countries where free citizens, governed by just laws, are happy and united, and seek the esteem and affection of their fellow citizens.' For some of the *philosophes* France was included within that definition. Diderot wrote in the first volume of the *Encyclopédie* that under the House of Bourbon France enjoyed a regime of freedom which encouraged the development of patriotic feelings, the key to freedom being the government's recognition of the rule of law. Montesquieu went further, arguing that in a legally regulated monarchical regime there was no need for patriotism at all. Similarly the article on 'Patriotism' by Louis de Jaucourt in the *Encyclopédie* extends the concept to a commitment to worldwide human rights. All these observations implied a passive role for patriotic citizens in well-regulated monarchical regimes. However, a more active, and to later generations a more familiar interpretation of patriotism, was ready to emerge. Montesquieu accepted that such an heroic virtue would be called for if law and order broke down and the community was left in peril. Jaucourt recalled the patriotism of Greece and Rome, 'this sacred fire', which rejected universality in favour of imperial glory. That was also Voltaire's position. The high priest of the Enlightenment produced a characteristically no-nonsense definition in his *Philosophical Dictionary* of 1764:

> It is sad that men often become the enemies of the rest of mankind in order to be good patriots ... To be a good patriot is to want one's town to enrich itself by commerce and to be powerful in war. It is clear that one country cannot gain without another country's losing and that it cannot conquer without producing miserable men. This, then, is the human condition: to wish for the greatness of one's country is to wish evil to one's neighbours.

In the first version of his *Social Contract*, written around 1760, Jean-Jacques Rousseau proposed that every citizen should be required to profess their love of country in an annual ceremony designed to bind them to the service of the state.[34]

This second interpretation of patriotism was more problematic for Louis XV since it implied positive political action by non-governmental agencies, and a role for the nation or the *patrie* that would loom larger even than that of the monarchy. Shortly before the Maupeou revolution, the king had once again reminded the members of the Paris parlement that the rights and interests of the nation were inseparable from his own, and were his responsibility alone. The coalition making up the Patriot party included liberal-minded noblemen, disaffected judges and embittered Jansenists, and its constituency was that educated minority, largely based in the capital, who had embraced the new ideas of the enlightenment.[35] They were not yet a revolutionary group. The intellectual debate in which they were involved – and that is what it remained for the moment – was on the face of it a rerun of the age-old confrontation between crown and parlement. That was why for the most part they gave their backing to a legal body whose political authority had always depended upon the king's will. Most saw no alternative way to end Maupeou's proclamation of royal despotism. A few far-sighted individuals, including Malesherbes, a representative of the great *robe* family of Lamoignon, thought of the estates general, which had not met since 1615. But until the new vocabulary gave birth to new political aspirations the king would remain firmly in control of the situation. He resolutely backed his chancellor for the remaining years of his reign, which he spent in further damaging his reputation in the eyes of his once admiring subjects.

Louis' compulsive need for sexual gratification remained with him in his mid-fifties. He now had access to what was in effect a private brothel at the Parc-aux-Cerfs in Versailles, which he acquired in 1755 and continued to visit until 1771. The girls who lived there, the *petites maîtresses*, are for the most part unknown, except for Mary-Louise O'Murphy, La Belle Morphise. The daughter of an Irish immigrant, she bore the king at least one son who became a general. She herself, or another representative of the sisterhood of the Parc-aux-Cerfs, was painted into immortality by François Boucher.[36]

   Louis sold the Parc-aux-Cerfs at the request of Madame du Barry, with whom he formed the last, and most notorious, liaison of his life. It is Pompadour's misfortune to be eternally coupled with du Barry as the two great courtesans of eighteenth-century France, for the marquise was incomparably the more significant and impressive figure. Du Barry's origins were even humbler than Pompadour's, though she shared the latter's ambition and physical allure. She was personally amiable but no intellectual or aesthete. She began her working life as Jeanne Bécu, a high-class prostitute in Paris, before becoming the mistress of count du Barry who introduced her to a succession of aristocratic lovers. Louis himself became infatuated with her during 1768 but was prevented from declaring her *maîtresse en titre* by the hypocritical protocol of the court, which required the successful candidate to be the wife of a nobleman. This detail was quickly taken care of, Jeanne Bécu entering a marriage of convenience with du Barry's obliging brother. The ribald reaction at court to the new favourite's arrival is captured in the gleefully related but entirely apocryphal conversation between the king and one of his courtiers: 'They say that I am succeeding Sainte-Foix in Du Barry's affections. Yes, Sire, as Your Majesty succeeds Pharamond!'(the legendary founder of the French monarchy). Du Barry was also the subject of a campaign of vitriolic pornography, inspired by the duke of Choiseul who blamed the new *maîtresse en titre* for his dismissal in 1770. This was another sign of the potential threat posed to the establishment by the swelling influence of public opinion. It was inconceivable that Gabrielle d'Estrées or Athénaïs de Montespan could have been similarly vilified.

In fact, Du Barry's part in Choiseul's fall was minimal. In a world dominated by faction her position at court inevitably made her an important go-between in political intrigue. She joined the anti-Choiseul camp because that was where the king found himself, infuriated by a minister who appeared to be unable or unwilling to challenge *parlementaire* pretensions. Louis also had a second reason for mistrusting his secretary of state for war and foreign affairs. By 1770 the king was anxious for peace at all costs, but Choiseul's characteristically hard-line rivalry with Britain seemed calculated to provoke war. Louis had taken an interest in French foreign policy for many years, but it was an idiosyncratic interest, typical of the withdrawn nature of his kingship and of his inability to govern decisively.

The *secret du roi* was the phrase used to describe the unofficial foreign policy conducted by the king and his cronies behind the backs of his ministers. This bizarre diplomacy, which began in the 1740s, had as its main objective the succession of the king's cousin, the prince of Conti, to the Polish throne, together with the reestablishment of traditional French alliances with Turkey and Sweden. A network of secret correspondents was set up, centred on the French ambassador in Poland, the count of Broglie. Each of them reported privately to Louis via de Broglie, enclosing copies of the dispatches sent to them by the king's own secretary of state. It was Louis' way of persevering with his royal responsibilities in attenuated form, spiting the warring parties at court by creating a little faction of his own. Like his performance at the *lever* and *coucher*, the *secret du roi* reveals Louis acting out the role of king without exercising real authority.

The Diplomatic Revolution of 1756 saw the *secret* adjusted to take account of the new alliances with Austria and Spain, and later, following the disastrous peace of Paris, further adjusted to prepare for a war of revenge against Britain. With this latter initiative the *secret du roi* descended into farce. Louis' chief agent in this cloak and dagger serial was the Chevalier d'Eon, a secretary in the French embassy in London. With the king's close involvement, plans were put in hand for an invasion of England. However, d'Eon fell out with Versailles and threatened to leak the king's instructions to the British government. Having survived a French attempt at kidnapping him, d'Eon agreed to return the compromising documents in exchange for an annual pension of 12,000 livres. For all the time and effort, not to mention correspondence involved in the *secret*, it yielded very few results: Turkey's declaration of war on Russia in 1768 and the 1772 *coup d'état* in favour of Gustavus III in Sweden, were the only successes. It continued in operation until Louis XV's death, though even de Broglie wanted to abandon it. Then his successor handed all the documentation to the new secretary of state for foreign affairs, Vergennes, who was himself in on the secret, 'so that in him official and secret diplomacy may be said to have come together at last'.[37]

The end of Louis XV's reign carried with it echoes of his great-grandfather's last years. Death, which had always obsessed this brooding personality, took its toll of his family. In 1765 he lost his only son, the dauphin, and two years later his daughter-in-law, Marie-Josèphe. His queen, Maria Lesczinska, died in 1768, having enjoyed a closer relationship with her husband after La Pompadour's death. Women continued to dominate his court, however, as they had done habitually under the Bourbons, though comparisons with the conclusion of the previous reign founder on the contrasting influence of Mesdames du Barry and Maintenon.

During the early 1770s the king seemed intent on highlighting the disparity between the conspicuous consumption of the royal family and the near bankruptcy of the nation. In May 1770 his eldest grandson, now the dauphin, married Marie-Antoinette, the fifteen-year-old daughter of the Austrian empress, Maria Teresa. No expense was spared to mark that occasion, or the marriages of the dauphin's two younger brothers, destined in another world to become kings as Louis XVIII and Charles X. In June 1773 the new dauphine made her official entrance into Paris, and in the following year headed the court's attendance at the Paris opera for the premiere of *Iphigénie*, by her countryman, Christoph Gluck. All these grand and expensive occasions would later help to feed the terrible anger of the Revolution, as would the heady, gem-laden opulence of the favourite, du Barry. One aristocratic observer of the scene, the duke of Croÿ, reflecting on the scale of the problem of restoring the nation's finances, commented wryly: 'as if one went in for retrenchment at Versailles!'[38]

The king's mistress and the prospective queen of France, Marie-Antoinette, provided Versailles with a final opportunity in Louis' reign for gossip on a grand scale, one more example of the irrelevance and artificiality of the king's world in the eyes of almost all his subjects. Daughter of a Holy Roman Emperor and wife of the heir to the French throne, the new dauphine was a proud young woman who was unwilling to be upstaged as the first lady of the court by such a socially inferior rival as the king's *maîtresse en titre*. Her solution was simple but, in the context of the etiquette-ridden world of Versailles, devastating: she refused to speak to du Barry, thereby failing to recognize her privileged status and even her existence. The situation became so fraught that even the Franco-Austrian alliance, which the dauphin's marriage to Marie-Antoinette was intended to strengthen, seemed to be at risk. Maria Teresa was forced to write to her wayward daughter, pointing out that since the king had chosen to admit Madame du Barry into the court she deserved to be treated with respect. With ill grace Marie-Antoinette gave way, and on New Year's Day 1772 aimed the banal though eagerly recorded observation in the direction of her enemy: 'There are a lot of people at Versailles today.' She did not speak to her again from that day until 1793, the year in which Madame Guillotine claimed them both in the Place de la Révolution.[39]

The age of Louis XV drew to a close in an atmosphere of political, financial and moral crisis. In April 1774 the king was taken ill with smallpox. He died a fortnight later, on 10 May, at the age of sixty-four. Two days before his death Madame du Barry left Versailles to allow Louis to make his peace with God, as the duchess of Châteauroux had withdrawn from Metz all those years before. Louis XV's human foibles have been fully catalogued; his inadequacies as king are less easily identified. Essentially Louis failed because as a personality he was ill-suited to adapt to the challenges of his generation. It was not enough to copy his great-grandfather. In seeking to do so his talents were sabotaged by his temperament, and he found himself increasingly out of his depth and out of his time.

7

Louis Capet

The last of the Bourbons to rule France before the Revolution, Louis XVI, was baptized Louis-Auguste, after the most revered of his ancestors, the saint-king Louis IX. For the first time since the death of Henry IV, France had avoided a period of minority rule, though at nineteen the new ruler had little experience in the political arts. Indeed, like his late grandfather, he had not been expected to become king. His elder brother, the duke of Burgundy, died in 1761 and four years later his father, Louis XV's only surviving son, succumbed to tuberculosis at the age of thirty-six. The latter's posthumous influence over the new king was reflected in the return to power of the minister whom he had considered best equipped to tutor the inexperienced young man. One of Louis XVI's first acts was to write to the count of Maurepas, who had been exiled from the court for the previous twenty-five years following an indiscreet attack in verse on Madame de Pompadour. Born in 1701, Jean Frédéric Phélypeaux was the most senior living representative of the great *robe* dynasty that had served in the king's ministries for a century. Jean Frédéric inherited the office of secretary of state from his father, and was minister for the navy for twenty-six years before his disgrace in 1749. By 1774, therefore, he appeared the ideal candidate to initiate Louis into the mysteries of kingship. A venerable figure with a wealth of experience, Maurepas' long exile had lifted him above faction. He could be expected to offer disinterested advice, and although it was not part of the new king's thinking, there was merit in having the well-intentioned aspirations of the young ruler tested against the cynical views of this witty, worldly-wise professional.

When Louis XVI succeeded his unpopular grandfather the monarchy was facing a low-key crisis. It was not yet a crisis for the monarchy per se, but it was a challenge to the new king to show his worth by restoring faith in the system. What precisely that system was, or should be, was the question reflected in the rapidly growing number of publications rehearsing the views of the educated elite and providing the basis for an embryonic public opinion. In particular, the age-old question of the extent to which the king was obliged to put the interests of his people before those of his House became more focused and challenging. The de facto shift from personal ownership to executive responsibility remained difficult for some in the royalist camp openly to acknowledge. Louis XV's historiographer royal, Jacob Nicolas Moreau, wrote a tract for the education of the dauphin, shortly to become King Louis XVI, which was entitled *Les devoirs du prince*. In it he insisted that the new monarch would acquire the crown as an inherited possession, ownership of which would bestow on him the sole right to govern. He admitted that, in ruling, kings should seek the happy medium separating 'irreligious indocility from blind and superstitious obedience'. Nevertheless, they alone had the right to decide the precise location of the happy medium; that could not be the subject of a dialogue with the people. Here was the difficulty in acknowledging the idea of the king as the state's chief executive officer: acting in that capacity carried a presumption of national consent.[1]

There were signs at the beginning of his reign that Louis XVI intended to take his executive role seriously. He went along with Maurepas' suggestion that senior government ministers should once again be members of the *robe* nobility, men trained for a career in royal administration and not grandees whose qualification for service rested exclusively on their ancient lineage. He insisted, too, on taking his own decisions in government, resisting Maurepas' advice that a chief minister should be appointed, preferably himself, to coordinate official business on the king's behalf. The first major decision facing him, and one of the most crucial of his reign, concerned the draconian reform of the parlements undertaken by his chancellor, Maupeou, in the last years of his predecessor's reign.

For most of those who were politically aware, Maupeou's actions smacked of despotism, for the parlement of Paris in particular, despite its unhistorical assertion that it spoke for the nation, had for centuries legitimized and tempered the application of royal power. Maurepas believed that the restoration of the parlements would restore confidence in the monarchy and balance to the old political order. He viewed these judicial organizations of hereditary office-holders as a force for stability in politics. The king was less sure, and characteristically inclined to temporize. But he did find it unacceptable that the magistrates had been deprived of their offices in 1771 without any financial compensation. The purchase of office was after all a family investment in property which, on the basis of his own possessory rights, the king had no authority to confiscate.

Here was the nub of the problem facing the king's government. For all that the *robe* professionals had contributed towards modernizing the state, ultimately, like the feudal knights gathered around their chief, the king, they remained stakeholders in a highly personal enterprise. Though not a root and branch reformer, Chancellor Maupeou had opened a small window of opportunity for royal government to move to another level. The king could have become more avowedly the chief executive of the state, working with civil servants who had received his commission rather than with officers who had invested in the Bourbon business. But seeking to respond to the public's view that Maupeou's reforms represented a flight to despotism, Louis was persuaded to annul them and restore the parlements to their traditional place. Though taken with the best of intentions, it was a decision that would permanently weaken his government. This was not because the courts were emboldened to resume their anti-government campaign – on the contrary, the magistrates appeared traumatized for a decade by their unhappy experience – but because the king's mind, and that of his chief adviser, Maurepas, was incapable of comprehending how traditional Bourbon kingship might be transmuted into enlightened state absolutism.[2]

Not that Louis' mind was closed to new ideas; but their often dangerous implications passed him by. That was true in the area of state finance, where for generations kings of France had struggled to raise adequate taxes and to justify doing so. As the owner of the crown, the king alone was assumed to have the right to tax his subjects, but they too had their property rights and excessive taxation might lead them eventually to challenge the king's. Indeed, at that very moment the American colonists were rejecting the taxation demands of the British parliament. Though this occurrence greatly encouraged the Choiseulistes in the French government, who saw the opportunity to take revenge for the humiliations of the Seven Years War, it also resonated with those who believed in the need for an intermediary body to reconcile the interests of the king and his people.[3]

True to his reforming instincts, Louis appointed a new controller general of finance after only three months of his reign. The new man was Anne Robert Jacques Turgot, formerly intendant of Limoges, a leading light among the group of economic reformers known as the Physiocrats, and a contributor to the *Encyclopédie*. Turgot's plans for radical reform began, where John Law's had also begun, with the land. But whereas the Scotsman shifted his focus to bullion, Turgot persisted in his belief that economic expansion, and therefore increased national wealth, depended exclusively on profits derived from the land. A tax on the net income of landowners should therefore constitute the government's sole tax, direct or indirect. All the existing taxes which inhibited capital investment in the land, including the *taille*, should be abolished. As for how this new tax was to be assessed, that would be the responsibility of representative assemblies of landowners meeting on four levels, from the parochial to the national. Nothing of this was established during Turgot's brief ministry.[4] Nor, unsurprisingly, was his plan to introduce a state-sponsored uniform system of education, which would inculcate feelings of patriotism in every citizen. Such schemes would have required the king to embrace unequivocally his role as chief executive of the state of France, and cast aside any residual ideas of royal ownership. They had not reached the point of formal submission when the controller general was dismissed in May 1776.

What Turgot did achieve pointed in that direction, but not sharply enough to disconcert the king. He had the forced labour obligation to maintain the king's highways, the *corvée*, which had previously fallen on commoners alone, commuted into a payment levied on all non-clerical landowners, including members of the second estate. This was in keeping with Turgot's primary objective, to maximize the economic value of the land. Louis offered his support, observing that:

> I have no intention of blurring the distinctions between the Estates nor of depriving the nobility of my kingdom of the distinctions it has acquired by its services ... which I shall always maintain. It is not a question here of a humiliating tax but of a simple contribution which everyone should take a pride in sharing, since I am myself setting the example by contributing in virtue of my domains.[5]

But in fact Turgot was indeed challenging the established order in which individuals functioned only as members of their corporate estate. The parlement of Paris fairly pointed out the significance of what was being proposed, drawing its own conclusions about the likely consequences:

> The kingdom of France is made up of a number of distinct and separate estates ... Any system which, under a seeming humanity and beneficence, would tend to establish between men an equality of duties and to destroy these necessary distinctions would soon bring about disorder, the inevitable consequence of absolute equality, and accomplish the overthrow of civil society, the harmony of which is maintained only through this gradation of powers, authorities, preeminences, and distinctions which keeps everyone in his place and safeguards all estates against confusion.[6]

Turgot's abolition of the craft guilds was similarly aimed at providing individuals with an opportunity to exploit their talents unhampered by corporate restrictions: 'all persons of whatever quality and condition' should be free to practise whatever craft or crafts they chose.[7]

Turgot's dismissal was less the consequence of his failure to win the ideological case which he was in the process of presenting than of his lack of inter-personal skills. His unsubtle demands for action alienated his ministerial colleagues and ultimately the king, causing Louis plaintively to remark that 'M. Turgot wants to be me and I don't want him to be me'.[8] Nevertheless, for the first time since John Law's 'reign' over half a century earlier, a minister of the crown had espoused an economic reform programme which was little short of revolutionary.

Undoubtedly one of the factors contributing to Turgot's disgrace was his opposition to French involvement in the revolt of the American colonies, an intervention which he believed would be disastrous. He would be proved right in a manner beyond his own imagining, for the war 'would serve to put a torch to the "gothic" superstructure of the Ancien Regime, fragile and fossilized as it had become'.[9] In the context of France's Great Power status, however, the colonists' revolt offered an early opportunity to redress the balance so catastrophically tilted in Britain's favour at the peace of Paris in 1763. The king was an enthusiastic supporter of French involvement, as he indicated in June 1776 to his Bourbon cousin, Charles III of Spain: 'I think the time has now come to concentrate exclusively on taking the measures most appropriate to humiliating this Power which is our national enemy and the rival of our House.'[10] Incidentally, this observation also reveals the continuing dichotomy in Louis' thinking about the nature of his kingly role: protecting the family's *gloire* appeared to be as important as safeguarding the national interest.

France began by providing unofficial support to the colonists – men, money and arms – and then in 1778 formally recognized the independence of the United States of America. In the subsequent war France held to a naval strategy which was ultimately crowned by the decisive Franco-American victory at Yorktown in 1781. The treaty of Versailles (1783), though offering relatively unspectacular gains to France, was hugely satisfying to the king who had all along supported the strong naval effort. France's war aims were largely achieved: the independence of the United States with the consequent humiliation of her British rival, the reconquest of the West African territory of Senegal and the West Indian island of Tobago, and the recovery of French fishing rights in Newfoundland. Thus the shame attaching to the treaty of Paris, signed only twenty years before, was assuaged. An earlier humiliation, imposed on France at the peace of Utrecht in 1713, was also ended: no longer would a British commissioner be entitled to reside in Dunkirk to prevent the port's refortification. France's last major conflict under the ancien régime seemed to have gone some way towards redressing the lost balance of power with Britain which in hindsight had been steadily tipping against France since the climactic war of the Spanish Succession.[11]

Sadly for Louis XVI this was a pyrrhic victory on several levels. First, the cost of the war came to about one billion *livres*. To put that figure into context, the state's normal annual revenue amounted to 475 million *livres*, and three years after the peace had been signed annual expenditure was still not far short of 600 million *livres*. There were two reasons for this dire state of affairs. The first was what has been called the eternal question facing the old regime: 'Would the rich finally agree to pay taxes?'[12] The second was the manner in which the war had been funded. Turgot was succeeded as finance minister by the unlikely figure of Jacques Necker, a Protestant Swiss banker who had made his fortune out of loans to the struggling Compagnie des Indes, the creation of an earlier foreign banker in charge of French finances, John Law. Necker's chief priority upon assuming office was to find a method of financing the French war effort in support of the American colonists. In the light of his successful career as a banker, he decided on a policy of raising loans rather than taxes. He was also a reformer by inclination, convinced that taxes, which were already too high, would be unsustainable if increased further.

Necker's wartime concern, however, was to increase the king's ordinary revenue by cutting waste and improving the efficiency of the collection. He knew that the accurate predictability of this fund would make borrowing on the international market that much easier. Similarly, he believed that more dramatic reform of ancien régime finances would depend on instilling into the population the crucial business attribute of confidence. That implied harnessing the nascent public opinion which was beginning to impinge on French political life. He was a strong supporter of the British system which gave maximum publicity to the budget each year, thereby proclaiming the country's creditworthiness.[13] What was possible under the British parliamentary monarchy, however, could not happen in France without radical restructuring: certainly Necker did not consider that the French parlements had a credible role. His solution was to introduce two experimental provincial assemblies, in Berry and in Haute-Guienne, consisting of landowners from all three estates with representation two to one in favour of the third estate and with voting by head. These notables were set such fundamental tasks as examining how the contentious *taille* might be reformed. In this piecemeal fashion Necker hoped to introduce a reform programme which, because it bore the imprimatur of enlightened public opinion, would be confidently accepted by the whole nation. But this was a slow and by no means universally popular way of proceeding, and meanwhile the country's debts continued to mount.

On another level too the winning of the war against the British proved to be a pyrrhic victory, as Necker's preoccupation with public opinion increasingly demonstrated. For one effect of this war was to radicalize public opinion as European, including French, sympathizers returned across the Atlantic bearing notions of popular sovereignty and the rights of man, which the burgeoning presses of Europe were quick to disseminate.

Necker was certainly playing with fire in claiming that only by embracing public opinion could the French monarchy adopt rational, workable policies which eschewed both despotism and excessive liberty.[14] His *pièce de resistance* in this area was his famous *Comte rendu au roi*, which he published in 1781. This purported to be a full and transparent statement of the king's ordinary income and expenditure. Whether it was an entirely accurate account has been the subject of much scholarly debate, but its greater significance lay in the mere fact of its publication. For it revealed the mysteries of government for the first time, including the cost of pensions to the privileged, and the amounts spent on maintaining the extravagant lifestyle of the royal courtiers. The *Comte rendu* was an instant publishing success: three thousand copies were sold on the day of publication and over twenty thousand were in circulation shortly afterwards. Necker had certainly succeeded in whetting the public's appetite for information about government finance, but how the public would interpret that information remained to be seen. Louis XIV had worked hard to distance the crown, both physically and psychologically, from the people by inhabiting a separate world at Versailles. His successors followed his example, with the brief exception of Philippe of Orléans's regency when that astute politician brought his charge, Louis XV, back to the capital. Necker's *Comte rendu* effectively dragged the king and his court into the market place, their value for money to be assessed by the citizenry. It was possible to discover, for example, that the daughter of Queen Marie-Antoinette's favourite, the duchess of Polignac, received a dowry of 800,000 *livres*, by no means an unusual amount in the context of the royal court but enough to pay the annual wage of two thousand Parisian workmen.[15]

By this time, Necker's personal credit had begun to run out, unlike that of the kingdom if he was to be believed. The king, who had himself appealed to the court of public opinion when dismissing Chancellor Maupeou and reversing his reforms, now began to doubt the wisdom of his minister's full-blooded anglophilia. Consequently, he was not minded to protest when Necker resigned in May 1781, peeved at his failure to be granted additional financial powers for the duration of the war. In November Louis' long-time mentor, Maurepas, died, and Louis was left alone to face a financial disaster which he dimly recognized was threatening to turn into a constitutional crisis.

In the aftermath of the American War the desperate state of the nation's finances became apparent, despite Necker's public relations campaign arguing the contrary. In 1786 the king finally recognized the dimensions of the crisis and became a revolutionary. His accomplice was his controller general, Calonne, the former intendant of Metz, who set out proposals which Louis enthusiastically endorsed. These proposals drove a coach and horses through the political, social and economic structures of the ancien régime. The objective, for so long a mirage for French kings and their financial advisers, was the influx of tax revenue into the royal coffers unrestricted by privilege and evasion. In words which echoed the views of his notorious but sharp-minded predecessor, John Law, Calonne observed that 'One cannot take a step in this vast kingdom without encountering different laws, conflicting customs, privileges, exemptions … rights and claims of all kinds'.[16] To impose order on chaos and to introduce equity into the system of taxation, Calonne proposed the establishment of a land tax to be levied across the whole kingdom on all landowners, whatever their social status. In addition all internal customs barriers were to be dismantled and the ancient forced labour tax, the *corvée*, finally abolished. Some semblance of national support for these root and branch reforms was to be provided by a network of landowners' assemblies operating in those areas not covered by provincial estates, and by the decision to have the whole package approved by an assembly of notables.

Calonne expected a hand-picked assembly to be far more compliant than the long-dormant estates general or the troublesome parlement of Paris. The latter in particular would have been an extremely unlikely accomplice in this daring initiative. For centuries it had maintained that the legality of the French state lay in the crown's acceptance of discrete relationships with the various orders of society, thereby guaranteeing a range of liberties which the controller general was now seeking to remove. That traditional view was also at the root of the concept of personal kingship, of the crown belonging to the House of Bourbon. The underlying effect of Calonne's reform proposals would have been to reiterate the alternative view, namely that the king was the chief official of the state, dedicated to its service as were all his subjects without discrimination. Such a vision of uniformity evoked ideas of a role for the nation, which was acceptable so long as the monarchy continued to hold centre stage and was not challenged by some alternative emanation of the national spirit: in that context it was not entirely reassuring for Calonne to be congratulated on his patriotic reforms by the distinctly radical count of Mirabeau.

In fact, by seeking both to dismantle and reconstruct the established order without disturbing the crown's pre-eminence, Louis XVI and his minister had opened the door to increasingly uninhibited criticism from every quarter. The assembly of notables started the rot by refusing to endorse Calonne's proposals. With deep disquiet Louis was forced to dismiss him, and to replace him by the notables' effective leader and a protégé of Queen Marie-Antoinette, the archbishop of Toulouse, Loménie de Brienne. Brienne was not among the king's favourites, Louis having already denied him promotion in the French church with the wry observation that 'An Archbishop of Paris must at least believe in God!' The new chief minister made clear his mistrust of equality at the expense of ancient liberties, commenting that what worked in republics and despotisms, in Philadelphia or Constantinople, was not acceptable in France where the *Grands* provided both the people's support and the monarchy's.[17] It was too late, however, for the genie was out of the bottle and nobody, including Louis himself, knew how events would unfold. Brienne's attempt at compromise failed, and in May 1787 the assembly was dissolved. The king's most recent biographer has argued convincingly that 'in the history of Louis XVI the Ancien Regime ended with his decision to convoke the Notables and the Revolution began when he was forced to sacrifice Calonne.'[18]

In the absence of the makeshift assembly of notables Brienne was forced to fall back on the parlement of Paris in his efforts to gain support for the new land tax, and unsurprisingly he was rebuffed. If the magistrates' opposition was predictable, however, their reasoning was far less so. Their new revolutionary vocabulary appeared to compromise their traditional stance, enabling them to deploy their forensic skills to reach quite contradictory conclusions. These advocates of a society of orders or estates began to espouse the idea of the citizen's individual rights and by inference therefore the rights of the nation at large. In opposing the proposed land tax in July 1787, the court proclaimed that 'those taxes which he [the French tax payer] pays to the king are a subvention which he owes only to the state ... the sovereign is merely the dispenser of such funds'. Perversely, and in total antithesis to the law enshrined in its registers, the parlement was espousing the idea, in the words of one recent commentator, 'that the monarch in France was unavoidably becoming little more than a distinguished servant of a dynamic and evolving master, the impersonal historic collectivity manifesting itself alternately as the "state" or as the "nation"'[19]. According to the magistrates' confused logic therefore, they were entitled on one and the same occasion to maintain 'that the nation, represented by the estates general, alone has the right to grant to the king the necessary aid'.[20]

As a result of its posturing the parlement became the idol of Parisian public opinion, persuaded that the magistrates were acting in the people's best interests to prevent large-scale fiscal exploitation. Although the court was briefly exiled to the town of Troyes, Brienne's nerve failed as he realized the extent of the parlement's popular support: in the autumn of 1787 it was recalled to the capital and the land tax proposal dropped. A new trial of strength between the king's minister and his sovereign court rumbled on through the winter and spring of 1788, until in the high summer the government finally ran out of credit and became insolvent. Faced with this crisis, Loménie de Brienne had no alternative but to announce that the estates general would meet in the following year, 1789. The deception behind the parlement's language was finally unmasked when it proposed that the estates general should convene according to the forms observed in its previous meeting in 1614. The court's popularity drained away overnight and was never regained. Its final act, in October 1790, was to draw up a protestation against the decisions of the National Assembly: 'in the midst of the ruins of the monarchy there still stands a monument preserving the principles by which that monarchy has been regulated for so many centuries'.[21] Half of the signatories would later pay for their defiance with their lives. By that time the legal framework which they were defending had been swept away, and there would be no role in the new France for the parlement of Paris.

The history of the Bourbon kings of France is interwoven with that of the lives of a handful of women – mothers, wives, mistresses – whose names continue to resonate across the generations. They include Jeanne d'Albret, Anne of Austria, Madame de Maintenon, the marquise de Pompadour, and finally Louis XVI's wife, born the Archduchess Maria Antonia but from the time of her marriage known by the French version of her name, Marie-Antoinette. Her immortality has been curiously established. She revealed neither the political will and robustness of Jeanne or Anne of Austria, nor the subtlety of Maintenon, nor the taste and refinement of Pompadour. She was of limited intellect and perception, somewhat giddy and empty-headed, spiteful and self-indulgent, but low down any league of public evildoers. Yet the damage inflicted on this otherwise unremarkable woman's reputation by the power, the inventiveness and the invective of the media helped to justify the introduction of state violence of a kind incomprehensible to her husband or his predecessors. She was one of the first victims of the new world order in which state control depended on the manipulation of public opinion.

That end product was the result of a long gestation, yet its portents became suddenly and dramatically apparent. Like his reviled predecessor, Louis XVI ascended the throne with a good deal of popular support and adulation, a welcome fulsomely extended to his queen. The Austrian ambassador recorded a visit by Marie-Antoinette to the Paris opera in January 1775 when 'The people, crowding on her route, cheered her so as to give the most visible and extraordinary proofs of their love'.[22] But this was a false and fleeting love affair soon to be replaced by a degree of national loathing incommensurate with the queen's actions and personality. The transformation was fashioned by the pamphlet press whose growth reflected that of the reading public as well as the dramas of Louis XV's declining years. Few aspiring young writers were able to fulfil their true aspiration to become *philosophes*, the new celebrities of the eighteenth century. Instead, embittered by their lack of success, they became *libellistes*, determined to traduce and undermine that *grand monde* which had denied them access. Their targets were the court, the church, the nobility and the royal family itself, amongst whom Marie-Antoinette was their star victim.[23] The reasons for that virulent hostility are complex.

Since the days of the sun king, Louis XIV, the Bourbons had used ceremonial to maintain their authority and disguise their humanity. As Versailles became increasingly remote from the people, both psychologically and physically, its royal tenants continued to be protected from political dangers by a surreal detachment from the real world. Any flouting of the rituals of Versailles would, however, surely undermine this state of affairs, and Marie-Antoinette's initial culpability lay in this area. This spirited young woman, the Empress Maria Teresa's daughter, who became mistress of Versailles in 1774, was intolerant of the formal rules of behaviour to which she was expected to adhere, the expression of a culture quite alien to her. Her resentment no doubt owed something to unhappiness in her private life. For some years her husband was unable to consummate their marriage. She eventually became pregnant for the first time in 1778 after Louis had undergone a minor restorative operation. Meanwhile, she remained rebellious, christening her lady-in-waiting, the countess of Noailles, Madame l'Etiquette, and seeking to circumvent the regulations she found most irksome. At first, her lapses seemed small-scale, though it was in the nature of life at Versailles that even the most trivial rules had to be obeyed. Marie-Antoinette was intent upon maximizing the privileges and pleasures available to her as queen without accepting the accompanying dreary routines. By ignoring the finely tuned social mechanisms regulating the political life of the court, she risked sacrificing her royal immunity and attracting an unprecedented degree of resentment and criticism. Her style was to avoid public duties by withdrawing into a private world inhabited by her chosen friends, to the detriment of the customary obligations imposed on the wife of the king. For example, the Austrian ambassador in Paris, Mercy-Argentau, reported to Maria Theresa as early as April 1776 on the queen's new-found enthusiasm for horse races which 'often take place on Tuesday, and the queen then fails to receive the ambassadors … who recently were prevented from paying court to the queen during three entire weeks'. He added the telling observation that 'The queen excuses everything from those who amuse her. The more or less favourable way she receives people depends almost entirely on this'. In the following year this opinion was reinforced by Marie-Antoinette's own brother, Emperor Joseph II, in letters to their brother Leopold. 'The desire to have fun is very powerful in her', he wrote, 'and since people are aware of it, they prey on that weakness, and those who give her the largest amount of, and the most varied pleasure are listened to and treated well.' And again, with prescience,

> The queen … thinks only of having fun … she is tied down by no etiquette, she goes out, she runs around alone or with a few people without the outward signs of her position, she looks a little improper, and while this would be all right for a private person, she is not doing her job, and that may well have consequences in the future.[24]

Antoinette's friends were headed by two young women, the princess of Lamballe, chief lady-in-waiting in the queen's household, and the duchess of Polignac, who became governess of the royal children in 1782. The favourite meeting place of the queen's *société* was the elegant mini-château, the Petit Trianon, constructed by Gabriel in the gardens of Versailles for Madame de Pompadour. Antoinette had asked her husband for her own house as soon as she became queen, an early sign of her intention to redefine the role of royal consort. Neither the long-suffering Maria Lesczinska nor any of her predecessors as queen of France would have dreamt of seeking such independence. Only royal mistresses had previously been accommodated in this fashion. Indeed, Antoinette's relationship with Louis XVI, though characterized by mutual fidelity, was paradoxically more reminiscent of that of a *maîtresse en titre*. Her brother certainly thought so. In June 1777 Joseph II confided to Leopold of Tuscany that 'Her situation with the king is very odd; he is only two thirds of a husband, and although he loves her, he fears her more; our sister has the kind of power to be expected from a royal mistress, not the kind a wife should have, for she forces him to do things he doesn't want to do'.[25]

The queen did indeed dominate her husband, but for some time her political successes, like the exile to his estates of her enemy, the former foreign minister d'Aiguillon in 1775, were simply acts of personal spite. Her domination lay in the king's recognition of her independence as mistress of the Petit Trianon, where, surrounded by her chosen courtiers, she was free to indulge her extravagant lifestyle and evade the obligations which Versailles had traditionally imposed on the ruler's wife. There she could enjoy the private company of her friends without the need for formality in dress or manners. This life of 'back to nature' simplicity did not, however, check Marie-Antoinette's financial profligacy or her liking for expensive jewellery. Mercy-Argentau reported on the public's displeasure at the cost of the new English-style garden created at the Trianon, and on the queen's escalating gambling debts. He also recorded her insatiable desire for diamonds at whatever cost. Although her husband gave her precious stones costing 300,000 *livres* in the course of 1775, she could not resist diamond earrings costing 600,000 *livres* at the beginning of 1776, though she did decide to pay for them by instalment.

This scenario of the queen acting scandalously outside her allotted role gave the pamphleteers *carte blanche* to destroy her character and create an enduring caricature. She was reborn as a whore, an insatiable harlot, an indiscriminate lover of men and women, the Messalina of her age. Her extravagance was converted into callous indifference for the suffering of her husband's subjects: she is still best remembered for a single sentence that never crossed her lips: 'Let them eat cake!' The final component in the vitriolic assault upon the queen was the subject of her nationality. The idea of patriotism, which had emerged at the end of the previous reign, now threatened to acquire greater definition through attacking the enemy within. Marie-Antoinette became *l'Autrichienne*, the representative of a foreign power who was therefore by definition the enemy of the people of France. There was a grain of truth in this allegation, for her marriage had been designed to shore up the Franco-Austrian alliance, the so-called 'Diplomatic Revolution', which was no longer popular in France by the time of her wedding in 1770. Conversely, there were hopes in Vienna that the queen would become a valuable secret weapon in the prosecution of Austrian foreign policy. That expectation foundered upon her limited strategic sense. Although Marie-Antoinette flirted with political decision-making, her actions were invariably governed by her attitude to individuals. Only towards the end of the reign, from 1787, did her political influence begin to flower.

In 1783 her enemies were given a unique opportunity to castigate Marie-Antoinette for being both promiscuous and foreign. In the Salon exhibition of that year a new portrait of the queen, by Elisabeth Vigée-Lebrun, was put on show. It depicted her wearing a simple white muslin gown, and a straw hat. This famous painting, of *Marie-Antoinette en chemise*, caused such consternation that Vigée-Lebrun was pressed to withdraw it. It represented the height of fashion in England but in France was considered too informal, immodest even, to be worn in public by the queen. The artist later recalled that some critics accused her of painting the queen in her underwear! However absurd that accusation, Marie-Antoinette's portrait *en chemise* made a statement about the role of the queen of France which related to the Trianon rather than to Versailles, and it further inflamed the imaginings of *libellistes* keen to depict the little château as a lesbian lair. It also allowed them to stress the queen's Austrian preferences: had she not restyled the Petit Trianon as Little Vienna or Little Schönbrunn, and did not her *robe en chemise* threaten the French silk-making industry of Lyon? The salon of 1783 marked an important stage in the process of demonizing the queen.[26] That process was carried much further two years later during the last great scandal of the Bourbon monarchy, the affair of the diamond necklace.

That Marie-Antoinette was susceptible to diamonds was a given in court society. So when the royal jewellers found themselves with a necklace to dispose of with a value of over 1.5 million *livres*, it was assumed that the queen would be the most likely purchaser. She proved to be uncharacteristically resistant, however, probably because the original intended recipient had been the disgraced former mistress of Louis XV, Madame du Barry, whom Antoinette thoroughly despised. This was the backdrop to an extraordinary charade in which the queen played a central role, though without any knowledge of what was happening. The two chief actors were Jeanne de la Motte and Louis, cardinal of Rohan. In one respect they were ideally suited to work together: as confidence trickster and gullible victim. They had nothing else in common. By persuading the king's sister, Elisabeth, that she was a descendant of the Valois kings fallen on hard times, Jeanne, baronne of la Motte de Valois, to give her full bogus title, acquired a foothold on the edge of Versailles society. Rohan belonged to the distinguished family of Rohan-Soubise and numbered among his forbears Henri who had caused Louis XIII so much trouble as leader of the Huguenot rebels early in the previous century. He was desperate to improve his chances of political advancement and was easily persuaded that his best chance lay in performing a signal service for the queen. That service was to act as her intermediary in purchasing the diamond necklace. He was set up by La Motte and her cast of assistants. These included a Marie-Antoinette lookalike shrouded in white muslin, who under cover of darkness briefly met the cardinal in the gardens of Versailles. The dénouement was entirely predictable. The necklace was handed over to the conspirators and immediately broken up and sold off in London. Rohan received no money from the queen to pay off the jewellers, who then contacted the queen's lady-in-waiting and the whole deception was exposed. The swindlers and their dupe were arrested, Rohan to his great embarrassment on 15 August as he was about to celebrate the Assumption Day mass. During the following months leading up to the trials and verdicts, the popular press had a field day. Who could doubt that the queen was indeed involved in the whole shady business, or that her real relationship with Rohan and La Motte was a sexual one? Her alleged lesbianism fitted neatly its contemporary description of 'the German vice', indicating where her true allegiance lay. In the year before the necklace scandal broke, Marie-Antoinette was involved in a violent dispute with the foreign minister, Vergennes, in support of her brother, Joseph II, who was attempting to open the River Scheldt in the Austrian Netherlands to free navigation: the queen of France once again showing her true colours as *l'Autrichienne*.[27] The verdict of the parlement of Paris, that Cardinal de Rohan was not guilty, and the popular enthusiasm which greeted his release, left Marie-Antoinette humiliated and her reputation further tarnished.[28]

The summoning of the estates general marked the effective fall of the Bourbon monarchy, for the 'bankruptcy of the monarchy was … not only financial, but political and intellectual, too. It had collapsed in every sense, leaving an enormous vacuum of power.'[29] At first Louis did not suffer anything like the degree of national hostility visited upon his wife. Nevertheless, the constant ridiculing of the monarchy, and its exposure to public criticism as never before, had taken their toll. It was becoming apparent that the 'magic had gone out of the Bourbons by the reign of Louis XVI'.[30] The king contributed to the crisis by his own chronic indecision, though it has to be said that no amount of firm decision-making could have managed the French Revolution. But unfortunately for Louis, who was seriously committed to reform, his brooding introspection led to damaging suspicions that he was not. The key issue dominating the newly constituted estates general was whether they should meet as a single body and vote by head rather than by estate. The king had already revealed his reformist instincts by accepting that the Third Estate should be represented by twice as many deputies as each of the other two. But on the matter of voting by head or by estate he prevaricated, and events began to create their own momentum. To compound Louis' anxieties his elder son, the dauphin, died early on the morning of 4 June 1789; a fortnight later the Third Estate, frustrated by the lack of royal support, finally took matters into its own hands and proclaimed itself the National Assembly. Still distraught at the death of his son, the king revealed his state of mind by dismissing the 'National Assembly' as a mere phrase.

Disappointment at Louis' lukewarm reaction so far turned to deep suspicion when a royal visitation to the meeting of the estates was announced for 20 June. It appeared to the deputies that the intention was to dissolve the meeting, especially since the queen and Louis' youngest brother, the count of Artois, were supporting an increase of the military presence around the capital. In order to pre-empt royal action against the Assembly the deputies moved to a nearby tennis court where they enacted the first set-piece of the Revolution, the Tennis Court Oath, commemorated only a few yards from the original site, in David's sketch in the museum at Versailles. Pulled in different directions by those advising him, the king predictably adopted mutually exclusive positions. On the same day, 27 June, he ordered the representatives of the First and Second Estates to join the National Assembly, at the same time tightening the military ring around Paris and Versailles. With the collapse of royal authority, the way was open for violence to fill the vacuum left by the disintegrating status quo. Paris seethed with rumour and fear and popular fury. At last, on 14 July 1789, one of the most powerful symbols of ancien régime power, the prison of the Bastille, was captured by a Parisian mob. The head of its governor, de Launay, was hacked from his body with a pocket knife and paraded in triumph through the streets on the end of a pike. This was the second set-piece of the Revolution, and sadly more characteristic of what was to follow than the Tennis Court Oath had been. Ritualized violence was to become not only the Revolution's signature but also its justification.[31]

The king realized that the game was up and on the following day announced the withdrawal of the troops threatening the capital. Two days later he visited Paris to make his peace with its turbulent citizens, appearing wearing the city's red and blue cockade in his hat. On the same day his young brother, Artois, left the country, followed by Marie-Antoinette's friends, the duke and duchess of Polignac. The National Assembly, now restyled the National Constituent Assembly, was ready to resume its reforming work, 'but the identity of the figure that was advancing through the door seemed somehow different, its shape and size uncertain and vaguely menacing.'[32]

The sole objective of the Constituent Assembly was to promulgate a constitution worthy of the French nation. Unlike the American republican model, which had so greatly influenced the proto-revolutionaries, the French equivalent was expected to incorporate a role for the king. Despite his tergiversations, Louis remained part of the proposed patriotic union of all Frenchmen and women. That was very much the aspiration expressed in the *cahiers de doléances*, which had been prepared for the meeting of the estates. In them Louis XVI appeared as an essential element in the national revival, some of the *cahiers* even recommending that a monument be erected in his honour, with the inscription, 'Louis XVI, le français'.[33]

How was the king to interpret this new patriotic kingship so alien to his Bourbon predecessors? Even the role of inherited chief executive of the family business was strikingly different from what was on offer to the king after 1789. Since the early 1770s patriotic sentiment had begun to alter the perception of the ruler's role. At first patriotism was a narrow concept identified only with opposition to the alleged ministerial despotism of Maupeou, but gradually it became the bond which made all Frenchmen and women shareholders in a great national enterprise. If the king was to remain the chief executive he would have to represent unequivocally the nation's interests, rather than those of his own House. The evidence suggests that neither Louis XVI nor his queen ever fully grasped the fact that the two interests were ultimately irreconcilable.

The dilemma presented itself immediately, in August 1789, when the National Assembly produced both the rallying cry of the new order and the final denunciation of the old. In the Declaration of the Rights of Man and the Citizen, Louis was faced with a direct challenge. Article 3 proclaimed that 'The fundamental source of all sovereignty resides in the nation. No body nor any individual may exercise any authority which does not derive explicitly from the sovereign nation'.[34] At the same time the government of France was declared to be monarchical and the crown hereditary in the Bourbon line. In separate decrees the Assembly abolished the feudal system, the sale of judicial and municipal offices, all forms of financial privilege relating to taxation, as well as all the other special privileges enjoyed by provinces, regions, towns and village communes.

Louis did not respond at once, though the auguries were not good. In a letter to the archbishop of Arles he persisted in talking about the sacrifices made by the first two orders of the state, despite the declaration's ringing endorsement of equal rights for all citizens. When he eventually replied to the Assembly it became clear that his reservations far outweighed his support, to the extent that he would only agree to publish rather than promulgate the legislation. He also revealed his total lack of understanding of the role of patriot king, which he was now expected to play, by expressing particular concern for the feudal rights of foreign princes owning lands in Alsace.[35] In fact, as he was later to avow in the declaration issued as he sought to flee the country in June 1791, Louis' exclusion from the constitutional debate had left him with only the vain shadow of royalty. In the end, his mind would not allow him to embrace such a drastic transformation.

The king's intellectual position was, however, of little relevance in the autumn of 1789. The reality was that royal authority had collapsed and the country was in chaos. The 'Great Fear' was sweeping the land, as hungry peasants sought to destroy all the physical vestiges of the feudal regime, provoking in turn a mass paranoia aimed against fictitious gangs of brigands bent on the destruction of all property. In Paris, where emotions were already inflamed by the events of 14 July, bread was in particularly short supply. In such a situation the restoration of authority would depend on the certain unpredictability of violence. Both sides acted accordingly. The minister for the Royal Household, the count of Saint-Priest, summoned the Flanders Regiment to Versailles to protect its occupants. This move, threatening enough in itself, was exacerbated by exaggerated accounts of a grand banquet held to welcome the regiment, during which white and black cockades, representing the king and queen, were substituted for the patriotic Parisian red and blue. The response was another of the Revolution's set-pieces, the October Days (5 and 6 October). Led by the capital's market women, some thousands of demonstrators set out for Versailles, to demand bread and retribution. The mood of the mob was ugly and became more so after their arrival before the gates of the château. The motif of force, which ultimately defined the French Revolution, persuaded the king to announce his unequivocal acceptance of the August decrees, and to agree to the invitation, realizing that he was in no position to refuse it, to return to Paris with his unwanted visitors. Violence had come within a hair's breadth of the hated queen, and the heads of the two bodyguards who had saved her bobbed along on the end of pikes, a macabre escort for the royal family as Louis XVI and Marie-Antoinette left Versailles for the last time en route to their unwelcoming capital. Over a century earlier Louis XIV's Versailles project had reinvigorated the House of Bourbon. The departure of his successor five generations later was a symbol of the family's decline.

In his new home in the Tuileries Louis struggled to make sense of the disorientating world around him. Shortly after his arrival the National Assembly amended his title from 'Louis, by the grace of God, King of France and Navarre', to 'Louis, by the grace of God and the constitutional law of the state, King of the French', in order to emphasize to the world, and to the king, that he owed such authority as he still possessed to the nation rather than to the Almighty.[36] In July 1790 the Festival of Federation was celebrated, to mark the anniversary of the storming of the Bastille. The king was given a prominent position in the ceremony, though he had to share it with the president of the National Assembly, and both were subordinated to the altar representing France, *la patrie*, to whose service Louis XVI and all his subjects were recruited. At this time the objective of patriotism was still being portrayed as the acquisition of political liberty for mankind in general, but that generous interpretation was soon to be replaced by a narrower definition which would provide the ideology for the new world order coming into existence on the streets of Paris, and justify the violence of its birth.

There had long been an undercurrent of hostility towards foreigners stretching back to the designation of Marie-Antoinette as *l'Autrichienne*. She was seen as the enemy within, now joined by a host of *émigrés* without, headed by the king's brother, Artois, and the latter's chief adviser, the former controller general Calonne. These hostile groups around the nation's frontiers were regularly added to by new dissidents disillusioned with the latest Revolutionary turn of events, their expectations buoyed in 1790 by the publication of Edmund Burke's swingeing attack on the Revolution in France. Their best hope of turning the tide or the clock back lay with recruiting the active support of the European Powers, headed by Marie-Antoinette's brother, Emperor Leopold II. Louis himself, who was virtually a captive in his own capital, eventually decided that the only course of action left open to him was to become an *émigré* also. He prepared the ground in November 1790 by appointing a former minister who had escaped to Switzerland, Breteuil, as his plenipotentiary to negotiate with foreign powers. Then on the night of 20 June 1791 the royal family, king, queen, Louis' sister, Madame Elisabeth and the royal children, made an ill-fated dash for freedom, but succeeded only in ensuring that the obscure town in Lorraine where they were captured, Varennes, would have an enduring footnote in history.

News of the flight turned national unease about the foreign threat into something approaching panic. It confirmed two disturbing facts. First, that the king, whose public role in the new regime was intended to justify its title of constitutional monarchy, had been revealed as the leader of the opposition, intent on pursuing a revisionist policy that would restore at least some of the monarchy's lost rights.[37] That put him firmly with the *émigrés* plotting counter-revolution, and their number was increasing dramatically. Indeed, at the time of the king's capture at Varennes, the elder of his two younger brothers, the count of Provence, was reaching the sanctuary of the Austrian Netherlands. This was widely seen as unpatriotic behaviour amounting virtually to treason by the royal family and its allies. Secondly, since the ruling houses of Europe were traditionally united by ties of kinship, they were more likely to come to Louis' aid now that his unwilling participation in the Revolutionary drama had been revealed. Suddenly the banner of patriotism as a rallying cry for all oppressed humanity seemed grotesquely indulgent when the nation itself was at risk. Voltaire's narrow definition of 1764, with its hint of force, made far more sense to those political activists in Paris who felt increasingly under siege during the summer of 1791. A victim of that changing perception was a Prussian nobleman, Anarchasis Cloots, who found himself in Paris shortly after the fall of the Bastille. He became one of the chief advocates of that generous-spirited patriotism which would lead to universal brotherhood. He spoke at the first Festival of Federation:

> A number of foreigners from all the countries on earth ask to line up in the midst of the Champs de Mars; and the cap of liberty that they will raise with such enthusiasm will be the pledge of their unfortunate fellow citizens' approaching deliverance.

Cloots was elected to the National Convention in 1792, but by then ideas of universal *fraternité* had lost their appeal in the face of enemies abroad. In 1793 the Convention decreed that no individual born abroad could represent the French nation. Cloots came under suspicion, attracting the enmity of another member of the Convention: 'Can we regard a German baron as a patriot?', demanded Maximilien Robespierre rhetorically. Cloots was arrested. At his trial it was perversely alleged by his accusers that his idea of a universal republic had provided the crowned heads of Europe with a pretext for attacking France. He was sent to the guillotine in March 1794.[38]

Initially the government overcame the embarrassment of the Varennes episode by maintaining the ludicrous fiction that the royal family had not fled but had been kidnapped. Louis was suspended from performing the royal duties which had driven him to flight in the first place. That was to be the situation until he formally accepted the new constitution, an amalgam of earlier legislation which the Assembly was on the point of finalizing. He duly ratified it in September 1791. The work of the Constituent Assembly was now finished and elections for a new body were held. The Legislative Assembly held its opening session on 1 October 1791.

By this time the sense that the Revolution was under siege was becoming more palpable. Just over a month earlier the emperor and the king of Prussia had issued a manifesto declaring their willingness to join with other European powers to restore the fortunes of the king of France. Though this was in fact a means of avoiding action, because both rulers knew that there was little international support for such a crusade, it didn't feel like that in Paris. Besides, there were well-founded suspicions, frequently aired in the Legislative Assembly and in the press, that the queen was acting out her hated role as *l'Autrichienne*, conspiring against the Revolution. The more extreme voices in the new Assembly, headed by the journalist, Jacques-Pierre Brissot and his Girondin group, responded by calling for action against the *émigrés*. The result was a series of decrees: the count of Provence was to be stripped of his rights of succession to the throne if he failed to return to France within two months; *émigrés* refusing to return would be deemed conspirators against the state, and their land sequestrated; even the land of their relatives remaining in France would be confiscated. By the year's end feelings in the Tuileries riding school where the Legislative Assembly conducted its business had reached fever pitch, whipped up by the oratorical brilliance of another of the Girondin deputies, Vergniaud. He contrasted the *émigrés*, 'The audacious satellites of despotism, carrying fifteen centuries of pride and barbarism in their feudal souls', with 'the representatives of free France, unshakably attached to the constitution ... led by the most sublime passions beneath the tricolor flag'.[39]

Warmongering was becoming irresistible, further encouraged by the unexpected support of the king and queen, who in their increasingly anomalous and hazardous situation calculated that war was unlikely to make their lot worse and might considerably improve it. It was an understandable but fatal miscalculation.[40] On 20 April 1792 France declared war on Austria, and almost at once Prussia joined the anti-French coalition. The fate of the Revolution now hung in the balance, and the nature of the new order began to evolve. Force and violence had been at the heart of events since 1789, and patriotism had been increasingly defined in those terms. Now in the light of the combined assault on the Revolution, from enemies within and without, patriotism became the only justification for political action. A permanent state of emergency was introduced, beginning in July with the implementation of the new law, *la patrie en danger*. Under the old regime kings had been willing, in extremis, to ignore the law when the security of the state was at risk. But such moments had always been viewed as temporary and undesirable aberrations. In the new world order, however, patriotism would become the heartbeat of the nation, and the essential task of government would be to define and represent that power, at the same time demanding the citizens' loyalty as a sign of their patriotic intent. In Paris in the summer of 1792 that idea was still germinating as the capital was taken over by patriotic forces out for blood: militant *fédérés*, arriving from the provinces to join the 14 July anniversary celebrations (including among the late arrivals at the end of July, the Marseille contingent entering Paris to the strains of their newly adopted battle hymn), and politically minded *sans culottes* from the various Parisian sections. In the following years their patriotic fervour would be channelled through the mechanisms of state Terror: 'The government of the Revolution', proclaimed Robespierre in 1793, 'is the despotism of liberty against tyranny.'[41] The inevitable consequence of that vision was the unbridled and irresistible expansion of state power, for patriotism was becoming whatever the government said it should be. As Cardinal Richelieu had foreseen a century and a half before, 'Qui a la force a souvent la raison en matière d'Etat.'[42]

In the combustible atmosphere of Paris in July 1792 the Brunswick Manifesto provided the spark for the explosion which finally destroyed the Bourbon monarchy. Issued in the name of the commander of the allied forces but in fact the work of *émigrés*, this document threatened Paris with draconian reprisals if any harm befell the royal family. The effect was to fortify the already widely held belief that Louis and his queen were involved in an international conspiracy to bring the Revolution down. On 10 August under the leadership of the so-called Insurrectionary Commune the royal palace of the Tuileries was stormed and in an orgiastic display of violence some six hundred of the king's Swiss Guard were killed. Louis and Marie-Antoinette together with the king's sister, Elisabeth, took refuge in the Legislative Assembly. Appointed by the most militant elements in the Parisian sections, the Insurrectionary Commune included Robespierre and Hébert, working closely with Paris's deputy attorney, Danton. All of them, the king's family and its sworn enemies, would be dead before the end of 1794, the victims of state patriotism in one form or another.

The events of 10 August made it dramatically clear that constitutional monarchy had become an irrelevance to the political life of the French nation. Not only Louis XVI himself but the Legislative Assembly too had ceased to matter, a fact which the latter immediately recognized by suspending the king from the exercise of his functions, and voting for its own replacement by a National Convention which would have the task of drawing up a new constitution. The king and his family were committed to the Temple prison in the north east of the city, and the last rites of the Bourbon monarchy began.

In this world at least Louis did not expect a happy ending. Shortly before his arrival at the Temple, in refusing offers of money from his courtiers he responded, 'Keep your purses, gentlemen, you will need them more than we shall, as you will have longer to live, I hope.'[43] He was more optimistic about his chances in the next world, for the king was a genuine Christian whose personal standards at court had been in marked contrast with those of most of his forbears. Not surprisingly therefore his prison regime included ample time for the reading of devotional works like the *Imitatio Christi*, and for reflecting on the divine purpose behind his family's desperate predicament. For the first few weeks of their incarceration there was a curiously unnerving contrast between life within the Temple walls and what was happening outside. Insulated from the febrile world of the capital, the royal prisoners were able to lead a relatively structured life, allowing the king to tutor his son and the family to dine and take recreation together. But beyond the walls the bloodletting was reaching new levels of depravity. Well over a thousand inmates of the capital's prisons were killed in the September massacres by mobs convinced that they were extirpating counter-revolution. Among the victims was the queen's old friend, the princess of Lamballe whose blonde head and decapitated body were carried to the Temple by a frenzied crowd keen to confront Antoinette with their grisly trophies. The king had no doubt that in due course the demonstrations of hatred and rage on the streets outside would reach in and destroy him.

The National Convention met for the first time on 20 September 1792 and on the following day voted for the abolition of the monarchy. By a happy coincidence for the revolutionaries the opening of the Convention took place on the same day as the battle of Valmy at which the French decisively halted the Prussian advance. Consequently, it was not only possible to declare the monarchy irrelevant but also the ex-monarch, who was no longer needed as a political bargaining pawn. From that moment Louis' fate was sealed: it was simply a question of how he was to be condemned. That was not an easy question to answer and Louis was determined to make the Convention's task as difficult as possible.

In fact the king's demeanour and actions in the last months of his life were quietly heroic. He coped with the uniquely grim situation in which he found himself with courage and dignity, to the extent that his trial threatened to attract public support rather than condemnation.[44] Stripped of the trappings of power, he was revealed as a man of solid Christian virtues, a thoroughly decent individual. But of course it was impossible to view him apart from his kingly role, which was the focus of his defence and of the Convention's attack in his trial, which effectively began on 11 December 1792. The mayor of Paris was deputed to escort the king, whom he addressed as Louis Capet, from the Temple to the Tuileries where the Convention was in session. Louis took mild exception to the style of address, pointing out that Capet was a distant ancestral name of no significance for himself. The significance for the Convention no doubt lay in the fact that the monarchy was indeed a centuries-old institution, whose destruction would be truly revolutionary.

The position of the two sides was of course mutually incompatible: the king's acquittal would imply the Revolution's guilt. Louis' defence, which was entirely of his own devising, was based on the constitution of 1791, which pronounced the royal person to be inviolable and sacred. It followed therefore that there was no law under which the king could be found guilty. In addition, since the Convention was seeking to act as both judge and prosecutor there was no legal mechanism available which would not undermine due process. In other words the king was being denied both the prerogatives of kingship and the legal rights enjoyed by every citizen.[45] He was therefore, uniquely, a man without rights in his own country. Addressing the Convention in the previous month, the fearsome Saint-Just had come to the same conclusion, though from an entirely opposed perspective. For him Louis XVI had never belonged to the French nation, for the assumption of kingship at once made him an outlaw. In a famous phrase he summed up his draconian stance: 'No man can reign innocently.'[46] Saint-Just's conclusion was that, since the king was already condemned, only the death sentence remained to be pronounced.

The king himself continued to hold the view that he would perish at the Convention's hands. He told his defence lawyer, Malesherbes, 'I am sure they will make me perish; they have the power and the will to do so.' He understood that he was to be the victim of what later generations would call a show trial, and was determined to demonstrate that his enemies could only establish his guilt by flouting the law: he was looking to history for vindication. 'Let us concern ourselves with my trial', he continued to Malesherbes, 'as if I could win; and I will win, in effect, since the memory that I will leave will be without stain.'[47]

Though he maintained that he should not be condemned for playing the role forced upon him, Louis was fundamentally opposed to the Revolution, and was guilty of communicating with outside forces whom he hoped might ameliorate its effects. He remained a diehard supporter of divine-right kingship and of a reformed ancien régime, believing that he would answer to God and not to the nation for his stewardship. In his eyes that did not diminish his obligation of care for his subjects or turn him into a tyrant, but for the revolutionaries it excluded him from the ranks of the patriots and therefore turned him into an enemy of the people.

After many hours of legal wrangling and internecine struggle on the floor of the Convention between Jacobin and Girondin deputies, the question was eventually put on 15 January 1793: 'Is Louis Capet, ci-devant king of the French, guilty of conspiracy against the liberty and attempts against the security of the state? Yes or No.' The result was an almost unanimous 'Yes', 693 of the 745 members, almost all of those present, voting in favour and none against. The Convention reconvened on the following day to decide the king's fate. Late on 17 January after a further thirty-six hours of continuous debate, Louis was condemned to death, though only by a small majority. His execution was fixed for the morning of the following Monday, 21 January 1793. Having been separated from his family since the beginning of his trial, Louis sought permission to see them once more, on the evening of the 20th. During his time alone the king had composed his last will and testament with his family very much in mind. He chose to write it on Christmas Day 1792, the eight-hundred-and-fifth anniversary of the coronation of Hugh Capet's son, Robert, as co-ruler with his father. In his will Louis addressed his own son, the dauphin Louis, urging him,

> if he has the unhappy fate of becoming king, to think that he owes himself completely to the happiness of his fellow citizens; that he must forget all hatred or resentment, and especially everything that has to do with the misfortunes and afflictions that I have suffered.[48]

Louis also asked his wife's forgiveness for his share of the responsibility for the parlous state to which she had been reduced. He found the family gathering, with Marie-Antoinette, the dauphin, his daughter, Madame Royale, and his sister, Madame Elisabeth, so distressing that he could not bear to go through with a second, final meeting arranged at Marie-Antoinette's insistence for seven o'clock on the following morning. The last hours of the *ci-devant* king have been well documented: his meticulous instructions to his devoted manservant, Cléry, who had shared his master's lonely life in the Temple; his long drive in the mayor's coach through silent crowds to the Place de la Révolution; his own removal of his coat and collar before his hands were bound behind his back; his final protestation of innocence to the crowd drowned by the drum roll; the cry of his chaplain, 'Son of Saint Louis, mount to heaven', as the blade descended; the severed head of the king, part trophy part proof, triumphantly held aloft, the final set-piece of the French Revolution.

It would have taken a remarkable man to have made a success of Louis XVI's inheritance. In fact Louis possessed neither the personality nor the intellectual capacity to cope. Though well-meaning and anxious to introduce reform within the narrow limits prescribed by his view of the world, he proved indecisive and ultimately irrelevant in the face of the dramatic circumstances and unfamiliar attitudes which he quite simply failed to understand. But in human rather than princely terms his posthumous reputation is less unflattering. The leading historian of his trial has summed him up thus: 'He was a good man, a loving husband, a devoted father, a sincere Christian, a conscientious king, a loyal patron, and an incompetent prince.' Among Louis' contemporaries the regicide Lazare Carnot, later to be Napoleon's war minister, provided a fitting epitaph: 'The best has paid for the worst. Bad causes have their martyrs just like good ones.'[49]

The execution of the king did not save the Revolution; on the contrary it was relevant only in so far as it added to the vulnerability of the new regime. By the spring of 1793 France was at war with Prussia, Austria, Britain, Spain and the Dutch Republic. At the same time counter-revolution was getting into full swing in the west of France, in the Vendée. The Revolution was indeed in danger and its leaders prepared a desperate remedy to save it. Henceforth the executive would not be limited by any constitutional niceties; all its actions would be justified and dictated by the need to defend the Revolution. This was to be a moral crusade demanding unqualified support from the people, in whose name it was being conducted. It was led by the extraordinary figure of Maximilien Robespierre. Under the rule of virtue and terror all those from whatever political or social group who opposed the regime, or whose conduct undermined its authority, or were in any way less than enthusiastic about it, were deemed to be unpatriotic and wicked. Those who gave their unqualified support held the moral high ground. In time, following the French model, all those who perpetrated the crime of treason against the state would come to attract a peculiar moral obloquy, inviting a terrible retribution.

The Terror was the ultimate manifestation of reason of state, fraudulently but necessarily expressed in moral terms in order to disguise its inhumanity. Thus over a period of some nine months some 16,000 men and women were sent to the guillotine.[50] Most of their names are unknown; the handful of exceptions played their part in governing France. Danton and Desmoulins, who wanted a relaxation of the Terror; Saint-Just and Robespierre, whose executions brought it finally to an end; and the former queen, Marie-Antoinette, who was the Terror's most sought-after victim.

After her husband's death Marie-Antoinette was separated from her two children and transferred to the Conciergerie, an insalubrious prison on the Île de la Cité. Inevitably, she was arraigned in due course before the instrument of the Terror, the Revolutionary Tribunal. Officially her offence was counter-revolutionary conspiracy, which in the light of her known views was not an unreasonable indictment. Yet the public prosecutor's main assault was upon her virtue, culminating in an accusation of incest with the dauphin, her son:

> the widow Capet, immoral in every way, a new Agrippina, is so perverse and so familiar with all crimes that, forgetting her quality of mother and the demarcation prescribed by the laws of nature, she has not stopped short of indulging herself with Louis-Charles Capet, her son, and on the confession of this last, in indecencies whose idea and name make us shudder with horror.

Such pornographic accusations had been customarily levelled against Marie-Antoinette even during her days as the reigning queen. Under the Terror they were guaranteed to establish her guilt. Her answer to this latest allegation was brief and dignified: 'If I have not responded, it is because nature refuses to respond to such a charge made against a mother'.[51]

The inevitable death sentence was pronounced on 15 October 1793. For her last journey she dressed herself in a plain white dress and bonnet. Her hair, which she had carefully groomed for her appearance before the Tribunal, was shorn in preparation for the knife, and her hands were tied behind her back. She went to her death in an open cart, deprived of the relative privacy afforded to her husband. Only her red, high-heeled shoes which, miraculously in view of the countless petty acts of cruelty inflicted on her, she had managed to hold on to, hinted at defiance. That and her proud bearing, marvellously caught in David's lightning sketch made along the route.

Thus the French nation took its revenge on *l'Autrichienne*. Marie-Antoinette never fully understood or tried to come to terms with the Revolution. She was far less accommodating than the king, though far more viciously traduced by their enemies. Like Louis, she achieved a degree of resignation and steadfastness in coping with her long ordeal, but at a cost. A lifetime rather than a decade seems to separate the two images of the queen, the portrait *en chemise* of 1783, and the sketch of the haggard old woman who would never reach her thirty-eighth birthday, captured by David on her journey to the Place de la Révolution.

Marie-Antoinette's son was left to suffer in prison. The authorities were minded to leave him there since, according to French monarchical law, he had become King Louis XVII at twenty-two minutes past ten on the morning of 21 January 1793, when his father succumbed to the guillotine. There was no enthusiasm for keeping the sickly, demoralised boy alive, and in 1795 he died at the age of ten in the Temple prison where he had spent the previous three years of his life. The Bourbon cause appeared to be irretrievably lost. Meanwhile the Revolution had moved on and young General Bonaparte was on the point of exporting it to the sound of the Marseillaise.

Epilogue

The Terror accounted for most of the royal family and for many of those who had been too closely associated with them. The latter included Louis XV's *maîtresse en titre*, Madame du Barry, and the distinguished magistrate and septuagenarian, Lamoignon de Malesherbes, who paid for his brave advocacy of Louis XVI at his trial. The king's sister, Madame Elisabeth, was executed in the spring of 1794. Only his daughter, Marie-Thérèse Charlotte, Madame Royale, survived the holocaust. She was exchanged for some revolutionaries incarcerated in an Austrian gaol, and lived into the second half of the nineteenth century. Two of the family's leading members survived, however, because they had escaped from the country in time. These were the king's two brothers, the counts of Provence and Artois. The younger, Artois, departed for Brussels shortly after the storming of the Bastille and became the leader of the *émigré* cause. In exile he continued to hold views which suggested that he believed a return to the old regime was both possible and desirable. As a political reactionary he was in a league of his own. His elder brother, the count of Provence, left France almost two years later, arriving in the Austrian Netherlands in June 1791. Though no less committed to counter-revolution than Artois, Louis-Stanislas-Xavier had a more realistic appreciation of what was politically possible, a useful ability should he ever have the opportunity to test it. Since he had claimed the title of King Louis XVIII immediately upon the death of the young prisoner in the Temple, his supporters hoped that he might.

The opportunity duly arrived in 1814 with the abdication of the emperor, Napoleon I. The triumphant allies, unable to agree on how France should be governed, decided to consult the French nation via its senate. The latter quickly produced a constitution which would protect the achievements of the Revolution, and announced that 'The French people freely call to the throne Louis-Stanislas-Xavier, brother of the last king'. On one level this was a gratifying summons for Louis, but on another a quite unacceptable one. For the implication was that he was to become Louis-Stanislas-Xavier I, the nation's nominee, whereas he knew himself to be Louis XVIII, king by divine right in the ancient line of Saint Louis. When the news of Napoleon's abdication emboldened one of his courtiers to tell him joyously that he was king of France, he replied coldly, 'Have I ever ceased to be?'[1]

As Louis made his way back to Paris from his English exile he understood the need for compromise. The Revolution had changed France for ever, and that had to be acknowledged. But at the same time his return had to indicate that the restoration of the Bourbons was also the restoration of divine-right monarchy, with all that implied for the authority of the king and his relationship with his people. His reign would be a series of attempts to reconcile the irreconcilable.

He got off to a good start. Arriving at Saint-Ouen on the northern edge of Paris he negotiated a deal with the senate. Their constitution was withdrawn and in its place Louis issued a charter in May 1814 which neatly confirmed most of the original constitutional proposals but wrapped them up in the white Bourbon flag which would shortly replace the tricolour as the emblem of the new regime. Thus the charter guaranteed the Revolutionary principles of liberty, equality and the inviolable rights of property owners, a modest freedom of the press, an independent judiciary, freedom of worship and freedom from arbitrary arrest. It decreed the establishment of a bicameral assembly, a chamber of peers and a chamber of deputies, to approve legislation or not, but the king remained 'the supreme head of the state; he commands land and naval forces, declares war, makes peace treaties and treaties of alliance and trade, makes appointments to all posts of public administration, and makes regulations and ordinances necessary to the execution of the law and the safety of the state'.[2] That was a far more worthwhile constitutional role for the restored monarch than any offered to his unfortunate brother after 1789. Most significantly, on this occasion the offer was coming from the monarch, and was formulated in the unmistakeable language of divine-right kingship: 'Louis, by the grace of God, king of France and Navarre'.

At first the country seemed disposed to indulge this royal mystification. The carefully stage-managed ceremonial of the royal entry to the capital sought to emphasize the underlying continuity of the succession. A new statue of Henry IV stood on the Pont-Neuf where its bronze predecessor, melted down during the Revolution, had once stood. Its inscription read, *Ludovico reduce, Henricus redivivus*: 'Through Louis' return Henry lives again'. It would have been impossible to find a less convincing role model for the new king than the charismatic warrior who had fought to unify his kingdom. Louis XVIII was a returning *émigré* who had watched helplessly as his kingdom was taken over by an ambitious Corsican subject. Also, unlike the physically impressive *Vert Galant*, Louis was almost too corpulent to move unaided. Nevertheless, Parisians appeared happy to overlook the obvious discrepancies and gave him a warm welcome.[3] Perhaps more surprisingly, there was no hostile reaction either when he decided to spend a small fortune renovating the old palace of Versailles, the iconic embodiment of the ancien régime, announcing his intention to spend six months of every year there.

The situation suddenly deteriorated in March 1815, however, with the news that Napoleon had escaped from Elba and was intent on reestablishing his power base in France. The unfortunate Louis became an *émigré* once more, fleeing to Ghent and then to Brussels. After a hundred days and Napoleon's defeat at Waterloo the Bourbon monarchy was again restored, for the last time. The Hundred Days did not generate a national backlash in favour of Louis XVIII's government. It provoked a savage campaign of terror in the south, waged by extreme royalist supporters of Artois, the heir to the throne, while the nation at large was forced to suffer the presence of foreign troops until 1818 and pay a massive new war indemnity.

For his part, the king had family debts to honour: the memory of his brother, sister and sister-in-law, Louis XVI, Elisabeth and Marie-Antoinette, all of them martyrs to the Revolution. He ordered a search for the remains of his decapitated brother. This was no easy task, for the king had been buried in the Madeleine cemetery in an uncovered coffin liberally laced with quicklime. Although a body was exhumed there could be no certainty about its identity. It could be that the inscribed coffin now lying in the crypt of the great Gothic basilica of Saint-Denis, purported to contain 'the body of the exalted, all-powerful and excellent prince Louis, sixteenth of that name, by the grace of God King of France and Navarre', is in fact the final resting place of one of the king's Swiss Guardsmen, murdered in the Tuileries gardens on 10 August 1792.

Be that as it may, Louis XVIII did his best to restore honour to his brother's memory. In 1816 he declared that as part of an 'expiatory celebration', the anniversary of the king's execution, 21 January, would become a national holiday, marked by a solemn service in every French church, at which the late king's last will and testament would be read out from the pulpit.[4] Marie-Antoinette's body was reinterred next to her husband's in Saint Denis. The tombs of all their royal predecessors remained empty, their contents pillaged during the Revolution.

Louis XVIII's charter stipulated that Catholicism was to be the official state religion; and indeed the revival of the Catholic Church was the necessary concomitant of the restored ideal of divine-right monarchy. In its new form, the alliance of throne and altar, the old diarchy of religion and politics was threatening once more to become the *sine qua non* of French government. The king was more subtle than either of his brothers, and while he remained in charge a kind of constitutional monarchy based on the charter seemed not incompatible with the rhetoric of the old regime. Louis' younger brother and heir to the throne, the count of Artois, was, however, anything but subtle. His views had changed very little since the time of his flight into exile on the eve of the Revolution. He remained a diehard reactionary in Restoration France, supported in the chamber of deputies by the ultra-royalists, or *tout court*, the ultras. Their position was strengthened in 1820 when the duke of Berry, son of the count of Artois, was assassinated and emergency measures to protect the monarchy could be justified.

In 1822 the limited freedom of the press was further reduced by legislation making it an offence to publish criticisms of divine-right kingship. Then in September 1824 Louis XVIII died, and Artois succeeded him as Charles X.

Louis XVIII had never been crowned and consecrated as king as his predecessors had been, an omission which Charles X was determined to remedy. The last coronation of a Bourbon king took place in May 1825 in its traditional setting, the cathedral church of Notre Dame in Reims. In order to bridge the political chasm which separated the third decade of the nineteenth century from 1775, the year of the preceding ceremony, the ritual was to a limited extent updated. In his coronation oath the new king swore 'to govern in conformance with the laws of the kingdom and the constitutional charter'. That affirmation was not in conflict with Charles's belief in the divine right of kingship, the charter having been originally granted to the people by their God-given sovereign; nor for that matter with the presiding cardinal's solemn summons to 'Charles X, whom God has given us for king'.[5] On one level the coronation ceremony, rooted in medieval tradition, appealed to the new Romantic Movement which was firing the European imagination. Viewed in those terms it appeared less threatening, more an historical confection than a policy statement. What would be decisive was the extent to which Charles's interpretation of the charter reconciled it with the past rather than with the present.

The defining moment occurred in 1829. While the chamber of deputies was prorogued the king decided to form a new ministry. The charter had always been ambiguous about the relative powers of the various elements of the constitution, the king, the two chambers and the ministers. Article 13, for example, pronounced that the king's person was sacred and inviolable, and that he alone possessed executive authority, adding mysteriously, 'Ses ministres sont responsables.'[6] Responsible to the king presumably, but had they no responsibility to the legislature as a whole? Such questions became more strident when the king revealed the identity of his new prime minister, Prince Jules de Polignac. Polignac had spent most of his life outside France. The son of Marie-Antoinette's close friend the duchess of Polignac, his lineage as well as his personal inclinations made him a fierce enemy of the Revolution and of popular sovereignty. Those who feared that Charles was committing himself irrevocably to the past knew that Polignac had no time for charters and believed that God intervened directly in human affairs.[7]

The liberal press was emboldened to take up the *émigré* gauntlet. The historian, journalist and politician, Adolph Thiers, much later to become president of the French republic, used his newspaper the *National*, to define an alternative view of constitutional monarchy:

The king reigns, the ministers govern, and the chambers judge. When the leadership falters, the king or the chamber dismisses the ministry which is doing a poor job of managing state affairs, and the chamber presents a new list of candidates from the prevailing majority.[8]

Nothing was further from Charles's mind than such a dilution of his powers; on the contrary he was determined, with Polignac's assistance, to increase them.

The new legislative session opened in March 1830, providing the first opportunity for the assembled chambers to react to the Polignac ministry. The king's speech from the throne was as menacing as many of the deputies feared. Charles referred enigmatically to the good measures he intended to take in order to fulfil his obligations under the charter, and to the powers he would find to overcome any obstacles placed in the way of government by what he called culpable manoeuvres. In response the chamber of deputies subtly challenged the king's right under the charter to govern independently, and hinted that it feared a *coup d'état*:

Sire, the charter ... consecrates as a right the participation of the country in the discussion of public affairs. That intervention ... is based on the permanent accord between the political views of your government and the wishes of your people, the indispensable condition of the normal conduct of public affairs. Sire, our loyalty, our devotion compel us to tell you that this accord does not now exist. An unwarranted mistrust of the feelings and thoughts of France is today the fundamental attitude of the Administration. Your people are distressed by this because it is an affront to them; they are worried by it because it is a threat to their liberties.[9]

Some deputies were blunter: 'the crown must appoint ministers who inspire confidence in the Chambers ... when they lose this confidence their duty is to resign'; and 'There are two methods of governing – one by law, the other by terror. To govern by law it is necessary to renounce coups d'état'.[10] The end-game was beginning.

Charles's response was to prorogue the assembly and call new elections for the chamber of deputies in the hope of securing a more compliant membership. These took place in July 1830 and resulted in an even more hostile chamber. The king's reaction was to publish on 26 July the four ordinances which in effect sealed the fate of the Bourbon monarchy. They suspended the freedom of the press, dissolved the newly elected chamber, and reduced both the number of deputies and the size of the electorate. Few doubted that this was the long-expected coup which would lead to the destruction of national liberties and to the full-blown revival of the ancien régime.

Events moved quickly. On 27 July the barricades went up in Paris, and on the following morning the commander of the royal troops informed the king, 'This is no longer a riot, it is a revolution.'[11] By the 29th Charles had lost his capital.

Louis XVIII's grand illusion was at last revealed as simply that; the crown had no capacity left for magic. Charles X knew that the game was up. At a meeting of his cabinet on that day he made an emotional speech revealing the extent to which the coming of the great Revolution still haunted him:

> Gentlemen, they force me to dismiss the ministers who have my confidence and affection and replace them with men named by my enemies. I am in the same position as was my unhappy brother in 1792, except that I have the advantage of having suffered for a shorter period of time; in three days it will be all up for the monarchy; as for the monarch, his end will be the same.[12]

It was not clear whether at that moment Charles feared a fate comparable with that visited upon Louis XVI, or simply expected to be removed from office. He abdicated on 1 August in favour of his young grandson, the duke of Bordeaux, the 'miracle child' born after the assassination of his father, the duke of Berry; and nominated the duke of Orléans as lieutenant general of the kingdom. Shortly afterwards, the last of the three royal brothers embarked on his melancholy progress through Normandy en route to Cherbourg, where he boarded ship and left France to begin his third and final exile.

Meanwhile, the Orléanists, who had been close to the throne for a long time, found themselves in pole position to take the ultimate prize. Louis Philippe, great-great-grandson of Louis XV's regent, decided to accept the crown rather than temporary governance and with it the title of 'king of the French'. This was no political earthquake; the restored House of Bourbon had only been accepted *faute de mieux* by a political nation struggling to identify its future direction.[13] The events of 1830 simply represented another step in that process.

A member of the chamber of peers, the viscount of Chateaubriand, statesman and diplomat but also one of the great wordsmiths of the Romantic Movement, offered a fitting epitaph on this race of kings:

> I did not go and bivouac in the past under the old flag of the dead – a flag which is not without glory but which droops along its pole because no breath of life flutters it. Were I to disturb the dust of the thirty-five Capets, I would not raise a single argument that would so much as be listened to. The idolatry of a name is abolished; monarchy is no longer a religion.[14]

Notes

Notes to Chapter 1: Antecedents

1   F. Lot and R. Fawtier, *Histoire des institutions françaises au moyen âge*, 3 vols (Paris 1957–62), ii, p. 138.

2   R. Mousnier, *The Institutions of France under the Absolute Monarchy, 1598–1789*, 2 vols (Chicago, 1979–84), ii, pp. 94–95.

3   Richard A. Jackson, *Vive le Roi!: A History of the French Coronation from Charles V to Charles X* (Chapel Hill, North Carolina, 1984), passim.

4   The classic work on this subject remains that of Marc Bloch, *Les Rois thaumaturges* (Paris, 1924); Louis de Rouvroy, duc de Saint-Simon, *Mémoires*, 7 vols (Paris, 1948–61), iii, p. 32.

5   This topic is the subject of stimulating analyses by E.H. Kantorowicz, *The King's Two Bodies: A Study in Medieval Political Theology* (Princeton, 1957), and by H.H. Rowen, *The King's State: Proprietary Dynasticism in Early Modern Europe* (New Brunswick, 1980). See also J.H. Shennan, *Liberty and Order in Early Modern Europe: The Subject and the State, 1650–1800* (London, 1986).

6   R. Fawtier, *The Capetian Kings of France* (London, 1960), pp. 185–87.

7   J.B. Henneman, *Royal Taxation in Fourteenth-Century France* (Princeton, 1971), p. 323.

8   Henneman, *Royal Taxation*, pp. 324–25. See also P.S. Lewis, *Essays in Later Medieval French History* (London, 1985), p. 110.

9   For an historian's view of modern French regionalism, see the engaging volume by Theodore Zeldin, *The French* (London, 1984), pp. 22–25.

10 Lewis, *Essays in Later Medieval French History*, pp. 191–92.

11 Henneman, *Royal Taxation*, pp. 155–57; G. Cabourdin and G. Viard, *Lexique historique de la France d'ancien régime* (Paris, 1978), pp. 148–50.

12 For a summary of the government's financial organization, see J.H. Shennan, *Government and Society in France, 1461–1661* (London, 1969), pp. 49–52.

13 Joseph R. Strayer, 'France: the Holy Land, the Chosen People, and the Most Christian King', in T.K. Rabb and J.E. Siegel (eds), *Action and Conviction in Early Modern Europe* (Princeton, 1969), pp. 3–16; Colette Beaune, *The Birth of an Ideology*, trans. Susan Huston (Berkeley, 1991), p. 19.

14 Strayer, 'France: the Holy Land, the Chosen People, and the Most Christian King', pp. 7–8.

15 J.H. Shennan, *The Parlement of Paris* (Stroud, 1998), pp. 50–52, 158–59. See also Charlotte C. Wells, *Law and Citizenship in Early Modern France* (Baltimore, Maryland, 1995), pp. 23–24.

16   Howell A. Lloyd, *The State, France, and the Sixteenth Century* (London, 1983), p. 76.

17   Mousnier, *The Institutions of France under the Absolute Monarchy*, i, p. 555.

18   Mousnier, *The Institutions of France under the Absolute Monarchy*, i, pp. 517–28; Lloyd, *The State, France, and the Sixteenth Century*, p. 31.

19   Shennan, *The Parlement of Paris*, pp. 165–66.

20   John A. Lynn, 'Recalculating French Army Growth during the *Grand Siècle*, 1610–1715', in *The Military Revolution Debate*, ed. Clifford J. Rogers (Oxford, 1995), p. 122.

21   David Potter, *A History of France, 1460–1560: The Emergence of a Nation State* (London, 1995), pp. 366–68; David Buisseret, *Henry IV* (London, 1984), p. 152.

22   Rowen, *The King's State*, p. 34; Jackson, *Vive le roi!*, pp. 85–93.

23   J.H. Shennan, *The Origins of the Modern European State, 1450–1725* (London, 1974), pp. 11–24.

24   Janine Garrisson, *A History of Sixteenth-Century France, 1483–1598* (London, 1995), p. 213.

25   Robert Knecht, the leading British historian on the subject of Francis I and the Renaissance court, has written extensively on the period: R.J. Knecht, 'Francis I: Prince and Patron of the Northern Renaissance', in *The Courts of Europe*, ed. A.G. Dickens (London, 1977), pp. 99–119; R.J. Knecht, *Francis I* (Cambridge, 1982), pp. 253–73; R.J. Knecht, *The Rise and Fall of Renaissance France* (London, 1996), p. 266. See also the comments in Frances A. Yates, *Astraea* (London, 1975), pp. 121–26.

26   Shennan, *The Parlement of Paris*, pp. 182–83.

27   Shennan, *The Parlement of Paris*, pp. 193–97. See the classic study by Roger Doucet, *Etude sur le gouvernement de François Ier dans ses rapports avec le parlement de Paris*, 2 vols (Paris, 1921–26), i, pp. 77–124. See too the article by R.J. Knecht, 'The Concordat of 1516: A Re-Assessment', *University of Birmingham Historical Journal*, 9 (1963), pp. 16–32, which evaluates the Concordat's historical significance.

28   Knecht, *Francis I*, p. 65.

Notes to Chapter 2: France in Peril

1   Janine Garrisson, *Les Protestants au XVIe siècle* (Paris, 1988), p. 186.

2   R.J. Knecht, *The Rise and Fall of Renaissance France* (London, 1996), pp. 306, 315; J.H. Shennan, *The Origins of the Modern European State, 1450–1725* (London, 1974), p. 71.

3   N.M. Sutherland, *The Huguenot Struggle for Recognition* (New Haven and London, 1980), p. 101.

4   Garrisson, *Les Protestants*, pp. 229–44.

5   Nancy Lyman Roelker, *Queen of Navarre: Jeanne d'Albret, 1528–1572* (Cambridge, Massachusetts, 1968), p. 18.

6   Myriam Yardeni, *La Conscience nationale en France pendant les guerres de religion (1559–1598)* (Paris, 1971), pp. 183–99; J.W. Allen, *A History of Political Thought in the Sixteenth Century* (London, 1960), pp. 292–96, 314–31.

7   Howell A. Lloyd, *The State, France, and the Sixteenth Century* (London, 1983), pp. 153–63; J.H. Shennan, *The Origins of the Modern European State, 1450–1725* (London, 1974),

pp. 74–75. For an interesting discussion on the complexity of Bodin's theory of sovereignty, see Nannerl O. Keohane, *Philosophy and the State in France: The Renaissance to the Enlightenment* (Princeton, 1980), pp. 67–73, and H.H. Rowen, *The King's State: Proprietary Dynasticism in Early Modern Europe* (New Brunswick, 1980), pp. 40–42.

8   Roelker, *Queen of Navarre*, p. 381.

9   Alan James, *Navy and Government in Early Modern France, 1572–1661* (London, 2004), pp. 15–19.

10 Quoted in Janine Garrisson, *A History of Sixteenth-Century France, 1483–1598: Renaissance, Reformation and Rebellion* (London, 1995), p. 368.

11 The review article by M. Greengrass, 'The Sixteen: Radical Politics in Paris during the League', *History*, 69 (1984), pp. 432–39, illuminates aspects of this once mysterious group.

12 E. Le Roy Ladurie, *The Royal French State, 1460–1610* (Oxford, 1994), p. 222.

13 Knecht, *The Rise and Fall of Renaissance France*, pp. 477–78, 512–29.

14 Yardeni, *La Conscience nationale en France*, p. 210.

15 David Buisseret, *Henry IV* (London, 1984), pp. 18–19.

Notes to Chapter 3: Henry IV

1   Nancy Lyman Roelker, *Queen of Navarre: Jeanne d'Albret, 1528–1572* (Cambridge, Massachusetts, 1968), pp. 99, 398.

2   F. Bayrou, *Henri IV: le roi libre* (Paris, 1998), p. 518.

3   Myriam Yardeni, *La Conscience nationale en France pendant les guerres de religion (1559–1598)*, (Paris, 1971), p. 173.

4   David Buisseret, *Henry IV* (London, 1984), p. 10.

5   Printed in *The French Wars of Religion: Selected Documents*, ed. and trans. David Potter (London, 1997), p. 166.

6   Buisseret, *Henry IV*, p. 25.

7   Yardeni, *La Conscience nationale en France*, p. 271.

8   J.H. Shennan, *The Parlement of Paris* (Stroud, 1998), p. 278.

9   Nancy Lyman Roelker, ed., *The Paris of Henry of Navarre as Seen by Pierre de l'Estoile* (Cambridge, Massachusetts, 1958), pp. 255–56; Buisseret, *Henry IV*, pp. 51–53.

10 N.M. Sutherland, *The Huguenot Struggle for Recognition* (London, 1980), p. 332.

11 Shennan, *The Parlement of Paris*, pp. 230–32.

12 Buisseret, *Henry IV*, pp. 72–73.

13 R. Mousnier, *L'Assassinat d'Henri IV* (Paris, 1964), p. 297. The edict is printed in full, pp. 294–334.

14 The precise nature of patron–client relationships has been the subject of some scholarly disagreement. See, for example, Sharon Kettering, *Patrons, Brokers and Clients in Seventeenth-Century France* (Oxford, 1986), pp. 18–22.

15 The magisterial work by R. Mousnier, *La Vénalité des offices sous Henri IV et Louis XIII* (Paris, 1971), is an indispensable guide.

16 Buisseret, *Henry IV*, p. 131.

17   Orest Ranum, *Paris in the Age of Absolutism* (New York, 1968), pp. 68–82; David Buisseret, *Sully* (London, 1968), pp. 133–37.

18   Buisseret, *Sully*, pp. 105–19, 126.

19   Buisseret, *Henry IV*, pp. 83–86; Mark Greengrass, *France in the Age of Henri IV* (London, 1984), pp. 188–92.

20   Buisseret, *Henry IV*, p. 180.

21   The leading historian in this field is David Buisseret. See, for example, 'The cartographic definition of France's eastern frontier', *Imago Mundi*, 36 (1984), pp. 72–80; and *The Mapmakers' Quest: Depicting New Worlds in Renaissance Europe* (Oxford, 2003), pp. 64, 129–31.

22   Bayrou, *Henri IV*, p. 461.

23   Bayrou, *Henri IV*, pp. 458–59.

24   Bayrou, *Henri IV*, p. 478.

25   Jean-Pierre Babelon, *Henri IV* (Paris, 1982), p. 848.

26   Buisseret, *Henry IV*, p. 173.

27   Babelon, *Henri IV*, pp. 970–71.

28   E. Le Roy Ladurie, *The Royal French State, 1460–1610* (Oxford, 1994), p. 246.

29   Buisseret, *Henry IV*, p. 176.

30   Mousnier, *L'Assassinat d'Henri IV*, pp. 235–36.

31   Yardeni, *La Conscience nationale en France*, p. 329.

32   Bayrou, *Henri IV*, p. 518.

Notes to Chapter 4: Louis XIII: the Implacable

1   J.H. Shennan, *The Parlement of Paris* (Stroud, 1998), pp. 241–42; Sarah Hanley, *The Lit de Justice of the Kings of France* (Princeton, 1983), pp. 231–43.

2   A. Lloyd Moote, *Louis XIII: The Just* (University of California Press, 1991), pp. 19–38.

3   R. Mousnier, *The Institutions of France under the Absolute Monarchy, 1598–1789*, 2 vols (Chicago, 1979–84), i, p. 479.

4   Mousnier, *The Institutions of France under the Absolute Monarchy*, i, pp. 99–105. In her critique of Mousnier, Sharon Kettering, *Patrons, Brokers, and Clients in Seventeenth-Century France* (Oxford, 1986), p. 22, accepts the validity of his categorization but argues that it leaves out of account other less committed forms of relationship.

5   N. M. Sutherland, *The French Secretaries of State in the Age of Catherine de Medici* (London, 1962), pp. 150–57; David Potter, *A History of France, 1460–1560: The Emergence of a Nation State* (London, 1995), pp. 108–09.

6   J. Russell Major, *Representative Government in Early Modern France* (New Haven, 1980), pp. 398–400.

7   Moote, *Louis XIII*, p. 46.

8   J. Michael Hayden, *France and the Estates General of 1614* (Cambridge, 1974), p. 131.

9   Major, *Representative Government in Early Modern France*, p. 408.

10   E. Le Roy Ladurie, *The Royal French State, 1460–1610* (Oxford, 1994), p. 100.

11   R. Mousnier, *L'Assassinat d'Henri IV* (Paris, 1964), p. 245.

12 P. Chevallier, *Louis XIII: roi cornélien* (Paris, 1979), p. 206.

13 Chevallier, *Louis XIII*, p. 220; Moote, *Louis XIII*, p. 54.

14 Victor-L. Tapié, *France in the Age of Louis XIII and Richelieu*, trans. and ed. D. McN. Lockie (London, 1974), p. 120.

15 A.D. Lublinskaya, *French Absolutism: The Crucial Phase, 1620–1629*, trans. Brian Pearce (Cambridge, 1968), p. 211.

16 Moote, *Louis XIII*, p. 125.

17 David Parker, *La Rochelle and the French Monarchy* (London, 1980), p. 116.

18 Joseph Bergin, *The Rise of Richelieu* (New Haven, 1991), p. 82.

19 Bergin, *The Rise of Richelieu*, p. 152.

20 Tapié, *France in the Age of Louis XIII and Richelieu*, p. 146.

21 William F. Church, *Richelieu and Reason of State* (Princeton, 1972), p. 191.

22 Parker, *La Rochelle and the French Monarchy*, pp. 63–76.

23 J.H. Shennan, *The Origins of the Modern European State, 1450–1725* (London, 1974), pp. 90, 93.

24 Parker, *La Rochelle and the French Monarchy*, p. 77.

25 Parker, *La Rochelle and the French Monarchy*, p. 80.

26 Moote, *Louis XIII*, p. 274.

27 Orest Ranum, 'Richelieu and the Great Nobility: some aspects of early modern political motives', *French Historical Studies*, 3 (1963), pp. 188–89.

28 Church, *Richelieu and Reason of State*, p. 331.

29 On the subject of Richelieu's fortune, see the outstanding volume by Joseph Bergin, *Cardinal Richelieu: Power and the Pursuit of Wealth* (New Haven, 1985), passim.

30 Richard Bonney, *Political Change in France under Richelieu and Mazarin* (Oxford, 1978), p. 287. See also the important work by Robert R. Harding, *Anatomy of a Power Elite: The Provincial Governors of Early Modern France* (New Haven, 1978), passim.

31 Bonney, *Political Change in France under Richelieu and Mazarin*, pp. 290–92; Roger Mettam, *Power and Faction in Louis XIV's France* (Oxford, 1988), pp. 84–85.

32 Bonney, *Political Change in France under Richelieu and Mazarin*, pp. 90–96.

33 Orest Ranum, *Richelieu and the Councillors of Louis XIII* (Oxford, 1963), p. 189; J.H. Shennan, *Government and Society in France, 1461–1661* (London, 1969), pp. 132–33.

34 Ranum, *Richelieu and the Councillors of Louis XIII*, pp. 125–42.

35 Mousnier, *The Institutions of France under the Absolute Monarchy*, ii, pp. 144–45; Mettam, *Power and Faction in Louis XIV's France*, p. 96.

36 Shennan, *The Parlement of Paris*, p. 250.

37 David Parrott, *Richelieu's Army: War, Government and Society in France, 1624–1642* (Cambridge, 2001), p. 551.

38 James B. Collins, *The State in Early Modern France* (Cambridge, 1995), p. 48.

39 Georges Dethan, *The Young Mazarin* (London, 1977), pp. 89–90.

40 John Lynch, *Spain under the Habsburgs* (Oxford, 1969), ii, p. 68.

41 G. Pagès, *The Thirty Years War, 1618–1648* (London, 1970), p. 120.

42 Parrott, *Richelieu's Army*, p. 547.

43 E. Le Roy Ladurie, *The Ancien Régime: A History of France, 1610–1774* (Oxford, 1996), pp. 61–62; R.J. Knecht, *Richelieu* (London, 1991), p. 109.

44 Parrott, *Richelieu's Army*, p. 321.

45 Quoted in Moote, *Louis XIII*, p. 277.

46 The phrase is Pierre Goubert's, *The Course of French History* (London, 1991), p. 115.

47 Nannerl O. Keohane, *Philosophy and the State in France: The Renaissance to the Enlightenment* (Princeton, 1980), pp. 168–69.

48 Tapié, *France in the Age of Louis XIII and Richelieu*, p. 426.

Notes to Chapter 5: Apotheosis: the Sun King

1   A. Lloyd Moote, *The Revolt of the Judges: The Parlement of Paris and the Fronde, 1643–1652* (Princeton, 1971), p. 43.

2   Cited in J. H. Shennan, *The Origins of the Modern European State, 1450–1725* (London, 1974), p. 35.

3   Moote, *The Revolt of the Judges*, p. 44; J.H. Kitchens, 'Judicial *Commissaires* and the Parlement of Paris: The Case of the *Chambre de l'Arsenal*', *French Historical Studies*, 12 (1982), p. 338.

4   J. H. Shennan, *The Parlement of Paris* (Stroud, 1998), pp. 260–61.

5   Shennan, *The Parlement of Paris*, p. 263; Moote, *The Revolt of the Judges*, p. 113.

6   Orest Ranum, *The Fronde* (New York, 1993), p. 68; Richard Bonney, 'La Fronde des officiers: mouvement réformiste ou rébellion corporatiste?', *XVIIe Siècle*, 145 (1984), p. 339. But compare the comments of Moote, *The Revolt of the Judges*, pp. 170–72.

7   Shennan, *The Parlement of Paris*, p. 268.

8   Shennan, *The Parlement of Paris*, p. 271.

9   Philip A. Knachel, *England and the Fronde* (Ithaca, New York, 1967), pp. 53–54.

10 Geoffrey Treasure, *Mazarin* (London, 1995), p. 181.

11 Richard Bonney, *The Limits of Absolutism in Ancien Régime France* (Aldershot, 1995), p. 822.

12 Richard Bonney, *Political Change in France under Richelieu and Mazarin* (Oxford, 1978), p. 297; Richard Bonney, 'The French Civil War, 1649–53', *European Studies Review*, 8 (1978), p. 88. This article has been reprinted in Bonney's *The Limits of Absolutism*.

13 See for example the extract printed in J. B. Wolf (ed.), *Louis XIV* (London, 1972), pp. 199–221: 'A Tolerably Great King'. The references in the present volume are taken from the Pléiade edition of 1948–61.

14 Indeed, the most recent biographer of the king, Anthony Levi, *Louis XIV* (London, 2004), claims that Mazarin was probably Louis' father. The evidence remains entirely circumstantial and, though not without merit, is insufficiently compelling to support such a profound rewriting of French history.

15 J. B. Wolf, *Louis XIV* (London, 1970), p. 180.

16 Paul Sonnino, *Mémoires for the Instruction of the Dauphin* (New York, 1970), pp. 23, 35.

17 Sonnino, *Mémoires*, p. 102.

18 H. H. Rowen, *The King's State: Proprietary Dynasticism in early Modern Europe* (New Brunswick, 1980), p. 76.

19   L. Hautecoeur, *Histoire de l'architecture classique en France*, 3 vols (Paris, 1943–50), ii, pt 1,
     pp. 260–63, 277–82; Anthony Blunt, *Art and Architecture in France, 1500–1700* (London,
     1953), pp. 232–34.

20   Philippe Beaussant, *Louis XIV, artiste* (Paris, 1999), pp. 118–25.

21   Hautecoeur, *Histoire de l'architecture*, ii, pt 1, pp. 287–89.

22   Nathan T. Whitman, 'Myth and Politics: Versailles and the Fountain of Latona', in John
     C. Rule (ed.), *Louis XIV and the Craft of Kingship* (Ohio State University Press, 1969),
     p. 298.

23   Marcel Marion, *Dictionnaire des institutions de la France aux XVIIe et XVIIIe siècles* (Paris,
     1923; reprinted 1968), contains a wealth of detail on the *maison du roi*.

24   Saint-Simon, Louis de Rouvroy, duc de, *Mémoires*, 7 vols (Paris, 1948–61), ii, p. 317.

25   Saint-Simon, *Mémoires*, iii, pp. 190–91.

26   Saint-Simon, *Mémoires*, iii, p. 192.

27   Norbert Elias, *The Court Society* (Oxford, 1983), p. 150.

28   Ragnhild Hatton, *Louis XIV and his World* (London, 1972), pp. 39–45; Wolf, *Louis XIV*,
     pp. 140–56.

29   Anne Somerset, *The Affair of the Poisons* (London, 2003), pp. 320–22.

30   J. François Bluche, *Louis XIV* (Paris, 1986), pp. 292–93, 391.

31   Somerset, *The Affair of the Poisons*, p. 107. The words are those of the contemporary
     memorialist, *abbé* Choisy.

32   John A. Lynn, *The Wars of Louis XIV, 1667–1714* (London, 1999), p. 31.

33   M. Mignet, *Négociations relatives à la succession d'Espagne sous Louis XIV*, 4 vols (Paris,
     1835–42), ii, p. 82.

34   Lynn, *The Wars of Louis XIV*, pp. 184–85; John J. Hurt, *Louis XIV and the Parlements*
     (Manchester, 2002), pp. 56–57.

35   Shennan, *The Parlement of Paris*, p. 278.

36   Bluche, *Louis XIV*, p. 425.

37   Peter Burke, *The Fabrication of Louis XIV* (New Haven, 1992), pp. 104–5.

38   Janine Garrisson, *L'Édit de Nantes et sa révocation* (Paris, 1985), pp. 187–88.

39   Mark Jones, 'The Medal as an Instrument of Propaganda in Late Seventeenth- and Early
     Eighteenth-Century Europe', *Numismatic Chronicle*, 142 (1982), p. 122.

40   H.M.A. Keens-Soper, 'The French Political Academy, 1712: The School for Ambassadors',
     European Studies Review, 2 (1972), pp. 329–55.

41   Pierre Goubert, *Louis XIV and Twenty Million Frenchmen* (London, 1970), p. 217.

42   Lionel Rothkrug, *Opposition to Louis XIV* (Princeton, 1965), p. 266; Goubert, *Louis XIV
     and Twenty Million Frenchmen*, p. 220.

43   The diplomatic correspondence leading to the signing of the two partition treaties is to be
     found in Paul Grimblot (ed.), *Letters of William III and Louis XIV, and of their Ministers*,
     2 vols (London, 1848), passim.

44   Mark A. Thomson, 'Louis XIV and the Origins of the War of the Spanish Succession',
     in *William III and Louis XIV: Essays 1680–1720 by and for Mark A. Thomson*, edited by
     Ragnhild Hatton and J.S. Bromley (Liverpool, 1968), pp. 146–48. Thomson's pioneering
     work has made a substantial contribution to the reappraisal of Louis XIV's diplomacy in
     the last decades of the reign.

45   Saint-Simon, *Mémoires*, iii, pp. 83, 89.

46   Thomson, 'Self-Determination and Collective Security as Factors in English and French Foreign Policy, 1689–1718', *William III and Louis XIV*, pp. 277–78.

47   Joseph Klaits, *Printed Propaganda under Louis XIV* (Princeton, 1976), pp. 214–16.

48   Bluche, *Louis XIV*, p. 890.

Notes to Chapter 6: Louis XV

1   Saint-Simon, Louis de Rouvroy, duc de, *Mémoires*, 7 vols (Paris, 1948–61), iv, p. 381.

2   J.H. Shennan, *Philippe, Duke of Orléans: Regent of France, 1715–1723* (London, 1979), pp. 97–98.

3   John J. Hurt, *Louis XIV and the Parlements* (Manchester, 2002), p. 130.

4   Shennan, *Philippe, Duke of Orléans*, p. 107.

5   P. Harsin (ed.), *John Law: oeuvres complètes*, 3 vols (Paris, 1934), iii, pp. 39–61, 'Mémoire sur le denier royal'.

6   Saint-Simon, *Mémoires*, vi, p. 594.

7   Shennan, *Philippe, Duke of Orléans*, p. 115.

8   Shennan, *Philippe, Duke of Orléans*, p. 124.

9   M.A. Sallon, 'L'échec de Law', *Revue d'histoire économique et sociale*, 48 (1970), p. 190.

10   Shennan, *Philippe, Duke of Orléans*, pp. 51–75.

11   Shennan, *Philippe, Duke of Orléans*, pp. 33–50.

12   Michel Antoine, *Le Conseil du roi sous le règne de Louis XV* (Paris, 1970), p. 599.

13   Peter R. Campbell, *Power and Politics in Old Regime France, 1720–1745* (London, 1996), p. 181.

14   See the richly illustrated, monumental catalogue produced to accompany the exhibition marking the two hundreth anniversary of the king's death, *Louis XV: un moment de perfection de l'art français* (Paris, 1974), passim.

15   J.H. Shennan, 'Louis XV: Public and Private Worlds', in A. G. Dickens (ed.), *The Courts of Europe* (London, 1977), p. 321.

16   Shennan, *Philippe, Duke of Orléans*, p. 132.

17   Colin Jones, *Madame de Pompadour: Images of a Mistress* (London, 2002), pp. 19–21.

18   Shennan, 'Louis XV: Public and Private Worlds', p. 316; Jones, *Madame de Pompadour*, pp. 57, 67.

19   The writer was the marquis d'Argenson. Jones, *Madame de Pompadour*, p. 108.

20   John Rogister, *Louis XV and the Parlement of Paris, 1737–1755* (Cambridge, 1995), pp. 64, 69.

21   Rohan Butler, *Choiseul* (Oxford, 1980), pp. 894, 1067.

22   Butler, *Choiseul*, p. 4.

23   The title given to the exhibition marking the double centenary of Louis XV's death, held in the Hôtel de la Monnaie, one of the last buildings to be completed during the reign. Designed by Jacques-Denis Antoine to house the royal mint, the foundation stone was laid by the controller general of finance in May 1771. Under it was placed a cedar wood casket

containing gold, silver and copper coins of the period, together with medals engraved with the king's portrait on one side and the façade of the new building on the other.

24   Michel Antoine, *Louis XV* (Paris, 1989), p. 824.

25   This was the barrister, E.-J.-F. Barbier. See Shennan, 'Louis XV: Public and Private Worlds', p. 320.

26   Shennan, *The Parlement of Paris*, pp. xxxviii–xxxix, 301–6. Campbell, *Power and Politics in Old Regime France*, pp. 237–74, demonstrates the important role played in the conflict by the magistrates of the *parti janséniste*, whose opposition to *Unigenitus* provided them with the basis for a wider political campaign.

27   Shennan, *The Parlement of Paris*, p. 309.

28   Julian Swann, *Politics and the Parlement of Paris under Louis XV, 1754–1774* (Cambridge, 1995), pp. 219–20, 243.

29   J.H.Shennan, 'The Political Vocabulary of the Parlement of Paris in the Eighteenth Century', *Diritto e potere nella storia europea*, 2 vols (Florence, 1982), ii, pp. 951–64.

30   Shennan, *The Parlement of Paris*, pp. 308, 311.

31   Swann, *Politics and the Parlement of Paris*, p. 335; Shennan, *The Parlement of Paris*, p. 318.

32   Swann, *Politics and the Parlement of Paris*, pp. 82–85.

33   Swann, *Politics and the Parlement of Paris*, p. 84; the standard work on Damiens is by Dale Van Kley, *The Damiens Affair and the Unraveling of the Ancien Régime, 1750–1770* (Princeton, 1984), passim.

34   J.H. Shennan, 'The Rise of Patriotism in Eighteenth-Century Europe', *History of European Ideas*, 13 (1991), pp. 698–700.

35   E. Le Roy Ladurie, *The Ancien Régime: A History of France. 1610–1774* (Oxford, 1996), pp. 458–462. See also the highly illuminating volume by Daniel Roche, *France in the Enlightenment*, trans. Arthur Goldhammer (Harvard, 1998), passim.

36   Jones, *Madame de Pompadour*, pp. 109–10.

37   Alfred Cobban, *A History of Modern France*, 2 vols (London, 1965), i, p. 98.

38   Quoted in Shennan, 'Louis XV: Public and Private Worlds', p. 322.

39   Olivier Bernier, *Imperial Mother, Royal Daughter* (London, 1986), pp. 86–87.

Notes to Chapter 7: Louis Capet

1   H. H. Rowen, *The King's State: Proprietary Dynasticism in Early Modern Europe* (New Brunswick, 1980), pp. 146–47.

2   John Hardman, *Louis XVI* (New Haven, 1993), pp. 32–36.

3   Rowen, *The King's State*, pp. 147–48.

4   Robert D. Harris, *Necker: Reform Statesman of the Ancien Regime* (University of California Press, 1979), pp. 79–81.

5   Hardman, *Louis XVI*, p. 52.

6   R. Mousnier, *The Institutions of France under the Absolute Monarchy, 1598–1789*, 2 vols (Chicago, 1979–84), i, pp. 37–38.

7   Mousnier, *The Institutions of France*, i, p. 472.

8   Hardman, *Louis XVI*, p. 53.

9   E. Le Roy Ladurie, *The Ancien Régime: A History of France, 1610–1774* (Oxford, 1996), p. 498.

10   Hardman, *Louis XVI*, p. 92.

11   Bernard Fay, *Louis XVI*, trans. P. O'Brien (London, 1968), p. 278.

12   Pierre Goubert, *The Course of French History* (London, 1991), p. 176.

13   Harris, *Necker*, p. 121.

14   K.M. Baker, *Inventing the French Revolution* (Cambridge, 1990), p. 196.

15   Goubert, *The Course of French History*, p. 177.

16   Hardman, *Louis XVI*, pp. 106–7.

17   Loménie de Brienne's views, which are broadly progressive, are set out in his 'Memorandum on Provincial Assemblies', published in the *Journal de l'assemblée des notables de 1787*, (ed.) Pierre Chevallier (Paris, 1960), pp. 13–19.

18   Hardman, *Louis XVI*, pp. 125–26.

19   Bailey Stone, *The French Parlements and the Crisis of the Old Regime* (Chapel Hill, North Carolina, 1986), pp. 92–93.

20   J. H. Shennan, *The Parlement of Paris* (Stroud, 1998), p. 321.

21   Shennan, *The Parlement of Paris*, p. 323.

22   Olivier Bernier, *Imperial Mother, Royal Daughter* (London, 1988), p. 157.

23   Robert Darnton, *The Literary Underground of the Old Regime* (Cambridge, Massachusetts, 1982), p. 29.

24   Bernier, *Imperial Mother, Royal Daughter*, pp. 187, 216–17.

25   Bernier, *Imperial Mother, Royal Daughter*, p. 217.

26   Dena Goodman (ed.), *Marie-Antoinette: Writings on the Body of a Queen* (New York, 2003), pp. 45–61: Mary D. Sheriff, 'The Portrait of the Queen'.

27   Simon Schama, *Citizens: A Chronicle of the French Revolution* (London, 1989), p. 225.

28   For an analysis of the various hypotheses advanced to explain the affair, as well as an account of Marie-Antoinette's role in the Scheldt crisis, see Munro Price, *Preserving the Monarchy: The Comte de Vergennes, 1774–1787* (Cambridge, 1995), pp. 174–75, 180–83, 193–94.

29   William Doyle, *The Oxford History of the French Revolution* (Oxford, 1989), p. 85.

30   Darnton, *The Literary Underground*, p. 205.

31   Schama, *Citizens*, p. 637.

32   Alfred Cobban, *A History of Modern France*, 2 vols (London, 1965), i, p. 151.

33   J.H. Shennan, 'The Rise of Patriotism in Eighteenth-Century Europe', *History of European Ideas*, 13 (1991), p. 700.

34   The full text is printed in John Hardman, *The French Revolution Source Book* (London, 1999), pp. 117–20.

35   Schama, *Citizens*, pp. 441–42, 458.

36   Cobban, *A History of Modern France*, i, pp. 164–65.

37   Hardman, *Louis XVI*, p. 206.

38   Shennan, 'The Rise of Patriotism in Eighteenth-Century Europe', p. 701.

39   Schama, *Citizens*, pp. 594–95.

40   Schama, *Citizens*, p. 587.

41 Shennan, 'The Rise of Patriotism in Eighteenth-Century Europe', p. 702.
42 J. H. Shennan, *The Origins of the Modern European State, 1450–1725* (London, 1974), pp. 104, 127.
43 Hardman, *Louis XVI*, p. 222.
44 David P. Jordan, *The King's Trial* (University of California Press, 1979), p. 141.
45 Jordan, *The King's Trial*, p. 132.
46 In a speech delivered to the Convention on 13 November 1792. See Michael Walzer, *Regicide and Revolution* (New York, 1992), p. 124.
47 Jordan, *The King's Trial*, p. 127.
48 Jordan, *The King's Trial*, p. 90.
49 Jordan, *The King's Trial*, pp. 85, 91.
50 Doyle, *The Oxford History of the French Revolution*, p. 253.
51 Goodman, *Marie-Antoinette*, pp. 114, 118.

Notes to Epilogue

1 Alfred Cobban, *A History of Modern France*, 2 vols (London, 1965), ii, p. 71; G. de Bertier de Sauvigny, *La Restauration* (Paris, 1955), pp. 43–44.
2 François Furet, *Revolutionary France, 1770–1880* (Oxford, 1992), p. 272.
3 Bertier de Sauvigny, *La Restauration*, pp. 58–59.
4 David P. Jordan, *The King's Trial* (University of California Press), pp. 225–26.
5 Richard A. Jackson, *Vive le roi!: A History of the French Coronation from Charles V to Charles X* (Chapel Hill, North Carolina, 1984), p. 192.
6 The provisions of the charter are analysed by Bertier de Sauvigny, *La Restauration*, pp. 68–73.
7 Vincent W. Beach, *Charles X of France* (Boulder, Colorado, 1971), pp. 294–95.
8 Beach, *Charles X of France*, p. 304.
9 David H. Pinkney, *The French Revolution of 1830* (Princeton, 1972), p. 20.
10 Bertier de Sauvigny, *La Restauration*, pp. 428–29; Beach, *Charles X of France*, p. 311.
11 Bertier de Sauvigny, *La Restauration*, p. 447.
12 Beach, *Charles X of France*, p. 381.
13 Robert Tombs, *France, 1814–1914* (London, 1996), p. 352.
14 Furet, *Revolutionary France*, p. 325.

Bibliography

Allen, J. W., *A History of Political Thought in the Sixteenth Century* (London, 1960).

Allmand, C. T., *The Hundred Years War: England and France at War, c. 1300–c. 1450* (Cambridge, 1988).

Antoine, Michel, *Le Conseil du roi sous le règne de Louis XV* (Paris, 1970).

Antoine, Michel, *Louis XV* (Paris, 1989).

Babelon, Jean-Pierre, *Henri IV* (Paris, 1982).

Baker, K. M., *Inventing the French Revolution* (Cambridge, 1990).

Bayrou, François, *Henri IV: le roi libre* (Paris, 1998).

Beach, Vincent W., *Charles X of France* (Boulder, Colorado, 1971).

Beaune, Colette, *The Birth of an Ideology*, trans. S. Huston (Berkeley, California, 1991).

Beaussant, Philippe, *Louis XIV, artiste* (Paris, 1999).

Bergin, Joseph, *Cardinal Richelieu: Power and the Pursuit of Wealth* (New Haven, Connecticut, 1985).

Bergin, Joseph, *The Rise of Richelieu* (New Haven, Connecticut, 1991).

Bernier, Olivier, *Imperial Mother, Royal Daughter* (London, 1988).

Bertier de Sauvigny, G. de, *La Restauration* (Paris, 1955).

Bloch, Marc, *Les Rois thaumaturges* (Paris, 1924).

Bluche, J. François, *Louis XIV* (Paris, 1986).

Blunt, Anthony, *Art and Architecture in France, 1500–1700* (London, 1953).

Bonney, Richard, *Political Change in France under Richelieu and Mazarin* (Oxford, 1978).

Bonney, Richard, 'The French Civil War, 1649–53', *European Studies Review*, 8 (1978).

Bonney, Richard, 'La Fronde des officiers: mouvement réformiste ou rébellion corporatiste?', *XVIIe Siècle*, 145 (1984).

Bonney, Richard, *The Limits of Absolutism in Ancien Régime France* (Aldershot, 1995).

Buisseret, David, *Sully* (London, 1968).

Buisseret, David, *Henry IV* (London, 1984).

Buisseret, David, 'The Cartographic Definition of France's Eastern Frontier', *Imago Mundi*, 36 (1984), pp. 72–80.

Buisseret, David, *The Mapmakers' Quest: Depicting New Worlds in Renaissance Europe* (Oxford, 2003).

Burke, Peter, *The Fabrication of Louis XIV* (New Haven, Connecticut, 1992).

Butler, Rohan, *Choiseul* (Oxford, 1980).

Cabourdin, G. and Viard, G., *Lexique historique de la France d'ancien régime* (Paris, 1978).

Campbell, Peter R., *Power and Politics in Old Regime France, 1720–1745* (London, 1996).

Chevallier, Pierre (ed.), *Journal de l'assemblée des notables de 1787* (Paris, 1960).

Chevallier, Pierre, *Louis XIII: roi cornélien* (Paris, 1979).

Church, William F., *Richelieu and Reason of State* (Princeton, New Jersey, 1972).

Cobban, Alfred, *A History of Modern France*, 2 vols (London, 1965).

Collins, James B., *The State in Early Modern France* (Cambridge, 1995).

Darnton, Robert, *The Literary Underground of the Old Regime* (Cambridge, Massachusetts, 1982).

Dethan, Georges, *The Young Mazarin* (London, 1977).

Dickens, A. G., *The Courts of Europe* (London, 1977).

Doucet, Roger, *Etude sur le gouvernement de François Ier dans ses rapports avec le parlement de Paris*, 2 vols (Paris, 1921–26).

Doyle, William, 'The Parlements of France and the Breakdown of the Old Regime, 1771–1788', *French Historical Studies*, 6 (1970).

Doyle, William, *Origins of the French Revolution* (Oxford, 1980).

Doyle, William, *The Oxford History of the French Revolution* (Oxford, 1989).

Echeverria, D., *The Maupeou Revolution: A Study in the History of Libertarianism, 1770–1774* (Baton Rouge, Louisiana, 1985).

Egret, Jean, *La Pré-révolution française, 1787–88* (Paris, 1962).

Egret, Jean, *Louis XV et l'opposition parlementaire* (Paris, 1970).

Elias, Norbert, *The Court Society* (Oxford, 1983).

Fawtier, R., *The Capetian Kings of France* (London, 1960).

Fay, Bernard, *Louis XVI*, trans. P. O'Brien (London, 1968).

Furet, François, *Revolutionary France, 1770–1880* (Oxford, 1992).

Garrisson, Janine, *L'Édit de Nantes et sa révocation* (Paris, 1985).

Garrisson, Janine, *Les Protestants au XVIe siècle* (Paris, 1988).

Garrisson, Janine, *A History of Sixteenth-Century France, 1483–1598: Renaissance, Reformation and Rebellion* (London, 1995).

Goodman, Dena (ed.), *Marie-Antoinette: Writings on the Body of a Queen* (New York, 2003).

Goubert, Pierre, *Louis XIV and Twenty Million Frenchmen* (London, 1970).

Goubert, Pierre, *The Course of French History* (London, 1991).

Greengrass, Mark, *France in the Age of Henri IV* (London, 1984).

Greengrass, Mark, 'The Sixteen: Radical Politics in Paris during the League', *History*, 69 (1984).

Grimblot, Paul (ed.), *Letters of William III and Louis XIV, and of their Ministers*, 2 vols (London, 1848).

Hamscher, Albert N., *The Parlement of Paris after the Fronde, 1653–1673* (Pittsburgh, Pennsylvania, 1976).

Hanley, Sarah, *The Lit de Justice of the Kings of France* (Princeton, New Jersey, 1983).

Harding, Robert R., *Anatomy of a Power Elite: The Provincial Governors of Early Modern France* (New Haven, Connecticut, 1978).

Hardman, John, *Louis XVI* (New Haven, Connecticut, 1993).

Hardman, John, *The French Revolution Source Book* (London, 1999).

Harris, Robert D., *Necker: Reform Statesman of the Ancien Régime* (University of California Press, 1979).

Harsin, Paul (ed.), *John Law: oeuvres complètes*, 3 vols (Paris, 1934).

Hatton, Ragnhild, *Louis XIV and his World* (London, 1972).

Hautecoeur, L., *Histoire de l'architecture classique en France*, 3 vols (Paris, 1943–50).

Hayden, J. Michael, *France and the Estates General of 1614* (Cambridge, 1974).

Henneman, J. B., *Royal Taxation in Fourteenth Century France* (Princeton, New Jersey, 1971).

Holt, Mack P., *The French Wars of Religion, 1562–1629* (Cambridge, 2005).

Hudson, D., 'In Defence of Reform: French Government Propaganda during the Maupeou Crisis', *French Historical Studies*, 8 (1973).

Hurt, John J., *Louis XIV and the Parlements* (Manchester, 2002).

Jackson, Richard A., *Vive le roi!: A History of the French Coronation from Charles V to Charles X* (Chapel Hill, North Carolina, 1984).

James, Alan, *Navy and Government in Early Modern France, 1572–1661* (Woodbridge, Suffolk, 2004).

Jones, Colin, *Madame de Pompadour: Images of a Mistress* (London, 2002).

Jones, Mark, 'The Medal as an Instrument of Propaganda in late Seventeenth- and Early Eighteenth-Century Europe', *Numismatic Chronicle*, 142 (1982).

Jordan, David P., *The King's Trial* (University of California Press, 1979).

Kantorowicz, E. H., *The King's Two Bodies: A Study in Medieval Political Theology* (Princeton, New Jersey, 1957).

Keens-Soper, H. M. A., 'The French Political Academy, 1712: The School for Ambassadors', *European Studies Review*, 2 (1972).

Keohane, Nannerl O., *Philosophy and the State in France: The Renaissance to the Enlightenment* (Princeton, New Jersey, 1980).

Kettering, Sharon, *Patrons, Brokers, and Clients in Seventeenth-Century France* (Oxford, 1986).

Kitchens, J. H., 'Judicial *Commissaires* and the Parlement of Paris: The case of the Chambre de l'Arsenal', *French Historical Studies*, 12 (1982).

Klaits, Joseph, *Printed Propaganda under Louis XIV* (Princeton, New Jersey, 1976).

Knachel, Philip, *England and the Fronde* (Ithaca, New York, 1967).

Knecht, R. J., 'The Concordat of 1516: A Re-Assessment', *University of Birmingham Historical Journal*, 9 (1963).

Knecht, R. J., *Francis I* (Cambridge, 1982). An updated version of this work, *Renaissance Warrior and Patron: The Reign of Francis I* (Cambridge), appeared in 1994.

Knecht, R. J., *Richelieu* (London, 1991).

Knecht, R. J., *The Rise and Fall of Renaissance France* (London, 1996).

Knecht, R. J., *Catherine de' Medici* (London, 1998).

Knecht, R. J., *The French Civil Wars, 1562–1598* (London, 2000).

Knecht, R. J., *The Valois* (London, 2004).

Le Roy Ladurie, E., *The Royal French State, 1460–1610* (Oxford, 1994).

Le Roy Ladurie, E., *The Ancien Régime: A History of France, 1610–1774* (Oxford, 1996).

Levi, Anthony, *Louis XIV* (London, 2004).

Lewis, P. S., *Essays in Later Medieval French History* (London, 1985).

Lloyd, Howell A., *The State, France, and the Sixteenth Century* (London, 1983).

Lossky, Andrew, *Louis XIV and the French Monarchy* (New Brunswick, New Jersey, 1994).

Lot, F. and Fawtier, R., *Histoire des institutions françaises au moyen âge*, 3 vols (Paris, 1957–62).

Louis XV: Un moment de perfection de l'art français (Paris, 1974).

Lublinskaya, A. D., *French Absolutism: The Crucial Phase, 1620–1629*, trans. B. Pearce (Cambridge, 1968).

Lynn, John A., 'Recalculating French Army Growth during the *Grand Siècle*, 1610–1715', Rogers, Clifford J. (ed.), *The Military Revolution Debate* (Oxford, 1995).

Lynn, John A., *The Wars of Louis XIV, 1667–1714* (London, 1999).

Major, J. Russell, *Representative Government in Early Modern France* (New Haven, Connecticut, 1980).

Marion, Marcel, *Dictionnaire des institutions de la France aux XVIIe et XVIIIe siècles* (Paris, 1923, reprinted 1968).

Mettam, Roger, *Power and Faction in Louis XIV's France* (Oxford, 1988).

Mignet, M., *Négociations relatives à la succession d'Espagne sous Louis XIV*, 4 vols (Paris, 1835–42).

Moote, A. Lloyd, *The Revolt of the Judges: The Parlement of Paris and the Fronde, 1643–1652* (Princeton, New Jersey, 1971).

Moote, A. Lloyd, *Louis XIII: The Just* (Berkeley, California, 1991).

Mousnier, R., *L'Assassinat d'Henri IV* (Paris, 1964).

Mousnier, R., *La Vénalité des offices sous Henri IV et Louis XIII* (Paris, 1971).

Mousnier, R., *The Institutions of France under the Absolute Monarchy, 1598–1789*, 2 vols (Chicago, 1979–84).

Pagès, G., *The Thirty Years War, 1618–1648* (London, 1970).

Parker, David, *La Rochelle and the French Monarchy* (London, 1980).

Parker, David, *The Making of French Absolutism* (London, 1983).

Parrott, David, *Richelieu's Army: War, Government and Society in France, 1624–1642* (Cambridge, 2001).

Pinkney, David H., *The French Revolution of 1830* (Princeton, New Jersey, 1972).

Potter, David, *A History of France, 1460–1560: The Emergence of a Nation State* (London, 1995).

Potter, D. (ed.), *The French Wars of Religion: Selected Documents* (London, 1997).

Price, Munro, *Preserving the Monarchy: The Comte de Vergennes, 1774–1787* (Cambridge, 1995).

Ranum, Orest, 'Richelieu and the Great Nobility: some aspects of early modern political motives', *French Historical Studies*, 3 (1963).

Ranum, Orest, *Richelieu and the Councillors of Louis XIII* (Oxford, 1963).

Ranum, Orest, *Paris in the Age of Absolutism* (New York, 1968).

Ranum, Orest, 'Courtesy, Absolutism and the Rise of the French State, 1630–1660', *Journal of Modern History*, 52 (1980).

Ranum, Orest, *The Fronde* (New York, 1993).

Roche, Daniel, *France in the Enlightenment*, trans. A. Goldhammer (Harvard, 1998).

Roelker, Nancy Lyman, *The Paris of Henry of Navarre as seen by Pierre de l'Estoile* (Cambridge, Massachusetts, 1958).

Roelker, Nancy Lyman, *Queen of Navarre: Jeanne d'Albret, 1528–1572* (Cambridge, Massachusetts, 1968).

Rogister, John, *Louis XV and the Parlement of Paris, 1737–1755* (Cambridge, 1995).

Rothkrug, Lionel, *Opposition to Louis XIV* (Princeton, New Jersey, 1965).

Rowen, H. H., *The King's State: Proprietary Dynasticism in Early Modern Europe* (New Brunswick, New Jersey, 1980).

Rule, J. C. (ed.), *Louis XIV and the Craft of Kingship* (Ohio State University Press, 1969).

Saint-Simon, Louis de Rouvroy, duc de, *Mémoires*, 7 vols (Paris, 1948–61).

Sallon, M. A. 'L'échec de Law', *Revue d'histoire économique et sociale*, 48 (1970).

Salmon, J. H. M., *Society in Crisis: France in the Sixteenth Century* (London, 1975).

Schama, Simon, *Citizens: A Chronicle of the French Revolution* (London, 1989).

Shennan, J. H., *Government and Society in France, 1461–1661* (London, 1969).

Shennan, J. H., *The Origins of the Modern European State, 1450–1725* (London, 1974).

Shennan, J. H., *Philippe Duke of Orléans: Regent of France, 1715–1723* (London, 1979).

Shennan, J. H., 'The Political Vocabulary of the Parlement of Paris in the Eighteenth Century', *Diritto e potere nella storia europea*, 2 vols (Florence, 1982).

Shennan, J. H., *Liberty and Order in Early Modern Europe: The Subject and the State, 1650–1800* (London, 1986).

Shennan, J. H., 'The Rise of Patriotism in Eighteenth-Century Europe', *History of European Ideas*, 13 (1991).

Shennan, J. H., *The Parlement of Paris*, 2nd ed. (Stroud, 1998).

Somerset, Anne, *The Affair of the Poisons* (London, 2003).

Sonnino, Paul, *Mémoires for the Instruction of the Dauphin* (New York, 1970).

Stone, Bailey, *The Parlement of Paris, 1774–1789* (Chapel Hill, North Carolina, 1981).

Stone, Bailey, *The French Parlements and the Crisis of the Old Regime* (Chapel Hill, North Carolina, 1986).

Stone, Bailey, *The Genesis of the French Revolution* (Cambridge, 1994).

Strayer, Joseph R., 'France: The Holy Land, the Chosen People, and the Most Christian King', T. K. Rabb and J. E. Siegel (eds), *Action and Conviction in Early Modern Europe* (Princeton, New Jersey, 1969).

Sutherland, N. M., *The French Secretaries of State in the Age of Catherine de' Medici* (London, 1962).

Sutherland, N. M., *The Huguenot Struggle for Recognition* (London, 1980).

Swann, Julian, *Politics and the Parlement of Paris under Louis XV, 1754–1774* (Cambridge, 1995).

Tapié, Victor-L., *France in the Age of Louis XIII and Richelieu*, trans. D. McN. Lockie (London, 1974).

Thomson, Mark A., 'Louis XIV and the Origins of the War of the Spanish Succession', *William III and Louis XIV: Essays 1680–1720 by and for Mark A. Thomson*, (eds) Ragnhild Hatton and J. S. Bromley (Liverpool, 1968).

Tombs, Robert, *France, 1814–1914* (London, 1996).

Treasure, Geoffrey, *Mazarin* (London, 1995).

Van Kley, Dale, *The Damiens Affair and the Unraveling of the Ancien Régime, 1750–1770* (Princeton, New Jersey, 1984).

Walzer, Michael, *Regicide and Revolution* (New York, 1992).

Wells, Charlotte C., *Law and Citizenship in Early Modern France* (Baltimore, Maryland, 1995).

Wolf, J. B., *Louis XIV* (London, 1970).

Wolf, J. B. (ed.), *Louis XIV* (London, 1972).

Wolfe, M., *The Conversion of Henri IV: Politics, Power and Religious Belief in Early Modern France* (Cambridge, Massachusetts, 1993).

Yardeni, Myriam, *La conscience nationale en France pendant les guerres de religion, 1559–1598* (Paris, 1971).

Yates, Frances A., *Astraea* (London, 1975).

Index